THE EDGE OF LAW

The Edge of Law explores the spatial implications of establishing a new legal institution in the wake of violent conflict. Using the example of the establishment of the War Crimes Chamber of the Court of Bosnia and Herzegovina, Alex Jeffrey argues that legal processes constantly demarcate a line of inclusion and exclusion: materially, territorially and corporally. In contrast to accounts that have focused on the judicial outcomes of these transitional justice efforts, *The Edge of Law* draws on long-term fieldwork in Bosnia and Herzegovina to focus on the social and political consequences of the trials, tracing the fraught mechanisms that have been used by international and local political elites to convey their legitimacy. This book will be of interest to sociolegal and geographical scholars working in the fields of transitional justice, legal systems, critical geopolitics and criminology.

ALEX JEFFREY is a reader in human geography at the University of Cambridge and fellow of Emmanuel College. Following work for a youth nongovernmental organisation in Bosnia and Herzegovina, Alex's scholarly work has examined the politics of state formation after violent conflict. Alex is author of more than 40 papers and chapters on the political and legal geographies of the state and published *The Improvised State: Sovereignty, Performance and Agency in Dayton Bosnia* (2013). He sits on the Editorial Board of *Political Geography* and the *RGS-IBG Book Series*.

CAMBRIDGE STUDIES IN LAW AND SOCIETY

Founded in 1997, Cambridge Studies in Law and Society is a hub for leading scholarship in socio-legal studies. Located at the intersection of law, the humanities, and the social sciences, it publishes empirically innovative and theoretically sophisticated work on law's manifestations in everyday life: from discourses to practices, and from institutions to cultures. The series editors have long-standing expertise in the interdisciplinary study of law, and welcome contributions that place legal phenomena in national, comparative, or international perspective. Series authors come from a range of disciplines, including anthropology, history, law, literature, political science, and sociology.

Series Editors

Mark Fathi Massoud, *University of California, Santa Cruz*

Jens Meierhenrich, *London School of Economics and Political Science*

Rachel E. Stern, *University of California, Berkeley*

A list of books in the series can be found at the back of this book.

THE EDGE OF LAW
Legal Geographies of a War Crimes Court

Alex Jeffrey
University of Cambridge

CAMBRIDGE
UNIVERSITY PRESS

CAMBRIDGE
UNIVERSITY PRESS

University Printing House, Cambridge CB2 8BS, United Kingdom

One Liberty Plaza, 20th Floor, New York, NY 10006, USA

477 Williamstown Road, Port Melbourne, VIC 3207, Australia

314–321, 3rd Floor, Plot 3, Splendor Forum, Jasola District Centre, New Delhi – 110025, India

79 Anson Road, #06-04/06, Singapore 079906

Cambridge University Press is part of the University of Cambridge.

It furthers the University's mission by disseminating knowledge in the pursuit of education, learning, and research at the highest international levels of excellence.

www.cambridge.org
Information on this title: www.cambridge.org/9781107199842
DOI: 10.1017/9781108186018

© Alex Jeffrey 2020

This publication is in copyright. Subject to statutory exception and to the provisions of relevant collective licensing agreements, no reproduction of any part may take place without the written permission of Cambridge University Press.

First published 2020

Printed and bound in Great Britain by Clays Ltd, Elcograf S.p.A

A catalogue record for this publication is available from the British Library.

ISBN 978-1-107-19984-2 Hardback

Cambridge University Press has no responsibility for the persistence or accuracy of URLs for external or third-party internet websites referred to in this publication and does not guarantee that any content on such websites is, or will remain, accurate or appropriate.

CONTENTS

Acknowledgements		*page* vi
List of Abbreviations		ix
1	The Edge of Law	1
PART I	PRODUCING THE EDGE OF LAW	25
2	Making a Court	27
3	Court Materiality	56
PART II	POLITICS AT THE EDGE OF LAW	77
4	Public Outreach	79
5	Law and Citizenship	106
PART III	CONTESTING THE EDGE OF LAW	133
6	Rules of Law	135
7	Entrance Strategies	153
8	Conclusion	180
Bibliography		188
Index		206

ACKNOWLEDGEMENTS

This book is a consequence of the assistance and encouragement of a wide cast of people over the past decade, for which I am very grateful. The initial research project *Localising International Law* was funded by the ESRC (RES-061-25-0479); this was a superb opportunity to examine the social and political consequences of relocating war crimes trials from The Hague to Sarajevo. I would like to thank Michaelina Jakala for her assistance on the project and Lejla Mamut, Asim Mukić, Selma Korjenić and Refik Hodzić for their support in formulating ideas, gathering data and discussing results. Zlatan Musić was a great help in the earliest phases of planning for the work, while the final stages benefitted from Saša Buljević's advice and research assistance. I would like to thank all those who participated in the empirical work, in particular the members of non-governmental organisations, victim associations, the Public Information and Outreach section of the Court of Bosnia and Herzegovina, and international organisations. The dissemination event in Sarajevo was a key moment in clarifying the impact and outcome of the project. I would like to thank TRIAL (Tracking Impunity) Sarajevo for helping to co-organise this event and for co-authoring the follow-up report.

Participation in the European Research Council grant *Youth Citizenship in Divided Societies: Between Cosmopolitanism, Nation, and Civil Society* (ERC 295392), led by Lynn Staeheli, helped to develop some of the main conceptual contributions of the book. I am grateful to Lynn for all her support and encouragement, and to the wider project team: Sandy Marshall, Vanja Čelebičić, Chloé Buire, Konstantin Kastrissianakis and Dan Hammett. I was also supported through an ESRC Impact Acceleration Grant *Communicating Law, Creating Citizens* at the University of Cambridge; I would like to thank participants in the workshops hosted in Cambridge and HMP Wandsworth, in particular Ann Griffin, Jessica Jacobson, Rachel Whitlock, Penelope Gibbs, Justice Tankebe, Phil Bowen and Ian Bickers. This impact work was only possible through help and assistance of Amy Ludlow and Ruth

Armstrong at the Institute of Criminology at the University of Cambridge; I am very appreciative of their help.

I have benefitted from a number of supportive contexts that have made finishing this book possible. The first is the collegial environment of the Department of Geography at the University of Cambridge. While there are too many colleagues and students to name each one, I am grateful for the support, advice and friendship of Bill Adams, Harriet Allen, Ash Amin, David Beckingham, Charlotte Lemanski, Emma Mawdsley, David Nally, Sue Owens, Sarah Radcliffe, Bhaskar Vira and Liz Watson. Fran Moore has been a constant source of ideas and encouragement, in particular through our co-convening of the *Legal Geographies* paper, launched in 2018. I also want to thank the students who – as I sit here – are completing its inaugural year; their curiosity and creativity are a source of inspiration. I also want to thank graduate students past and present, in particular the recent cohort of Makoto Takahashi, Judit Kuschnitzki, Tom Jackson, Ed Bryan, Debolina Majumder and Dino Kadich; their energy and ideas have kept me on my toes. António Ferraz de Oliveira and José Martinez have been valuable postdoctoral interlocutors and I am grateful for their advice.

Emmanuel College has provided another productive and welcoming place to write this book. I would like to thank Philip Howell for welcoming me to the college back in 2012 and his wise counsel in the years since. I am particularly grateful to his reading of the book manuscript and suggestions. The wider fellowship at the college have been a tremendous support. I am particularly grateful to the support, friendship and advice of Alex Archibald, Peter Burke, Robert Macfarlane, John Maclennan, Fiona Reynolds and Corinna Russell. I would like to thank the College Research Committee for providing funding that supported aspects of the research and dissemination.

I am lucky to be part of a thriving global community of geographers, with regular opportunities to share ideas and offer suggestions for emerging work. I want to thank to scholars who have visited Cambridge and shared ideas and advice, in particular Nick Blomley, Derek Gregory and Merje Kuus. A number of key workshops and conferences have helped to shape the argument in the book. I am especially grateful to John Morrissey for organising the *Haven Project Symposium* at the National University of Ireland, Galway in 2016; this was a superb opportunity to develop ideas that have finally emerged in Chapters 6 and 7. The invitation to speak at the *Redress and the International* workshop at the Australian National University in Canberra in

ACKNOWLEDGEMENTS

2018 provided an excellent opportunity to refine some of the key arguments and legal claims. I am grateful in particular to Rachel Hughes, Maria Elander, Lia Kent, Nesam McMillan and Michelle Burgis-Kasthala for the invitation, company and helpful discussion. Some of the early ideas for the book were forged through an invitation to give a plenary talk at the 2014 Warwick Postgraduate Political Geography Conference, and I would like to thank the organisers and participants for the feedback at this event and the opportunity to present the nascent ideas. The ideas in the book have also benefitted from presentation at a series of departmental or research group seminars, including at London School of Economics, Nottingham University, Newcastle University, Oxford University, University College London, University of East Anglia and Zurich University. The continued support and advice of friends and colleagues has been much appreciated, including Colin McFarlane, Alex Vasudevan, Fiona McConnell, Rachael Squire, Joe Painter, Stuart Elden, Matthew Bolton, Stuart Dawley, Nick Gill and Katherine Brickell.

In places, the book adapts material published elsewhere, some elements of Chapter 3 were published in 'Legal Geography 1: Court Materiality' from *Progress in Human Geography* (2019); Chapter 4 has material previously published in 'The Political Geographies of Transitional Justice' from *Transactions of the Institute of British Geographers* (2011, 36[3]: 344–359); Chapter 5 has material previously published in 'Using Courts to Build States: The Competing Spaces of Citizenship in Transitional Justice Programmes' from *Political Geography* (2015, 47: 43–52); Chapter 6 has some elements that appeared as 'International Humanitarian Law and the Possibility of the Commons', in A. Amin and P. Howell, eds., *Releasing the commons rethinking the futures of the commons* (Routledge, 2016). I am grateful to the publishers and editors for the permission to use this material.

I would like to thank the editors at Cambridge University Press, in particular Finola O'Sullivan and Marianne Nield for their encouragement, patience and advice. I would like to thank the anonymous referees for their valuable inputs through the project and, especially, to the editorial board members at the Cambridge Law and Society Series.

Finally, thanks to my parents, Pru and David; to Craig Jeffrey and Jane Dyson for their ideas and help; to my sister Eve for the music; and – most significantly – to Laura, Rufus and Clemence for all the love and support.

ABBREVIATIONS

ARBiH	*Armija Republike Bosne i Hercegovine* (Army of the Bosnian Republic)
BiH	Bosnia and Herzegovina
CBiH	The Court of Bosnia and Herzegovina
CCI	*Centri civilnih inicijativa* (Centre for Civil Initiative)
CSN	Court Support Network
DP	Displaced Person
EU	European Union
FRY	Federal Republic of Yugoslavia
GFAP	General Framework Agreement for Peace (Dayton Peace Accords)
GTZ	*Gesellschaft für Technische Zusammenarbeit* (German Technical Cooperation Agency)
ICG	International Crisis Group
ICTY	International Criminal Tribunal for the former Yugoslavia
IEBL	Inter-entity Boundary Line
I-For	Implementation Force
IHC	International Housing Commission
IPTF	International Police Task Force
IRC	International Rescue Committee
JNA	*Jugoslovenska narodna armija* (Yugoslav People's Army)
MZ	*Mjesna zajednica* (local community association)
NATO	North Atlantic Treaty Organisation
NGO	Non-Governmental Organisation
OHR	Office of the High Representative
OSCE	Organisation for Security and Co-operation in Europe
OZNa	*Odeljenje za zastitu narodna* (Department for the People's Defence)
PIC	Peace Implementation Council
RRTF	Return and Reconstruction Task Force

LIST OF ABBREVIATIONS

RS	Republika Srpska (subdivision of Bosnia and Herzegovina)
SDA	*Stranka demokratska akcije* (Party for Democratic Action)
SDP	*Socijaldemokratska partija Bosne i Hercegovine* (Social Democratic Party)
SDS	*Srpska demokratska stranka* (Serb Democratic Party)
S-For	Stabilisation Force
SIPA	State Investigation and Protection Agency
SNSD	*Savez nezavisnih socijaldemokrata* (Alliance of Independent Social Democrats)
UN	United Nations
UNDP	United Nations Development Programme
UNHCR	United Nations High Commission for Refugees
USAID	United States Agency for International Development
USDA	United States Department for Agriculture
VOPP	Vance Owen Peace Plan
VRS	*Vojska Republike Srpske* (Army of Republika Srpska)
WCC	War Crimes Chamber

CHAPTER ONE

THE EDGE OF LAW

This book argues that law is a form of practice that is productive of an edge. This edge is considered from the outset as a spatial phenomenon: a border, volume, limit or plane. The concept of jurisdiction – the territorial limits of legal authority – immediately puts us in mind of the production of a geographical extent to the exercise of law or a legal system. From this starting point, we can begin to see law as a productive force: it does not reflect preexisting spatial arrangements but brings them into the world through its enactment. But the edge of law is suggestive of more than a Euclidean imagination of spatial reach: it is also pointing to the ways in which law creates insiders and outsiders (often troubling the territorial characteristics of jurisdiction), produces specific sites of legal adjudication and presents the production of legal knowledge as a closed system separate from wider social formations. Rather than one boundary-making process, the edge of law becomes three: the designation of spatial limits to law; the constitution of certain sites, bodies and texts as containing legal expertise; and, finally, a set of mechanisms through which law seeks to obscure this boundary-making work. The production and enactment of law is not an exercise in encompassment, but the discursive, material and performative enactment of enclosure.

The scale on which the edge is considered over the course of the book is subject to multiple interpretations, reflecting the plural way in which 'law' may be understood. If we think of law in its very simplest terms as the 'rules of a legal system'[1] then we can consider the edge of law as coterminous with international boundaries, as we would assume in the case of a legal system that had exclusive jurisdiction over the territory of a nation-state. This is a powerful imaginary of the spatial characteristics of law and at the heart of accounts of *legal centralism*, reflecting a belief that 'law is and should be the law of the state, uniform for all persons, exclusive of all other law, and administered by a single set of state institutions'.[2] Of course, such a singular account of law has been the focus of sustained scholarly and practitioner critique, for both denying the existence of legal pluralism, or the coexistence of multiple agents of legal authority, while also overstating the uniformity of state legal processes. Such geopolitical imaginations of state preeminence are amplified in cases in which law is instrumentalised as a tool of state building after conflict. While the argument in this book will contribute to the well-established critique of state centralism, I also want to preserve a focus on its power as an ideology that shapes the behaviour of political and legal actors by projecting an image of how the world should be. In this sense I want to both challenge the empirical reality of legal centralism while also recognising its normative authority.

But defining law in a different way, or at least focusing on a different aspect of our brief definition, highlights a different edge of law. If we focus less on the abstract projection of rules over space and think instead of the legal system that is required to administer such rules, we are presented with an alternative edge. As opposed to the edge of the state, we can consider the spaces produced in the adjudication of law by legal officials and the mechanisms through which such sites are severed from the wider social field. Perhaps most explicitly, focusing on this edge of law considers the mechanisms – so prevalent in critical accounts of legal processes – through which the law has performed its fundamental autonomy as a closed system of knowledge and practice.[3] Enclosure is enacted through architectural norms (the designation of certain bounded sites as legitimate space of legal adjudication), practices of comportment (styles of dress and language that demarcate the legal official from wider society) and performance of legal trials

---

[1] Griffiths, J. (1979). Is law important? *NYU Law Review* 54: 339–374, p. 343.
[2] Griffiths, J. (1986). What is legal pluralism? *The Journal of Legal Pluralism and Unofficial Law* 18(24): 1–55, p. 3.
[3] Blomley, N. K. (1994). *Law, space, and the geographies of power*. New York: Guilford Press, p. 8.

(designating roles and established expected forms of practice). Rather than denying the existence of these edges and boundaries as significant social realities, I am seeking in this book to trace how they are sustained in practice, focusing on the everyday ways in which law's separation is performed. Of course, just as legal centralism highlights the actual existing legal pluralism present in any state territory, tracing the edges of a legal system draws attention to the institutions and actors that blur and challenge practices of legal distinction.

The edge of law, then, is an aspiration and a mercurial reality. It is both a normative ideal and the object of social activism. It exists as a singular imagination but in its realisation the edges of law can traced across spatial scales. But this is not to slip into relativism: the book's central concern is with the ways in which legal processes have been used to try and consolidate a post-conflict state but in doing so have been unsettled by law's pluralism and its embedded nature in wider social processes. The general theoretical perspective in this book, then, is one that emerges from critical human geography, work that has taken inspiration from scholarship in the fields of law-in-society, legal anthropology, sociolegal studies and criminology. As these opening remarks make clear, this is a book that considers law as a social construction but in doing so does not seek to undermine its significance to the organisation of both society and the state. There is a complex geometry to this conceptualisation of law, tracing how it emerges from, and acts upon, a social field. This seeming paradox is captured in Galligan's invocation of law as a 'distinctive social phenomenon' but also 'one that is yet closely entwined with other aspects of society'.[4] Focusing on the edge of law allows us to probe this paradox and examine law's distinctive role in post-conflict state formation.

Introducing the edge of law in these terms also gives the reader a sense of what this book does not aim to achieve. This is not a study in analytical jurisprudence, I am not seeking to meticulously scrutinise the nature of law and legal institutions to contribute to fundamental questions as to its characteristics. The methods involved in this study are not philosophical conjecture, carefully tracing the implications of specific claims to truth. It is closer to a legal anthropology, exploring how a legal institution has been socialised in a specific context and with what effects. Neither is this a treatise in moral philosophy,

---

[4] Galligan, D. (2006). *Law in modern society*. Oxford: Oxford University Press, p. 4.

outlining the different moral claims made in the performance of competing legal systems. This is not to say that justice is not an important factor within the operation of the legal systems under scrutiny, it is just a recognition that the focus of the analysis is on the authority of different justice claims and their ability to shape the operation of law. In particular, the privileging of retributive processes over restorative justice is an enduring refrain in the operation legal processes under investigation, but the evidence presented here does not lead to an ultimate designation of the worth of either. Like others, I am motivated instead to explore the myriad ways in which the operation of law is productive of uneven landscapes of power, but not in the simple relationship of sovereign–subject but rather in an illumination of the different embodied and agentic positions that exist at the edge of law.

SITING THE EDGE: THE COURT OF BOSNIA AND HERZEGOVINA

This book argues that tracing the edge of law helps explain the limits to legal redress and the subsequent challenges of using law as an instrument to establish justice. It advocates a materialist and ethnographic appreciation of the operation of law, drawing attention to its origins, enrolment of bodies, spatial reach and circulation within networks of associations and individuals. The empirical material centres on the process of establishing and operating the Court of Bosnia and Herzegovina (CBiH) 2005–2014, and in particular its increasing role in the prosecution, trial and conviction of those suspected of war crimes during the 1992–1995 conflict in Bosnia and Herzegovina (BiH). It is, then, an exploration of the legal geographies of transitional justice, a term that draws attention to the desire to seek judicial redress for crimes undertaken under a previous political regime.[5] From the outset, the CBiH held a dual objective: to adjudicate on crimes of the past while acting as a unifying institution for the fragmented post-conflict state.[6] It constitutes a rare example of a functioning state-level institution in a state where many powers have been transferred to devolved polities, in particular the two substate entities: the Federation of BiH (Federation) and the Republika Srpska (RS).

---

[5] Teitel, R. G. (2000). *Transitional justice*. Oxford: Oxford University Press.
[6] See Nettelfield, L. J. (2010). *Courting democracy in Bosnia and Herzegovina*. Cambridge: Cambridge University Press.

Contributing to the emerging field of critical legal geography,[7] I argue that exploring the origins, materials and bodies enfolded into the operation of the CBiH opens sightlines of the limits of legal responses after conflict and their varied political effects. This process involves an examination of the ways in which law denies its own origins, limits and exclusions – in doing so performing a constant process of imagined inclusivity, universalism and irrefutability. A key dynamic in this procedure is the requirement to render problems 'legible' to enact administration, a process often connected to the emergence of the modern state from the seventeenth century onwards.[8] For Scott, the legal systems of the state are directed towards a narrow set of objectives (taxation, political control and conscription), a process that always involves the reduction of social reality into a 'convenient, if fictional, shorthand'.[9] As Scott demonstrates in numerous empirical settings, governing through such simplifications requires a scientific attachment to the control of variables, where social contexts must be assumed to be constant to validate administration. But aspects of this image of legal categorisation have come under critical scrutiny. Blomley,[10] when examining Native American property rights in Vancouver, warns against rendering a neat distinction between a 'real' context and the virtual nature of the legal categories that enframe them. Instead, Blomley employs the term 'bracketing' to point to how legal property processes 'entail ... the drawing of a boundary that marks an inside that is detached or disentangled from that now identified as outside'.[11] In this sense – and this is at the heart of Blomley's project – the bracket

---

[7] Braverman, I., Blomley, N., Delaney, D. & Kedar, A. (eds.). (2014). *The expanding spaces of law: A timely legal geography*. Palo Alto, CA: Stanford University Press; Delaney, D. (2015). Legal geography I: Constitutivities, complexities, and contingencies. *Progress in Human Geography* 39(1): 96–102; Herbert, S. (2009). *Citizens, cops, and power: Recognizing the limits of community*. Chicago: University of Chicago Press.

[8] Foucault, M. (1979). On governmentality. *Ideology and Consciousness* 6: 5–21; Scott, J. C. (1998). *Seeing like a state: How certain schemes to improve the human condition have failed*. New Haven, CT: Yale University Press; Tilly, C. (1990). *Coercion, capital, and European states, AD 990*. Oxford: Basil Blackwell.

[9] Scott, *Seeing like a state*, p. 24.

[10] Blomley, N. (2014). Disentangling law: The practice of bracketing. *Annual Review of Law and Social Science* 10: 133–148; Blomley, N. (2015). The ties that blind: Making fee simple in the British Columbia treaty process. *Transactions of the Institute of British Geographers* 40(2): 168–179.

[11] Blomley, The ties that blind, p. 169.

serves an important performative role of summoning into being certain understandings of social relations, privileging them with stability in a dynamic social field.

In the case of BiH, we can see a series of stabilisations taking place where a legal institution is used to consolidate the state. In their enactment, these frameworks are neither distinct nor mutually exclusive, but they point to the contradictions at the heart of the use of law as a framework for the interactions of states, what Oomen terms 'the judicialisation of international relations'.[12] On one level, the desire for transitional justice for crimes of the past, and use of retributive means, invigorates a political discourse of victims and perpetrators in BiH. While providing a site of legal redress, this has had the effect of justifying the connections between ethnic identity and territory contained in the 1995 Dayton Agreement.[13] This exclusionary impulse is met with a secondary spatial framework that celebrates the strengthening of the state, reflecting a popular desire for a civic government capable of defending individuals from injustice. The existence of a universal rule of law across BiH territory cultivates the possibility of substantive citizenship rights conferred by the state. Finally, the requirement of the CBiH to be imposed by intervening agencies and the discourses of international humanitarian law that sustain its legal code points to more cosmopolitan affiliations stimulated through this institution. Such 'context transcending constitutional and international norms'[14] have energised civil society organisations working alongside the court, as human rights organisations and victims associations have relied upon resources, discourses and strategies from organisation beyond the borders of BiH to both support and contest the legal process.

While this is predominantly a study of the emphasis on state sovereignty within the operation of law and its consequences for subsequent legal action, it begins to highlight the empirical challenge of imagining a neat correlation between the creation of a legal system and its acceptance as a legitimate legal arbiter by a wider social field. This

---

[12] Oomen, B. (2005). Donor-driven justice and its discontents: The case of Rwanda. *Development and Change* 36(5): 887–910, p. 887.
[13] Campbell, D. (1998). *National deconstruction: Violence, identity, and justice in Bosnia*. Minneapolis: University of Minnesota Press.
[14] Benhabib, S. (2004). *The rights of others: Aliens, residents, and citizens* (vol. 5). Cambridge: Cambridge University Press, p. 19.

recognition of the significance of legitimacy to the authority of law orientates our attention to the material and social mechanisms through which law seeks to perform its authority. From the architectural aspects of court buildings through to the requirement to enrol civil society actors through outreach programmes, the performance of law is one of contradicting forces: autonomy and embeddedness. Towards the end of the chapter I turn to the empirical context of the book: the establishment of the Court of Bosnia and Herzegovina in the years since 2003, and in particular its imagined function as a successor to the International Criminal Tribunal for the former Yugoslavia (ICTY). The chapter concludes with a structure of the book and an outline of the methods of data collection. The edge of law poses a challenge to purely abstract accounts of the role of law in post-conflict environments and forces a consideration of the plural and embodied practices and imaginations of law and justice that coexist in any single setting.

THE EDGE OF LAW

These opening remarks combine a critical account of the geopolitics of law with a materialist examination of legal systems, where studying the edge is a recognition that law does not neatly with the boundaries of states while the material and social practices of law construct edges between legal rationalities and wider society. What is missing from these initial reflections is people and agency, how individuals navigate, reproduce and transgress these imaginations of law and space. Over the past three decades sociological, criminological and anthropological work has sought to trace the edges of law through studies of the motivations and experiences of risk-taking, thrill-seeking and criminal behaviour. This is, at first glance, at some remove from the considerations of establishing of legal systems. But these studies of *edgeworks*, as such behaviour has been called, provide an insight into not simply the delimitation of certain practices as legal and others as illegal, but why individuals are drawn to break the law, not for material gain, but for the bodily thrill of transgression. For Stephen Lyng, the sociologist who brought the term *edgeworks* to scholarly prominence,[15] such acts are not simply a question of individual identity, they are constitutive of new forms of solidarity, revealing 'a range of activities rooted in a common

---

[15] See Lyng, S. (1990). Edgework: A social psychological analysis of voluntary risk taking. *American Journal of Sociology* 95(4): 851–886.

attraction to exploring the limits of human cognition and capacity in search of new possibilities of being'.[16] They cast a light on an alternative account of legitimacy, not emanating from a sovereign and supported through officers of the state, but performed through a challenge to the perceived alienation of modernity and the law.

Considering the breadth of the concept it is no surprise that examples of *edgeworks* abound. Some are concerned less with law and more with the examples of high-risk behaviour (though this can clearly involve law breaking), for example exploring the motivations of extreme sports enthusiasts such as BASE or wing-suit jumpers.[17] Others have examined the research process as a form of *edgework*, investigating how processes of qualitative data gathering involve shifting between differing contexts of meaning making and morality. Probing specifically the transgression of law, graffiti has been identified as an example of *edgework*, where the liberating sensation of reconstituting the aesthetics of the urban landscape provides the grounds for the legitimacy of the action.[18] Traced phenomenologically, the act of undertaking graffiti illuminates this alternative moral and ethical adjudication where, in certain circumstances, illegality becomes an important aspect of the practice. In this sense, graffiti is an enactment deliberately located *out of place*, a transgressive intervention rooted in the rejection of bourgeois practices of urban consumption.[19] The responses of the state to such transgressions are not always straightforward, particularly in circumstances where graffiti is presented as a reflection of a vibrant cultural scene and thus instrumentalised as a mechanism for attracting investment and new residents to gentrifying neighbourhoods.

There is much to be drawn from such phenomenological accounts of practices that sit uncomfortably on the legal/illegal boundary. But in tracing the edge of law, this book is interested in a more expansive account of the performance of law, beyond its punitive or repressive

---

[16] Lyng, S. (ed.) (2004). Edgework and the risk-taking experience. *Edgework: The Sociology of Risk-Taking*. London: Routledge, pp. 3–16.

[17] See Allman, T. L., Mittelstaedt, R. D., Martin, B., & Goldenberg, M. (2009). Exploring the motivations of BASE jumpers: Extreme sport enthusiasts. *Journal of Sport & Tourism*, 14(4), 229–247.

[18] Ferrell, J. (2016). Foreword: Graffiti, street art and the politics of complexity, in Ross, J. I. (ed.). *Routledge handbook of graffiti and street art*. London: Routledge, pp. xxx–xxxviii.

[19] Cresswell, T. (1992). *In place–out of place: Geography, ideology, and transgression.* Minneapolis: University of Minnesota Press.

functions. If we think of law in terms of its protective and rights-giving functions, the nature of political struggles, and the demarcation of the edge of law, becomes more apparent. For example, there is an overlap in such accounts of *edgeworks* with other forms of human/material practices motivated through an alternative understanding of legitimacy beyond that of the state-sanctioned law. Work on insurgent citizenship has focused attention on collective practices that transgress the law for individuals and groups to secure their rights.[20] Rather than transgression as an embodied experience of thrill and release, these examples focus on the practical and material benefits yielded through targeted law breaking, whether reconnected essential services in situations of utility privatisation[21] or the act of squatting as a claiming of housing rights in moments of disposition and rent hikes.[22] One of the most often-cited examples of such acts of citizenship is James Holston's study of autoconstruction in the urban peripheries of Sao Paulo, Brazil.[23] Holston's work is an intricate study of the social life of law, where elite accounts of universal citizenship mask the discriminator implementation of law as a tactic of disposition and entrenched inequality. While Holston does not use the rubric of *edgeworks*, he is exploring the deliberate transgression of law through what is termed 'residential illegality', auto-constructed housing that galvanised a 'new civic participation and practice of rights', mobilising residents to 'demand full membership in the legal city that had expelled them through the legalization of their property claim and the provision of urban services'.[24] Refuting the commonly held belief that autoconstruction was a reflection of intrinsic lawlessness in Brazil, Holston argues that elites 'elites have used the law brilliantly – particularly land law – to sustain conflicts and illegalities in their favour, force disputes into extra-legal resolution where other forms of power triumph, maintain their privilege and immunity, and deny most Brazilians access to basic

---

[20] Holston, J. (2009). *Insurgent citizenship: Disjunctions of democracy and modernity in Brazil*. Princeton, NJ: Princeton University Press; Miraftab, F. (2009). Insurgent planning: Situating radical planning in the global south. *Planning Theory* 8(1): 32–50.

[21] Miraftab, F., & Wills, S. (2005). Insurgency and spaces of active citizenship: The story of Western Cape anti-eviction campaign in South Africa. *Journal of Planning Education and Research* 25(2): 200–217.

[22] Vasudevan, A. (2015). *Metropolitan preoccupations: The spatial politics of squatting in Berlin*. Oxford: John Wiley & Sons.

[23] Holston, *Insurgent citizenship*.

[24] Ibid., pp. 8–9.

social and economic resources'.[25] Far from a fixed boundary that clearly divides the legal from the illegal, the edge of law here is a blurred and indistinct frontier that may be utilised to protect advantage and entrench inequality.

The purpose of illuminating such *edgeworks* is to begin to think through the ways in which agencies, embedded in specific material circumstance, transgress state sanctioned rules through a claim to alternative – often purportedly 'higher' – accounts of justice. Such accounts could focus upon the right to shelter, self-expression or simply the freedom to push the boundaries of what is deemed, though social mores or norms, to constitute acceptable behaviour. This is not to defend criminality, but rather to illuminate socially mediated understandings of right and wrong that do not map on to legally constituted rules concerning acceptable and unacceptable behaviour. But perhaps more significantly, this work points to ways in which the edge of law may not be a barrier to certain practices; it becomes the site where individuals experiment with subjectivity and challenge the reproduction of the state. Law is, then, a productive force, one that reclassifies behaviour, shapes understandings of inclusion and unfolds within specific geographic environments.

Rather than an incidental outcome of legal practice, by examining the edge of law the distinction rendered through its operation becomes an object of study in its own right. Viewing law and legal institutions in these terms helps to illuminate the challenges of establishing new legal institutions and codes, while also highlighting the forms of exclusion – legal, social and political – that are present in the operation of law. Of course, the distinction between the law and non-law is not simply a practice of dispassionate categorisation, it is productive of hierarchies of moral worth. Just as science and technology studies scholars have traced the 'boundary work' undertaken by scientists to enforce a normative distinction between the imagined virtue of scientific knowledge in contrast to non-scientific knowledge, so legal institutions and actors establish and maintain the edge between law and non-law.[26] Consequently, focusing on the edge of law demands inhabiting a specific orientation, one that identifies from the outset law's alterity and its

---

[25] Ibid., p. 19.
[26] Gieryn, T. F. (1983). Boundary-work and the demarcation of science from non-science: Strains and interests in professional ideologies of scientists. *American Sociological Review* 48(1): 781–795, p. 781.

outsides. It is, in this respect, a contribution to the wider body of work within the social sciences and humanities that has sought to trace a critical account of the social life of law, unsettling an image of law as a set of disembodied codes or texts, exploring instead the production of law in specific social circumstances. This is a familiar anti-essentialist refrain and one that seeks to illuminate the fictional quality of knowledge categories, where their accomplishment is an effect of power rather than a reflection of an intrinsic status.[27] In its familiarity, such a constructivist approach could be taken for granted, where it is assumed that any social practice is a relational and unstable set of claims. But I am not making a morphological claim: in focusing on the edge I want to focus on the process rather than form, to point to the edgework that takes place through assertions of law. In this understanding, law is not an object with limits, it is a moral and aesthetic force that is productive of a range of barriers, extents and edges.

This argument is contributing to work on law in society, seeking to contextualise law as a social practice but also understanding its distinctive features and role in shaping social and political life.[28] It does so through a study of the production of the edge of law in a post-conflict, state-building scenario, that of the establishment of war crimes trials at the CBiH. It argues that studying this example helps explain the limits to legal redress, the political expectations of legal processes and the subsequent challenges of using law as an instrument to establish justice after conflict. Drawing on this example and following the approach of Galligan,[29] the book directly engages with two facets of the law and society field: understanding law as a social formation (tracing its origins, institutionalisation and performance) while also exploring its implications for other social formations (such as associative life, identity formation and understandings of citizenship). This analytical approach will contribute to a growing field of research that has adopted a law and society perspective to examine the establishment and operation of international, humanitarian or transitional legal processes; instances where the innovative or ad hoc nature of the institutions of law makes

---

[27] Brown, W. (2009). *Edgework: Critical essays on knowledge and politics*. Princeton, NJ: Princeton University Press, p. 62.
[28] Galligan, *Law in modern society*, p. 2.
[29] Ibid.

studying its social consequences all the more pressing.[30] A particular focus has been placed on the social legacy of law, either by studying the effectiveness of a particular legal reform,[31] measuring attitudinal changes brought about through a specific legal innovation[32] or reflecting on the opportunities for popular participation and local agency in new institutions of law.[33]

TERRITORIAL EDGE OF LAW

In making this argument I am keen to hold in tension the multiple interpretations that may be offered of the edge of law. Such plurality is a useful resource when considering how the spatial aspects of law inhabit both metaphorical and material sites. This reflects law's ability to be – in very rudimentary terms – both an abstract concern (a force of authority that shapes behaviour, organises the material world and produces affects) and a material process (involving investigative institutions, court systems and carceral regimes).[34] In abstract terms, the edge of law relates to the spatial extent of a particular legal code or legislative institution. It is an edge rather than a boundary as it is always productive of activities, bodies and associations that are rendered outside the law. In doing so, the discussion could follow a long tradition of legal study in thinking through the sites as of *jurisdiction*, where the territorial extent of law is communicated through the existence of legislation that covers a spatial extent, often coterminous with state territoriality.[35] Where the state is understood (after Weber) as the human community with a monopoly of legitimate violence, this close relationship between state authority and lawmaking is somewhat tautological, law constitutes one of the most prominent ways in which the state exhibits its legitimacy as a rule making and breaking organisation.

---

[30] Lundy, P., & McGovern, M. (2008). Whose justice? Rethinking transitional justice from the bottom up. *Journal of Law and Society* 35(2): 265–292; McEvoy, K. (2007). Beyond legalism: Towards a thicker understanding of transitional justice. *Journal of Law and Society* 34(4): 411–440.

[31] Hazan, P. (2004). *Justice in a time of war: The true story behind the International Criminal Tribunal for the Former Yugoslavia*. College Station: Texas A&M University Press.

[32] Nettelfield, *Courting democracy in Bosnia and Herzegovina*.

[33] Lundy & McGovern, Whose justice?, pp. 265–292.

[34] Hart, H. L. A. (2012). *The concept of law*. Oxford: Oxford University Press.

[35] Elden, S. (2013). *The birth of territory*. Chicago: University of Chicago Press.

We could trace this privileged authoritative role of the state through numerous social and political theorists, each tracing the ability of the sovereign to utilise law as a mechanism for both reproducing the power of the state and casting out alternative normative frameworks as illegal. Following this path, we could see state boundaries as neatly delineated edges of law, where one legal regime meets the next.

Of course, the reality of twenty-first-century lawmaking unsettles this image of a tessellated series of territorial jurisdictions.[36] The increased prominence of Carl Schmitt as a theoretical inspiration for scholars of law in society points to a more complex territoriality, as sovereign authorities project their power across international borders. Sovereignty is characterised by the ability to suspend law, to produce spaces of exception where human subjects are stripped of their rights and rendered as 'bare life'.[37] In these instances, characterised by the operation of international agencies in refugee camps, archipelagos of global prisons and the use of drone attacks on military targets across the world, the edge of law is more mobile and plural.[38] Certainly, the edge is no longer traced along international boundaries, but is found within a range of micro-geographies positioned in remote and, at times, contested locations. It is in these examples that it is profitable to trace the edge of law not as a stable legal fact but more as an assertion of moral validity in the face of competing claims to law.

While the unbundling of sovereignty from territoriality may explain the emergence of new forms of what have been termed 'imperial' or 'colonial' power, it does not account for the simultaneous emergence of forms of law that govern the behaviour of states. Over the course of the twentieth century, it has become clear that states alone are not the sole producers of law, with intergovernmental and international agencies playing a prominent role in the production of international law through treaties, conventions and, more recently, international legal institutions.[39] Of course, doubts persist within legal theory as to whether these practices of international law can be satisfactorily

---

[36] Elden, S. (2009). *Terror and territory: The spatial extent of sovereignty*. Minneapolis: University of Minnesota Press.

[37] Agamben, G. (1998). *Homo sacer: Sovereign power and bare life*. Palo Alto, CA: Stanford University Press.

[38] Jones, C. A. (2016). Lawfare and the juridification of late modern war. *Progress in Human Geography* 40(2): 221–239.

[39] Broomhall, B. (2003). *International justice and the International Criminal Court: Between sovereignty and the rule of law* (Vol. 1). Oxford: Oxford University Press.

equated with municipal or state law, drawing attention to the relative absence of threats or sanctions that may compel states to behave in certain ways.[40] But in some senses, this endorses the need to trace the edge of law as these institutions cultivate an ambiguity towards the sanctity of international boundaries: reasserting state territoriality while providing the means to assert a more cosmopolitan form of law. For example, work that has studied the outcome of interstate territorial disputes at the International Court of Justice (ICJ) has found the court's approach to international disputes relies on existing state boundaries: first by looking to treaty law to resolve the dispute, then by employing the principle of *uti possidetis* (territory remains with the possessor) and, finally, considering effective control.[41] In this sense we can see in the operation of international law a latent dependence on the status quo, and a consequent reliance on histories of military might and colonial possession in the governance of international legal norms.

It is this lingering landscape of power in the workings of international law that raises scepticism of the true neutrality of international agencies and the possibility of challenging the lawmaking capabilities of powerful states. Perhaps a clearer expression of this contestation is encapsulated by attempts to not simply hold states to account in a general sense, but to provide rights and redress to individuals within states to challenge the authority of their sovereign. The rise of international humanitarian law (IHL) speaks to these new forms of international legal redress, institutionalised through war crimes tribunals and the international criminal court, institutions that again redraw the edges of law as various territories, bodies, events and activities become objects of legal concern. Such initiatives, structured around the moral claims of a common humanity, are often characterised as a Kantian form of legal imaginary that centres on more cosmopolitan forms of belonging and moral concern.[42] Of course, and as I examine both later in this chapter and in the wider arguments of the book, such an approach does not deny the edge of law, but rather traces these through the careful demarcation of human rights concerns, as certain

---

[40] Hart, *The concept of law*.
[41] Sumner, B. T. (2003). Territorial disputes at the International Court of Justice. *Duke Law Journal* 53: 1779.
[42] Jeffrey, A. (2009). Justice incomplete: Radovan Karadžić, the ICTY, and the spaces of international law. *Environment and Planning D: Society and Space* 27(3): 387–402.

bodies are conceived as the objects of law while others cast out without claims to redress.

TRACING THE MATERIAL EDGE OF LAW

We see in these examples considerable contestation of the spatial 'edge' of law in its production through the concept of jurisdiction. But while the edge of law provokes a consideration of the abstract assertion of law's spatiality, it also necessitates a consideration of the material environments in which legal adjudication may take place. This is what is often termed the *second order* element of law: the legal system (regulatory, investigative and punitive) that is created to enforce the law. If we are thinking of foundational stories of the force of law, there is a requirement to materialise the punitive possibilities of a legal system to shape individual behaviour. If we take one influential theory concerning the origins of law, John Austin's (1932) sanction theory, we can immediately grasp the significance of materiality. Austin's approach was to see law as a product of the union of rules and sovereignty – thus 'what makes the law the law is its being the general commands issued by someone who is habitually obeyed by the bulk of the population and habitually obeys no one else'.[43] Obedience to the law is secured through the threat of a sanction should the law not be followed thus, when instructed by the sovereign, individuals are obligated to comply. This is clearly a simplification of the nature of complex mechanism through which obligations emerge and laws are (or are not) obeyed, but it does provide a useful starting point for thinking through materiality and the edge of law. There is a telling interpretation of Austin's thesis in Hart's *Concept of Law*. He traces sanction theory through an example of a person carrying a gun approaching a bank clerk and commanding 'Hand over the money or I will shoot'. Hart explains the relationship that emerges in this act:

> Its distinctive feature which leads us to speak of the [person carrying the gun] *ordering* not merely *asking*, still less *pleading with* the clerk to hand over the money, is that, to secure compliance with his expressed wishes, the speaker threatens to do something which a normal [person] would

---

[43] Shapiro, S. J., & Shapiro, S. (2011). *Legality*. Cambridge, MA: Harvard University Press, p. 54.

regard as harmful or unpleasant, and renders keeping the money a substantially less eligible course of conduct for the clerk.[44]

This very simplified account does not seem the basis for an analysis of law's materiality, but – as Hart does – let's work outwards from this binary relationship of securing compliance towards a story of the edge of law. The first issue to address is the motivation for the bank clerk to hand over the money – following Hart (after Austin) it is the threat of pain or death as consequence of a bullet injury. This threat is constituted through the bank clerk's awareness that a gun produces bullets, and these could cause pain. It is an assumption based on experience, perhaps seeing people shot in another context or talking to someone who had suffered the ordeal of a bullet injury. While pain is the threat it is now materialised in the gun, or even the threat of a gun if the weapon is concealed but physical gestures are made to its presence.

There are two initial points that stem from these statements. First, that visuality is important to the enforcement of law: a regime of law must be *seen* as a potentially retributive system where lack of compliance will lead to forms of punishment. This may seem self-evident, but it challenges a brand of legal positivism, best encapsulated by Max Weber's account of the establishment of bureaucratic power within the modern state, where the legitimacy of the modern state is enacted through the existence of the correct legal procedures.[45] While Weber was certainly interested in the institutions and practices through which such legitimation of state took place, it is from the social histories of Michel Foucault that scholars have considered the significance of visuality and law. Like others, Foucault was keen to trace the shifting modalities of power, reflecting on the implications for the organisation and conduct of society. One of the key technologies for Foucault that facilitated the emergence of the modern state was the development of *disciplinary* forms of power, where the use of spectacular punishment (such public executions) to garner compliance were replaced with the bureaucratic instruments to shape bodily behaviour. Famously this has led Foucault to examine the functioning of clinics, prisons and asylums

---

[44] Hart, *The concept of law*, p. 19.
[45] O'Neill, J. (1986). The disciplinary society: From Weber to Foucault. *British Journal of Sociology* 37(1): 42–60.

to trace 'the legal-rational accounting process in techniques for the administration of corporeal, attitudinal and behavioural discipline'.[46]

The visual implications of this apparently hidden enactment of power are not straightforward. While the specific object of legal retribution may be removed from public site (coming back to Hart's analogy: the gun) spectacular enactments of the presence of a legal system endure. The prominent positioning of a court building and its monumental architecture seek to convey the presence and legitimacy of a specific legal system. They are, in Jacques Rancière's terms, 'aesthetic acts',[47] disruptions in the urban landscape that are designed to convey the authority of a specific set of sovereign arrangements; in the terms of this book: a prominent and material edge of law. As I will demonstrate later in the book, the lure of the aesthetic is particularly strong in moments of rapid political transformation, where changing the aesthetics of the urban landscape becomes a key technique through which to embed a new set of sovereign arrangements. But we must be careful not to equate prominence and spectacle with the successful claim to legitimacy. Indeed, following the work of Wendy Brown on the bordering practices of contemporary states,[48] such exercises in projecting power through monumental architecture could be interpreted as a signal of the weakness of the state, its constant need to perform its power in the face of alternative and ever-present sources of legitimacy. It is here we must be careful to discern between disciplinary power as a transient enactment with a deterministic interpretation of power that drains and denies the significance of agency in reworking power relationships.

The second aspect of visuality that stems from Hart's story of the gun bearer and the bank clerk is one of separation. The sanction theory works on an intrinsic separation between the source of law (with a gun) and those compelled to obey its rules. Again, this may seem self-evident, but it carries a series of material implications. While the gun bearer is in a position of authority through the potential use of force, their wider authority stems from their ability to choose which bank to rob, which individuals to coerce. It is not the moment of potential

---

[46] Ibid., p. 45.
[47] See Rancière, J. (2004). *The politics of aesthetics: The distribution of the sensible*. London: Continuum; and Clarkson, C. (2014). *Drawing the line: Towards an aesthetics of transitional justice*. New York: Fordham University Press.
[48] Brown, W. (2010). *Walled states, waning sovereignty*. Cambridge, MA: MIT Press.

violence that underscores the authority of law, but its ability to be a site of authoritative knowledge production. For this to work, it follows that the bank clerk cannot participate in the formulation of the bank-robbing strategy, their separation is an axiomatic part of the enactment of law. While it is clearly problematic to draw too many general characteristics of law from this vignette, the sanction theory demonstrates the ways in which the authority of law is a product of a certain form of expertise, validated through the subject position of the lawmaker. This privileged position of knowledge production is then communicated through a series of visual strategies. Be this the wearing of distinct uniforms (e.g., judges in wigs) or the reorganisation of spaces of trials to denote the different subject positions of those involved (e.g., the bench, dock and public gallery).

I will, therefore, argue that courts, prisons and tribunals become the edge of law between the urban public sphere and sites of securitised adjudication. Within courts, space is further subdivided between public and private areas, while court rooms are carefully arranged to connect spatial division with individual role in the trial process. Space is, in this sense, an instrument of legal distinction, both performing the authority of law while cultivating expectations regarding individual subjectivity within legal processes. I will argue throughout the book that courts are interventions in the material landscape that seek to embed a legal system, not least by providing a prominent location where justice may be seen to be done. Trace either of these imagined modalities of law any further and we run into their essentially entwined character: we cannot speak of jurisdiction as an abstract (or singular) entity when its force is derived from material presences, whether bodily (the presence of legal officials) or architectural (the simple presence of courts). Similarly, we cannot think of the material achievement of law as 'simply' a physical process, rather it is one where the relative authority of those involved is derived from abstract codifications, affective atmospheres and performances of status. The edge of law, then, involves a hybrid process, a symbiosis between materials and authoritative force.

The Edge of Law?

Placing the edge of law in the singular rather than the plural (such as the edges of law or the edge of laws) is meant as a provocation, inviting scrutiny of the plural realities of law in practice and the blurring of the line between legal processes and wider social fields. In this respect, this book is a performance of *edgework*, probing the legal, political and material ways in which the limits of law are demarcated and policed, and with what social effects. As we will see, this sensibility towards the edge is particularly apparent where multiple sites of justice coexist, or where the novelty of a new legal regime casts ambiguity over the appropriate formulation of legal arrangements. Inventing a law or introducing a new legal system is a perilous moment where the authority of an institution to write the law is thrown into sharp relief, exposing the often-undemocratic nature of lawmaking and the struggles to perform legitimacy. Postcolonial legal scholars and legal anthropologists have provided many examples of the attempts to present law as the highest form of moral authority in the face of competing approaches to law or legality.[49]

Examining the edge of law in these terms is freighted with methodological implications. At its heart, it requires scrutiny of the practices, materials and bodies through which law is made, attentive to the role of place specificity in the production of legal authority. As a consequence, scholars have employed ethnographic methods,[50] alongside a feminist critical perspective that illuminates the bodily, institutional and discursive mechanisms through which power relations are stabilised and reproduced.[51] In what follows, I argue that integrating work within critical legal geography with critical legal studies provides new sightlines on the mechanisms of law in times of change. In particular, I want to focus on three areas that this theoretical synergy can invigorate legal geography. First, feminist geographers have orientated scholarly attention to the reproduction of power relations through the operation of everyday life. As a reflection of this influence a wealth of studies have explored how the spatial and political interact in quotidian arenas, such as the home, street and school. At the same time, scholars have sought to project the 'everyday' into their analysis of political organisations, unsettling the very notion of a coherent institution[52] and studying how particular spatial discourses are produced

---

[49] Comaroff, J., & Comaroff, J. L. (eds.). (2008). *Law and disorder in the postcolony*. Chicago: University of Chicago Press.

[50] Latour, B. (2010). *The making of law: An ethnography of the Conseil d'État*. Cambridge: Polity.

[51] Brickell, K., & Cuomo, D. (2019). Feminist geolegality. *Progress in Human Geography* 43(1): 104–122; Hyndman, J. (2004). Mind the gap: Bridging feminist and political geography through geopolitics. *Political Geography* 23(3): 307–322.

[52] Müller, M. (2012). Opening the black box of the organization: Socio-material practices of geopolitical ordering. *Political Geography* 31(6): 379–388.

through the operation of bureaucracies.[53] This approach speaks to work within critical legal studies and legal anthropology that has sought to study the social life of law, tracing the myriad materials and bodies through which law is made[54] and the social implications of legal processes, both in terms of knowledge effects and the conduct of trials.[55]

Second, critical scholarship has orientated attention to the embodied nature of political life, both in terms of differentiated subject experiences and the significance of bodily disposition and proximity to alternative understandings of security.[56] This field has subsequently traced the ways in which geographical differences and discrimination are stabilised through the projection of difference onto the human body, and the corporeal ways in which such frameworks of power may be transgressed. Similar narratives of the body can be found in critical legal studies, not least Alan Hyde's *Bodies of Law*,[57] a book that examines the textual construction of bodies as sites of investigation, materialisations of evidence, expressions of property and loci of deviance. Quickly such lines of inquiry decentre the unitary and pre-existing concept of 'the body', a point developed in Damir Arsenijević's study of the classification of human remains recovered from mass graves.[58] In this work, Arsenijević examines the collusion between scientist, bureaucrat and priest in the assignment of ethnic identity to bodies recovered from sites in BiH. Here, human flesh is assigned ethnic characteristics regardless of the living body's own self-identification. In this way, law assumes 'the perspective of the perpetrator[s] of the crime'.[59]

---

[53] Kuus, M. (2015). Transnational bureaucracies: How do we know what they know? *Progress in Human Geography* 39(4): 432–448.
[54] Jeffrey, A., & Jakala, M. (2014). The hybrid legal geographies of a war crimes court. *Annals of the Association of American Geographers* 104(3): 652–667.
[55] Felman, S. (2002). *The juridical unconscious: Trials and traumas in the twentieth century*. Cambridge, MA: Harvard University Press.
[56] Koopman, S. (2011). Alter-geopolitics: Other securities are happening. *Geoforum* 42 (3): 274–284.
[57] Hyde, A. (1997). *Bodies of law*. Princeton, NJ: Princeton University Press.
[58] Arsenijević, D. (2011). Gendering the bone: The politics of memory in Bosnia and Herzegovina. *Journal for Cultural Research* 15(2): 193–205.
[59] Ibid., pp. 193–205.

The final methodological consideration raised by a critical legal geography of law relates to the relative significance granted to normativity.[60] Of course, the roots of feminist theorising in social activism echoes into the present through a desire to enact political transformation rather than simply provide a site for critique. Such a normative commitment is keenly expressed in Mountz's ethnography,[61] where the concluding chapter asserts emphatically that a more nuanced understanding of the embodied nature of the immigration process – an approach that emphasises the personal biographies of the individuals involved – supports a commitment to the right to seek asylum. Such links to the lived experience are developed in Orzeck's historical exploration of land transfers in Palestine,[62] work that stresses the role of normative theorising in examining popular understandings of justice in times of political upheaval. This develops, historically, the role of qualitative approaches in narrating the interplay between imaginations of justice and the practice of law. Crucially, justice here is not understood simply as a resolution of past violence but also in relation to the nature and practices of authority to which individuals are subject. In so doing, I am interested in what Orzeck terms both the 'discourse and understanding of justice',[63] where elite narratives of resolutions of the past are affirmed, challenged or reworked by individual subjects of law. Justice in these terms is not simply a legal outcome, but a reflection of the legitimacy of law, or a particular legal code, as a site of arbitration.

Reflecting these underlying methodological philosophies, the research for this book took place over three phases of residential fieldwork in BiH, the first in 2009, the second in 2011–2012 and the third in 2016. These periods of research built on a long-term engagement with non-governmental organisation (NGO) and academic work in BiH going back to 1999. The field data was gathered through two methods: interviews (with court officials, agents within international organisations, representatives from victim associations and NGOs and

---

[60] Megoran, N. (2008). Militarism, realism, just war, or nonviolence? Critical geopolitics and the problem of normativity. *Geopolitics* 13(3): 473–497; Olson, E., & Sayer, A. (2009). Radical geography and its critical standpoints: Embracing the normative. *Antipode* 41(1): 180–198.
[61] Mountz, A. (2010). *Seeking asylum: Human smuggling and bureaucracy at the border*. Minneapolis: University of Minnesota Press, pp. 167–175.
[62] Orzeck, R. (2014). Normative geographies and the 1940 Land Transfer Regulations in Palestine. *Transactions of the Institute of British Geographers* 39(3): 345–359.
[63] Ibid., p. 356.

civil society actors working with the CBiH) and trial monitoring (largely in 2011–2012 and 2016, comprising attending trials at the court and analysing transcripts). The sample of interviewees was established through snowballing from one informant to the next, facilitated by the long-term nature of the data-gathering process. Alongside these field activities the research has involved collating textual material concerning the emergence of the court and the role of international and local political elites, drawn from online archives, websites and institutional reports. All interview material was analysed using NVivo discourse analysis software. Initial findings from the research were presented to court officials, NGOs, victim associations and international agencies at a workshop in Sarajevo in 2012, permitting participants to assist in drawing conclusions and building theory. It was in a stuffy conference suite in Hotel Europe, Sarajevo, where different participants argued over the perceived barriers to achieving justice and the seeming exclusions of the legal process that the edge of law emerged as the structuring logic for understanding the challenges of establishing new legal processes in wake of atrocities of the past.

THE STRUCTURE OF THE BOOK

By highlighting the edge of law I am interested in the productive force of legal systems, not simply as reflections of preexisting social or political landscapes, but rather as the site of *tactics*: where individuals and groups utilise the law as a means of garnering respect or changing their social conditions or status. The chapters are divided into three parts reflecting different aspects of the edge of law. Part I explores the *production* of the edge of law, examining the geopolitical and material processes through which the CBiH came into existence. The first chapter in this part (Chapter 2) examines the inception of the Court of BiH, focusing on its role as a central part of the completion process of the ICTY. The court, then, was enrolled in a geopolitical practice of localising responsibility for the investigation of war crimes trials within the borders of BiH. This was more than a geographical relocation; it was a move intended by international officials to consolidate the fragmented post-conflict state through the simplification of territorial jurisdiction and to democratise the judicial process by fostering local control over war-crimes processes. The following chapter (Chapter 3) examines the material aspects to this process, in particular the selection and conversion of a former army barracks near the centre of Sarajevo into a court, an act that was intended by international elites to provide a focal point for the production of a new legal regime in BiH. However, the building's past, and its contextualisation within the divided political landscape of BiH, led to protests and calls for boycotts from some segments of BiH society.

Part II examines the politics of the edge of law, looking in particular at the mechanisms attempting to strengthen the legitimacy of the BiH public for the CBiH. These discussions focus upon the forms of agency and subjectivity that have been fostered through the establishment of the new legal regime at the CBiH. The first chapter (Chapter 4) examines the role of NGOs as intermediaries 'between' the court and wider BiH society, a form of *edgework* as individuals navigate between legal and non-legal contexts. It specifically explores the implications of outreach for understandings of the locations of trial justice, challenging the neat separation of the court's activities from the political contestations within the wider social field. The political implications of the court are examined in further depth in the subsequent chapter examining the role of the court in attempts to consolidate the BiH state (Chapter 5). The chapter examines the forms of citizenship that have emerged in the wake of the establishment of the CBiH, focusing on the prominent role played by civil society agencies in securing individual rights. Rather than reifying a straightforward geometry between state-sanctioned notions of liberal democratic citizenship and the more activist practices found within civil society, the evidence from the establishment of the court points to a plural story, where individuals are using informal spaces and practices to seek access to rights that they believe to be the responsibility of the BiH state.

Part III explores at the legal mechanisms through which the new legal regime in BiH has been *contested*. I am interested in thinking through the alternative sites of legal legitimacy that coexist with the CBiH. The first chapter (Chapter 6) revisits debates concerning the origins of law, to think through how the legacy of previous legal regimes cannot be erased but rather memories of their judicial norms shape decision making, and understandings of justice, in the present. The specific focus is the shift from the 1976 Yugoslav Criminal Code to the 2003 Criminal Code for BiH, a manoeuvre that opened the CBiH to renewed legal and political scrutiny. The subsequent challenges to the sentencing decisions at a series of high-profile war crimes trials weakened public confidence in the court and further undermined its legitimacy as the ultimate arbiter of law. In the second chapter

(Chapter 7) I continue to examine the localised implications of the geopolitics of justice through an exploration of recent attempts to change laws of citizenship in BiH as a strategy for confronting Islamist terror. I want to examine, historically and spatially, the implications of attempts to use law as a means of casting out and excluding bodies considered a security threat to both the BiH polity and wider regional geopolitics. As will become clear, and reflecting the analysis in previous chapters, this is not a story that can be told solely through the political and judicial machinations with BiH. Processes of exclusion are resourced, materially and ideologically, through numerous transnational networks, not least the support of the US government for antiterror initiatives and purported Russian support for the Serb separatism. But they are also resisted on multiple spatial scales: from street protests against extrajudicial imprisonment through to challenges to the legal propriety of arrests at the European Court of Human Rights (ECtHR). Far from static dictates, citizenship laws reflect the oscillation between encompassment and closure that characterise legislative attempts to determine political membership. The conclusion allows the opportunity to think across the different parts of the book to draw out the wider implications for the study of law in society, legal geography and transitional justice.

PART I

PRODUCING THE EDGE OF LAW

CHAPTER TWO

MAKING A COURT

INTRODUCTION

The Court of Bosnia and Herzegovina (CBiH) occupies an unimposing building around five kilometres outside the centre of Sarajevo (Figure 2.1). In many respects it defies the assumed characteristics of public legal buildings, imagined to present an imposing presence on the urban landscape to symbolically embed a particular legal regime. On a cold October afternoon, sitting with a member of the Public Information and Outreach Service (PIOS) at the court, I asked about the selection of the building and, specifically, why this site had been chosen for the court. Finishing her cigarette with the hint of a smile, she replied that 'all the good buildings in the centre of town had been taken by other international agencies'. This dry remark reflects the timing of the CBiH's establishment in 2005, 10 years after the Dayton Agreement and late in the process of BiH state formation. It also points to a process of articulation, where a new institution inevitably reflects the existing landscape of governmental and legal authority. We cannot, then, understand the making of the CBiH without first grasping the geopolitical and historical circumstances that produced its mandate and structure.

The first edge of law is, then, the moment of creation, from the absence to the existence of a new legal institution. This transition is not, of course, straight forward, and in this chapter I investigate how the War Crimes Chamber (WCC) of the CBiH came into being. Too often the creation of an international court is assumed to be either a

Figure 2.1 The Court of Bosnia and Herzegovina, Sarajevo
(Photo: author's own)

product of a single declaration (often the passing of a UN Security Council Resolution) or evidenced by its legal function (the commencement of its first trial). These are important performative moments: they underscore the significance of declarations of existence and the force of new legal frameworks, but they do little to convey why and how a specific institution was established in place of many other alternatives. To understand the later discussions of the social responses to the court and its struggle alongside other legal and political responses to the violence we need to view its creation through the prism of prevailing geopolitical and historical forces encircling the former Yugoslav states.

Tracing the roots of the WCC in the streams of Yugoslav and pre-Yugoslav history opens the analysis to a near limitless set of possible antecedents. In a sense, this reflects the shifting position of law, and the stated primacy of specific legal systems, in struggles over sovereignty in Southeast Europe since the end of the nineteenth century. I could begin, as others have, with an account of the pre-Yugoslav Illyrianism as a form of anti-imperial struggle that sought to wed concepts of justice to the democratic will of the South Slav peoples.[1] While this was by no means a unitary movement – localised legal traditions varied greatly within the 1918 Kingdom of Serbs, Croats and Slovenes, for example – these initial attempts to form a unified state emphasised the perceived illegitimacy of the imposition of law from an external imperial power. Or, indeed, I could begin with an examination of the social significance of the judicial system within Tito's Yugoslavia, where critics have suggested that law served as an 'instrument of the ruling class'[2] rather than an independent realm of arbitration. This social positioning of law, encapsulated by the 1976 Yugoslav legal code, has shaped subsequent interpretation of both the function of law and the intentions of international legal institutions with jurisdiction over post-Yugoslav states.

These examples are not selected at random: they illustrate a central tension in the operation of law, between the legitimacy granted through the will of the people (a democratisation narrative) and the authority granted through the protection of the state (a sovereignty narrative). This restates a central tension in much work in international relations and political geography: between the right of self-determination and inviolability of state territoriality.[3] While this chapter is not going to rehearse this particular tension in detail, I am interested in examining the productive qualities of these two justifications for political and legal agendas in former Yugoslav space. The first section of the chapter explores these 'legitimation narratives' as geopolitical frames: arguing that they point to different interpretations of the *nomos*, the normative frameworks through which appropriate action may be framed. In line with the general theoretical approach of the book, I am concerned here with the spatial attributes of this process of creation; how the geographical representation of BiH as a particular kind of place shaped the final form, function and institutional setting of both the International Criminal Tribunal for the former Yugoslavia (ICTY) and the WCC.

---

[1] Prpa-Jovanović, B. (1997). The making of Yugoslavia: 1830–1945, in Udovički, J., & Ridgeway, J. (eds.), *Burn this house: The making and unmaking of Yugoslavia*. Durham, NC: Duke University Press, pp. 43–63.

[2] Saxon, D. (2005). Exporting justice: Perceptions of the ICTY among the Serbian, Croatian, and Muslim communities in the former Yugoslavia. *Journal of Human Rights* 4(4): 559–572.

[3] Elden, S. (2009). *Terror and territory: The spatial extent of sovereignty*. Minneapolis: University of Minnesota Press.

While the tension between democratisation and state sovereignty provide a discursive backdrop to the forms of intervention made in the fragmentation of Yugoslavia, they must be considered alongside a third legitimising narrative: that of humanitarianism. In a number of important respects humanitarianism encapsulates the tensions between these two terms, simultaneously gesturing at the solidarity between peoples and the clear inequality between care giver and recipient.[4] Humanitarianism is therefore a recognition of both the intrinsic horizontal ties between peoples and the enactment of forms of corrective that point to the exercise of sovereign power projected beyond the borders of individual states. The second section of the chapter examines how the justification for legal responses rested on various interpretations of legitimacy, a flexible and situated notion behind which sits a set of normative assumptions concerning both law and the state.[5]

The third section begins the task of examining how differing understandings of the *nomos*, and their attendant geopolitical storylines, shaped the judicial response to the war in BiH. One key narrative arc here is the creation – and later completion – of the ICTY. Innovating in many ways, and recovering ideas of transitional justice that stretch back through the twentieth century, the ICTY was created to respond to unfolding atrocities in BiH, though its jurisdiction spanned the states of the former Yugoslavia. The purpose is not to gauge the success or otherwise of the tribunal; this has been explored with vibrant detail in other studies.[6] Instead, I am seeking to examine how the ICTY accommodated varying interpretations of the violence and the subsequent compromises these necessitated. In its early years, while the conflict was still ongoing, the ICTY was justified as a humanitarian response to the unfolding violence, removing the locus of justice from the BiH state. The tribunal's activity was hampered by geopolitical tensions between its main architects, coupled with its role in the process of brokering peace in BiH. It is instructive to consider these formative years as moments that underscore the tensions and ambiguities that have defined both the quest for transitional justice in BiH and the struggles

---

[4] Fassin, D. (2011). *Humanitarian reason: A moral history of the present.* Berkeley and Los Angeles: University of California Press.

[5] See Jeffrey, A., McConnell, F. & Wilson, A. (2015). Understanding legitimacy: Perspectives from anomalous geopolitical spaces. *Geoforum* 66: 177–183.

[6] Nettelfield, L. J. (2010). *Courting democracy in Bosnia and Herzegovina.* Cambridge: Cambridge University Press.

to communicate the purposes and activities of international humanitarian law (IHL) to an often-sceptical public.

The final act of the ICTY's narrative is its completion, and this comprises the fourth part of the chapter. The creation of the WCC of the CBiH was designed by international sponsors, in part, as an important step in the completion of the ICTY. But this was not the sole legitimation strategy: justification for the establishment of the WCC also included the end of impunity for war criminals and the 'handing back' of responsibility for judicial responses to the violence of the 1990s. Again, we see a lingering tension between a narrative of democratisation (of giving people within BiH control over judicial processes) and sovereignty (the ability of the state to arbitrate on law within its own territory). The following chapters examine the ongoing implications of these divergent understandings of the WCC's purpose, tracing the political response and significance for local understandings of justice.

LEGITIMATION: DEMOCRACY AND SOVEREIGNTY

> *No set of legal institutions or prescriptions exists apart from the narratives that locate it and give it meaning. For every constitution there is an epic, for each decalogue a scripture. Once understood in the context of the narratives that give it meaning, law becomes not simply a system of rules to be observed, but a world in which we live.*[7]

Language is at the heart of law; not simply as a mode of communication of preexisting rules, but as a set of citational practices that summon such frameworks into existence. It is commonplace to view such declarations as 'performative', following Judith Butler,[8] that they are producing the effect that they name. But we need to be careful to make a clear connection between these apparently dematerialised notions of the legal and the creation of actual existing laws, institutions and officials. In orientating attention to language Cover was seeking to rehabilitate the concept of the *nomos*, taken from the Greek word for

---

[7] Pp. 4–5 in Cover, R. M. (1983). Foreword: Nomos and narrative. *Harvard Law Review* 97: 4–68.
[8] See Butler, J. (2013). *Excitable speech: A politics of the performative*. Abingdon: Routledge.

law and notably used by Carl Schmitt[9] as a means of explaining the early-twentieth-century rise of Western-centric international law. For Cover, *nomos* refers to a normative universe that gives meaning to language and action.[10]

This focus on representation is not restricted to legal theory, much of the scholarship on international intervention in conflict and emergency has explored the role of language, often referred to (as previously noted) as narrative or 'framing', in determining the appropriate course of action. Consequently, the quest to uncover the normative universe of language and practice has been central to critical accounts of international intervention in conflict and developmental environments. In keeping with this trend, much of the scholarship on the international response to the violence in BiH has focussed on its representation, arguing that how the war 1992–1995 was described influenced proposed solutions. There are no shortages of explanations for the violence, concentrating on the role of international actors (both within and beyond the former Yugoslavia), the significance of competing ethnic narratives of statehood, the economic inequalities of the republic of Yugoslavia, amongst many others. Scholars in critical international relations and critical geopolitics have focused on the spatial aspects of these representative strategies: that BiH was understood as a certain kind of *place* with specific qualities in terms of its location (near or far), its inhabitants (victims or aggressors) and its security (unstable or peaceful). Post-structural scholars argue that such representations (or *mis*representations) are detached from the material circumstances of the country in question, consequently the mediation of understandings of BiH through news agencies and government scripting makes establishing a singular narrative of the violence impossible. Perhaps the most renowned mobilisation of such ideas came in the work of French scholar of media and culture Jacques Baudrillard with his infamous assertion that the 1991 Gulf War 'did not take place'.[11] Despite frequent misappropriations, Baudrillard's

---

[9] Schmitt, C. (1950 [2003]). *The Nomos of the earth*. New York: Telos Press.
[10] Cover, Foreword, p. 5. See also Delaney, D. (2010) *The spatial, the legal and the pragmatics of world-making: Nomospheric investigations*. Abingdon: Routledge-Cavendish.
[11] See Baudrillard, J. (1995). *The Gulf War did not take place*. Bloomington: Indiana University Press.

point is not one of denial of the violence but rather that the presentation of a asymmetric military assault as 'war' grants it legitimacy in the eyes of the viewing public. While plural interpretations of the violence in BiH are inevitable, they do not have to lead to a relativism where any claim has equal veracity or significance. Instead, one of the first tasks in tracing the edge of law in BiH is to explore how and why certain understandings of violence have risen to prominence and with what consequences.

Discerning the underlying reasons for representative strategies requires a focus on the normative frameworks underpinning descriptions of the violence, the competing understandings or invocations of the *nomos*. As opposed to a descriptive exercise, this taps into the more challenging question of how certain interpretations and responses to violence have been presented as legitimate and to which audiences. Scholars of state theory are well versed in the canonical place of legitimacy in theorisations of sovereignty, most notably through Weberian understandings of the state as that 'human community that [successfully] claims the monopoly of *legitimate* use of physical force within a given territory.'[12] I have written elsewhere on the significance of this definition for assertions of state power after conflict, but I want to return to this here to make a specific point about representation, legitimacy and law. Both during and after the conflict in BiH there has been a struggle over the establishment of legal systems aimed to address atrocity crimes committed during the conflict, and in each case claims to the right to make law have rested on varied 'legitimation strategies'.[13] We will see over the course of the book how these claims to legitimacy have varied sources and are often combined, but it is worth outlining three that have become key grounds for claims to law.

The first representational strategy is to ground claims of legitimacy in practices of democracy. Alluding to the 'will of the people' or describing the formation of the state as 'bottom up' have become key phrases in the lexicon of interventions by Western states in conflict and

---

[12] Weber, M. (1958). Politics as a vocation, in H. H. Gerth & C. Wright Mills (eds.), *Max Weber: Essays in sociology*. New York: Oxford University Press, pp. 77–128; emphasis added.

[13] Goddard, S. E. (2009). When right makes might: How Prussia overturned the European balance of power. *International Security* 33(3): 110–142.

post-conflict environments. One of the origin points of this narrative can be found at the end of World War I when US President Woodrow Wilson (1918) enshrined peoples' right of self-determination as a central principle of international legitimation: '"Self-determination" is not a mere phrase. It is an imperative principle of action, which statesmen will henceforth ignore at their peril'.[14] Over the course of the twentieth century there have been many reassertions of this discursive strategy, from post-colonial independence movements in the wake of World War II to the theatres of conflict during the Cold War. Perhaps the most explicit recent invocation of 'democratisation' has occurred in the developmental and military pursuits launched in the wake of the fall of authoritarian regimes following the end of the Cold War and the breakup of the USSR. The fragmentation of Yugoslavia shares many aspects of these strategies, as external agencies both adjudicated the legitimacy of state claims and justified subsequent interventions based on the presence (or otherwise) of democracy.

The key rhetorical point here is what counts as 'democracy' is both plural and mutable. Certainly, we need to be attentive to the differences between 'procedural' (framed around elections and referenda) and 'substantive' (focusing on equality, justice and fairness) understandings of the term, and how these different interpretations interact with assertions of law and legality. For example, democratisation in central and eastern Europe following the end of the Cold War combined a promotion of democratic procedure alongside a more abstract desire to cultivate 'civil society', a realm of associative life between the state and the market. But concentrating on procedural/substantive distinctions can lead to us to interpret democratisation as a form of governance, ignoring more critical accounts that point to the appropriation of the language of democracy to bolster fundamentally undemocratic interventions.[15] In this optic, democratisation is understood as a tool of discipline, where interventions are directed to the organisation and priorities of state governance. The animus of democratisation is less a concern for the will of the people and more a preoccupation with

---

[14] Abulof, U. (2016). We the peoples? The strange demise of self-determination. *European Journal of International Relations* 22(3), 536–565, p. 536; Wilson, W. (1918). President's address to Congress. *The Washington Post*, 12 February.

[15] See Barnett, C., & Low, M. (eds.). (2004). *Spaces of democracy: Geographical perspectives on citizenship, participation and representation*. London: Sage.

the construction and maintenance of Western hegemony.[16] Such critical perspectives call into question the authorial position of those presenting interventions as 'democratising', setting these alongside the experience of those subjected to military, political or developmental campaigns.

The second – and connected – grounding of legitimacy is in the inviolability of state sovereignty. This is, of course, a key strand of international law and the basis of state territoriality; a disruption to the spatial ordering of a single state poses an existential threat to the wider state system. The material consequences of the sanctity of state territoriality are evident in the bordering practices of states, where securitising the outer limits of the state becomes a core symbolic and practical aspect of statecraft. Despite claims of increasing globalism and the celebratory rhetoric of the ending of divisions in Germany and South Africa in the late 1980s and 1990s, recent years have seen an unprecedented spate of wall-building and securitisation at international borders. These acts have stimulated an intriguing debate as to whether securitisation of borders constitutes a signal of state strength or a performance of its weakness in the face of globalising forces. For Wendy Brown it is the latter, as such practices of 'late modern walling' are evidence of the theatricality of states, as they 'project ... power and efficaciousness that they do not and cannot exercise and that they performatively contradict'.[17] By focusing on walling's theatricality we are forced to pose the question of who it is for: The defence of the state against unwanted intruders? Or a performance of state strength for an internal population experiencing a sense of vulnerability in a changing world? Securitisation serves both functions, signalling the legitimising value of territorial control to the enactment of state sovereignty.

But, as with democratisation, preserving state territoriality diverges, in practice, from its normative claims and illuminates the coexistence of competing sovereignty claims. The act of walling imagines a static and universally agreed state system, rather than the dynamic set of sovereignty assertions we see in the world today. A lexicon has emerged to describe the partial statehood that stalks each corner of the world, from the anomalous to the unrecognised, the non-state to

---

[16] See Abrahamsen, R. (2000). *Disciplining democracy: Development discourse and good governance in Africa*. London: Zed Books.
[17] Brown, W. (2010). *Walled states waning sovereignty*. Cambridge, MA: MIT Press, p. 25.

the state-in-waiting. Each of these claims to statehood convey different assertions of legitimacy, each seeking recognition and protection. Beyond the clear tension here between democratic will and the protection of state sovereignty, there is the paradox – most starkly illustrated in the United States' 2003 Operation Iraqi Freedom – where a violent transgression of a state's territory is legitimised as an act in preserving the sovereignty of the state.[18] As in the case of our discussion of democratisation, we could dismiss the elastic and contradictory use of sovereignty preservation as a mask for the operation of global power politics. But one of the more productive approaches has been to retheorise sovereignty, specifically unbundling sovereignty from the territoriality of the state. In this context, sovereignty is understood less as a contained authority and more as an abstract form of power that is expressed in a variety of spatial settings: from prison camps to refugee centres, securitised urban spaces to military bases. Disentangled from straightforward notions of territoriality, such enactments of sovereignty focus on the biopolitics of contemporary global power, how populations are managed and regulated through the practices of global institutions, both state and non-state. It such a recognition of the ability to project power beyond state borders that leads scholars and commentators to speculate on the emergence of new forms of empire and imperialism that defy isolation to an individual state bureaucracy and are rather distributed through networks of governmental and corporate actors.

HUMANITARIANISM: SOLIDARITY AND SOVEREIGNTY

If democratisation and the preservation of state sovereignty are two powerful legitimation strategies for international intervention, the third – the discourse of humanitarianism – sees them brought together through normative concerns for the plight of fellow humans. The antecedents of the international tribunal in practices of humanitarianism is neither incidental nor without legal significance. It reflects the shift that had taken place across the twentieth century in the form and function of international law, as the subject of legal processes moved from states to individuals. It is here that we see the significance of the Nuremberg trials, as culpability for atrocities was projected down to individual political and military leaders rather than to the German

---

[18] Elden, *Terror and territory*.

state. In legal terms, the Nuremberg trials were particularly significant in provoking debate concerning transnational jurisprudence, though rather than being framed in terms of jurisdiction (or the spatial limits of legal authority) these debates centred on the temporality of law. Legal positivists argued that adherence to the rule of law included recognition of antecedent law as valid, hence if the actions during World War II were legal under Nazi law there are no grounds to retrospectively undertake criminal proceedings. In contrast, legal idealists promoted a concept of substantive justice, where certain crimes existed that were of such severity that they necessitated breaking with prior (in this case Nazi) legal systems.[19] This friction between legal positivism (the absolute authority of existing rule of law) and idealism (the existence of 'crimes against humanity' that transcend any single jurisdiction) has shaped the subsequent form and discursive context of international courts and tribunals. In particular, political elites (at both global and national scales) have sought to carefully proscribe when and where the rule of law is absolute, and conversely identify which military or paramilitary actions can be considered 'crimes against humanity': positivist legal formalism for some, idealist humanitarianism for others.

The shift to retributive forms of transitional justice in the wake of World War II ensured that it was individual punishment and not state-level reparations that characterised legal redress in the wake of the Holocaust.[20] The 1948 Universal Declaration of Human Rights (UDHR) and the subsequent growing concern for humanitarian crises reflect the changing orientation of international law, as both culpability and suffering are projected onto individual human bodies. Following Mark Duffield,[21] we can describe this as a growing *biopolitics* of humanitarianism, where the management and regulation of human bodies becomes the primary focus of IHL. There is nascent anti-statism in the UDHR, where sovereignty is contingent and violable in circumstances of mass atrocity or humanitarian crisis. But, shifting the locus of moral responsibility does not mean law deterritorialises. Instead the rising prominence of IHL has produced new landscapes of legal authority; new claims to protecting the rights and lives of distant strangers.

---

[19] Teitel, R. G. (2000). *Transitional justice*. Oxford: Oxford University Press, p. 13.
[20] See Goldstone, R. (2000). *For humanity: Reflections of a war crimes investigator*. New Haven, CT: Yale University Press, p. 75.
[21] Duffield, M. (2001). Governing the borderlands: Decoding the power of aid. *Disasters* 25(4): 308–320.

Where humanitarian concern can be characterised as an aspatial sensitivity; its histories, institutionalisation within tribunals and its subsequent legal form reflect prevailing geopolitical hierarchies and arrangements.

The ethics of humanitarianism reflect this tension between idealism and pragmatism. In some respects, the establishment of *ad hoc* tribunals and juridical response to war crime seem to cohere with a Kantian ethics where the virtues of thinking beyond the narrow state interests may provide the conceptual basis to limit the excesses of sovereign violence.[22] But such species-level concerns should not be read off as a move to a more virtuous or morally – attuned foreign policy, rather it is a manoeuvre that must be set with the geopolitical frameworks that shape the colonial and post–Cold War world. It seems appropriate, therefore, that Didier Fassin should draw a distinction between 'humanitarian morals (the principle on which actions are based and justified) and humanitarian politics (the implementation of these actions)'.[23] This helpful dichotomy is one that appears in much writing on the validity of a Kantian humanitarian ethics: between the ideals and the practice, or what Seyla Benhabib calls 'the growing normative incongruities between international human rights norms, particularly as they pertain to the "rights of others" ... and assertions of territorial sovereignty'.[24] In a sense – and following the path set down by Fassin – the task at hand is to explore the relationship between these two fields: or, in other words, the ways in which the imaginaries of humanitarian ethics are institutionalised and practiced in particular local settings and with what political effects.

The potential distance between the ideals and practices of humanitarianism has provoked a range of scholarly enquires that seek to ground humanitarianism in actual existing political interventions. Chomsky's account of the 1999 NATO intervention in Kosovo stands as a critical touchstone for such work: a text that sought to challenge the accounts of London and Washington on the official purpose of the NATO intervention in Kosovo (a response to Serb atrocities in Kosovo), arguing instead that the intervention reflected a new unipolar

---

[22] See Hoffe, O. (1994). *Immanuel Kant*. New York: SUNY Press.
[23] Fassin, D. (2011). *Humanitarian reason: A moral history of the present*. Berkeley: University of California Press, p. 8.
[24] Benhabib, S. (2004). *The rights of others: Aliens, residents, and citizens*. Cambridge: Cambridge University Press, p. 7.

world where the US-led NATO would project its power through military adventurism.[25] Here, humanitarianism stands as a virtuous discursive frame, masking narrower sovereign interests pursued through aerial bombardment of an impoverished nascent state. Weizman's account of the ethics of modern military intervention makes a similar claim, though he traces this through a thickening web of agencies, norms, values and materials.[26] For Weizman, humanitarianism, human rights and IHL, 'when abused by state, supra-state and military action, have become the crucial means by which the economy of violence is calculated and managed'.[27] The monitoring of human life, calculating its vulnerabilities and weighing these into the nature and form of military incursions is the hallmark of what Weizman terms 'the humanitarian present'. The enactment of IHL lies at the heart of these processes, not least its emphasis on the proportionality of violence enacted during conflict. Weizman draws attention to two significant challenges in the implementation of IHL. First, that the upholding of IHL does nothing to try and limit war. It is directed solely at the appropriate forms of conduct during war. Second, the principle of proportionality provides 'no scale, no formulas and no numerical thresholds ... it demands assessment on a case-by-case basis, within parameters that are always relative, situational and immanent'.[28]

In the absence of immutable frameworks guiding the implementation of IHL there is a requirement to consider the moments and institutions through which such humanitarian law has been implemented and with what effects. Though a seeming contradiction, many of the studies tracing such implementations have focused their attention away from the process of law to look at the social contexts, political frameworks and inter-subjective relationships through which legal processes operate.[29] Reflecting this approach, Boyle and Kobayashi explore the outcomes of people-led war crimes tribunals (PLWCTs) and in

---

[25] Chomsky, N. (1999). *The new military humanism: Lessons from Kosovo*. London: Pluto Press.
[26] Weizman, E. (2011). *The least of all possible evils: Humanitarian violence from Arendt to Gaza*. London: Verso Books.
[27] Ibid., 3–4.
[28] Ibid., 12.
[29] See, *inter alia*, Hughes, R. (2015). Ordinary theatre and extraordinary law at the Khmer Rouge Tribunal. *Environment and Planning D: Society and Space* 33(4): 714–731; Jeffrey, A., & Jakala, M. (2014). The hybrid legal geographies of a war crimes court. *Annals of the Association of American Geographers* 104(3): 652–667.

particular the Russell Tribunal 1966–1967, set up to debate the actions of the US government in Vietnam.[30] This study does not centre on the legal implications of this initiative, but on the resources and ethical implications of attempting an extra-juridical justice instrument. This analysis deliberately oscillates at the meeting point of two interpretations of ethics, a *humanitarian ethics* delivered by 'neutral, cool, and disembodied actors who apply universal particulars', and *care ethics* practised by 'engaged, emotional, and disembodied actors who reach judgements in the context of complex relationships'.[31] But this distinction is difficult to sustain in practice. Instead, the forms of ethical judgement that emerge through the operation of PLWCTs are rejecting the colonial logics of the imagined neutrality of Kantian ethics, but simultaneously resisting sliding into ethical relativism. For Boyle and Kobayashi, this necessitates a focus on the practical reasoning through which ethical judgement comes into being, a product of historical and geographical relationships traced on the ground and through situated human bodies.

THE INTERNATIONAL CRIMINAL TRIBUNAL FOR THE FORMER YUGOSLAVIA

One of the signature traits of international judicial instruments is the somewhat ill-defined character of their creation. While it is commonplace to cite UN Security Council Resolution 827 as the legal grounds for the work of the ICTY and its publication date (25 May 1993) as its moment of inception, the material and political circumstances of its creation are more complex. As with any organ of international justice, the founding of the ICTY was shaped by the prevailing geopolitical forces of the time, some fleeting, others going on to shape its work for the subsequent decades. Perhaps most significantly, the ICTY was established while the fighting in the BiH war was still ongoing, hence this was not a tribunal facing a clearly demarcated past regime, but a legal instrument that was entering into the fray of the moral adjudication and – inevitably – the legal classification of an ongoing conflict. From the very start, the ICTY could not claim

---

[30] Boyle, M., & Kobayashi, A. (2015). In the face of epistemic injustices? On the meaning of people-led war crimes tribunals. *Environment and Planning D: Society and Space* 33(4): 697–713.

[31] Ibid.

some dispassionate separation. It was, even in its inaction, an active agent in the unfolding violence.

It would be tempting to try and parse the geopolitical context of the ICTY's creation into different spatial scales, imagining the events in the meeting rooms of the UN Security Council are in some ways at a scale apart from the bloodshed in the towns and villages of former Yugoslavia. But there was an assemblage of political and legal issues that each sought to challenge the ability of local legal actors to exert criminal responsibility for the events of the war. This was a moment of global triumphalism, where the end of the Cold War had provided 'a fertile environment for the renaissance of international criminal justice',[32] a reference to a rekindling of the rubric of humanitarian law that had framed the Nuremburg and Tokyo tribunals in the wake of World War II. But this renaissance had been in progress long before the fall of the Berlin Wall and the fragmentation of the USSR. Its roots can be found in the growing intellectual and political concern with human rights, both as a response to specific forms of militarism and as new field of international jurisprudence. One of the interesting characteristics of this emerging form of transnational legalism is that it was led by civil society actors, including new NGOs such as Amnesty International and Human Rights Watch; philanthropic foundations such as Soros and the MacArthur Foundations; and key human rights lawyers.[33]

The emergence of the ICTY came at a moment when international intervening agencies were struggling to define and categorise the violence spreading across the territory of the former Yugoslav Republic. It is here we can trace a struggle over representation: Was this a civil war, of little concern to outside powers? Or a war of aggression by a powerful state on a vulnerable and newly independent neighbour? Was the violence a consequence of 'ancient ethnic hatreds'? This crisis of narration is not surprising. The fragmentation of Yugoslavia confounded the normative underpinnings of the international system, as the democratic right of self-determination came into conflict with the desire to protect minority rights. This is best illustrated in the travails of the Arbitration Commission on the Peace Conference for Yugoslavia (commonly known as the Badinter Arbitration Commission) tasked with giving opinion on

---

[32] Schabas, W. (2012). *Unimaginable atrocities: Justice, politics, and rights at the war crimes tribunals*. Oxford: Oxford University Press, p. 14.
[33] Hagan, J. (2003). *Justice in the Balkans*. Chicago: Chicago University Press.

the major legal questions posed by the dissolution of Yugoslavia. Following referenda in the Yugoslav republics of Slovenia and Croatia the European Economic Community (the precursor to the European Union) granted recognition of their status as independent states based on the principal of self-determination. Democratisation, then, was at the heart of state recognition, where the holding of a popular vote constituted a reflection of the will of the people.

The situation in BiH, as is well documented, was more challenging than other Yugoslav Republics and presented greater legal ambiguity. This is not the place for a detailed explanation of these events, there are a multitude of detailed accounts of the unfolding violence across the territory of BiH between 1992 and 1995.[34] But we need to trace some of the key dynamics of the conflict to understand the subsequent contestation over legal redress. Democratic legitimacy, as with in the cases of Croatia and Slovenia, rested on an expression of the will of the BiH population to cede from what remained of Federal Republic of Yugoslavia. But the demographics of BiH did not suit this democratic proceduralism: the absence of a majority between the three main ethic groups (Bosnian Muslim, Serb and Croat)[35] and the growing alignment between party politics and ethnic identity meant that a straightforward majority outcome would not assuage the fears of emergent minority groups. This proved to be the case: a referendum on independence of BiH was held on 29 February 1992, with a turnout of 63.4 per cent and a positive vote in excess of 99 per cent. The relatively low turnout reflected the absence of voters loyal to Serb causes, some boycotting the vote and others prevented from participating by Serb authorities.[36] Despite this, one month later the European Community and the United States recognised Bosnia's independence, citing the majority vote at the referendum.[37]

---

[34] See, for example, Glenny, M. (1996). *The fall of Yugoslavia: The third Balkan war*. London: Penguin Books; Ridgeway, J., & Udovički, J. (2000). *Burn this house: The making and unmaking of Yugoslavia*. Durham, NC: Duke University Press; Silber, L., & Little, A. (1996). *The death of Yugoslavia*. London: Penguin Books.

[35] See earlier discussion for the problems that surround the uses of these identity labels.

[36] Zimmerman, W. (1996). *Origins of a catastrophe Yugoslavia and its destroyers – America's last ambassador tells what happened and why*. London: Times Books, p. 188.

[37] For a detailed discussion of the contestation around these processes see Rich, R. (1993). Symposium: Recent developments in the practice of state recognition. *European Journal of International Law* 36: 36–65.

Recognition, then, was a product of the appearance of democratic politics where the will of the people was captured by the outcome of the referendum. But, of course, there are other ways of interpreting democracy, in particular separating such procedural aspects of democracy from more substantive features, in particular equality, justice and the protection of minority rights.[38] The outcome of the referendum was interpreted by the Bosnian Serb military and political elite, led by Radovan Karadžić, as a threat to their national security as Serbs assumed a minority status within the newly recognised BiH state. In attempting to establish a Serb state, the Republika Srpska carved from the territory of BiH, Karadžić was seeking to claim the production of a new sovereign entity, independent of BiH. Realising this project would involve spectacular violence, not least because the population of BiH was, particularly in urban areas, highly mixed. Indeed the outbreak of war can be seen as a mass consciousness-raising exercise in the primacy of ethnic identity across the territory of BiH. Where it had been incidental or difficult to discern in the past it became the primary identity marker as military and symbolic violence spread across the BiH territory in 1992.[39]

Wielding this ethnic matrix as a tool to produce exclusive territorial control, Bosnian Serb leader, Radovan Karadžić, claimed that then, as in the past, the outside powers were bent against Serbian sovereignty.[40] These ethno-national proclamations were taken as a call to arms, as during April 1992 Serbian paramilitaries began fighting for territory across Bosnia. These efforts were aided by the Yugoslav People's Army (JNA), who had redeployed out of Slovenia and Croatia and had seen a vast swelling of their number in the Serb areas of Bosnia. In early April 1992, heavy artillery surrounded Sarajevo, and would hold this position until the signing of the Dayton Agreement three and a half years later.

External attempts to make sense of the violence in BiH placed a distinctive emphasis on its complexity. Repeated assertions were made

---

[38] For a detailed discussion of this distinction see Bell, J. E., & Staeheli, L. A. (2001). Discourses of diffusion and democratization. *Political Geography* 20(2): 175–195.
[39] Human Rights Watch (1992). *War crimes in Bosnia-Hercegovina*. New York: Human Rights Watch.
[40] P. 179 in Udovicki, J., & Stikovac, E. (2000). Bosnia and Hercegovina: The second war, in Udovicki, J., & Ridgeway, J. (eds.), *Burn this house: The making and unmaking of Yugoslavia*. Durham, NC: Duke University Press, pp. 175–216.

by intervening agencies from both Europe and the United States that this was a conflict that defied simple geopolitical logics; its roots were instead traced to deficiencies in the character BiH's people. This move involved two forms of erasure. First, the wider geopolitical dynamics of the fragmentation of Yugoslavia were underplayed, overlooking the growing economic inequality between the six republics, the increasing centralisation of power in the hands of Slobodan Milošević ignored; and the altered status of Yugoslavia in the post–Cold War world. The second was an appreciation of the banal roots of the violence, as it stemmed from the cultivation of ethno-national rhetoric in political parties, football hooligans and criminal gangs.[41] As opposed to analysis that coupled these wider geopolitical dynamics with the emergence of everyday and brutal violence, the conflict was interpreted as a consequence of the character of the people of BiH. Not a political or military strategy, but an expression of a Hobbesian state of nature.

As cultural studies scholars have noted, the underlying representative strategy here shares much with Said's *Orientalism*, as the violence in BiH was seen to stem from ancient ethnic hatreds, a primordial disposition towards violence intrinsic to the Balkan people. There is an established body of work tracing such *Balkanist* interpretations of the violence, in doing so inserting the conflict into a much longer lineage of cultural production of the Balkans as backwards and deviant in contrast to the civilised and progressive West.[42] Confusion, complexity and ancient enmity were intertwined in such interpretations, characterised by then UK Prime Minister John Major's description of the violence as an unexpected calamity, '[creeping] up on us while our attention was on the turmoil in the Soviet Union, and took us almost unawares.... Its roots were bewildering'.[43] One particular tactic was to draw a parallel between Northern Ireland (as opposed to the Falklands or Iraq) and Bosnia, thereby evoking the long-term 'quagmire' of military intervention.[44] The US administrations of George H. W. Bush and Bill Clinton, who were keen to draw parallels between Bosnia

---

[41] Andreas, P. (2004). The clandestine political economy of war and peace in Bosnia. *International Studies Quarterly* 48(1): 29–51.
[42] See Todorova, M. (2009). *Imagining the Balkans*. Oxford: Oxford University Press.
[43] Major, J. (1999). *John Major: The autobiography*. London: Harper Collins, p. 532.
[44] Simms, B. (2001). *Unfinest hour: Britain and the destruction of Bosnia*. London: Penguin Books Ltd., p. 5.

and Vietnam, echoed this policy.[45] Crucially for this study, Balkanist interpretations of the violence obscured legal categories of perpetrator and victim, focusing instead on the general suffering of the BiH population.

It seems surprising considering the precedent of Slovenia and then Croatia that the international community found it so difficult to predict this emerging conflict in Bosnia. Government ministers in the United Kingdom continued to draw upon the rhetoric of regional complexity and 'ancient ethnic hatreds' to justify a policy of non-intervention. On countless other occasions during the Bosnian war, the UK government, and other members of the international community, would reproduce this strategy of casting confusion over this 'bewildering' conflict. What was avoided within these geopolitical scripts was any suggestion of the 'banality' of the conflict and the possibility that it was driven not by a frenzy of mass ethnic-based nationalism but 'largely by small groups of politically empowered thugs (substantially drawn from the ranks of bands of soccer hooligans, criminal gangs and released prisoners)'.[46] Instead it seems that Balkanism had a pervasive effect on UK policy making. Non-intervention was justified through a portrayal of the events in Bosnia as a collective 'moral sickness'.[47] At this crucial stage in the destruction of Yugoslavia, the foreign policy of the United Kingdom appeared to be dictated by a dispassionate realism. This position is perhaps exemplified in the case of the reports on Omarska concentration camp broadcast in the summer of 1992 by the journalists Ed Vulliamy, Penny Marshall and Ian Williams. The images of gaunt men standing behind barbed-wire fences raised the spectre of genocide on the European continent and sparked global public consternation at the lack of punitive measures against those that were responsible. While Western leaders individually spoke of the need to hold individuals to account for war crimes, the prospect of an international judicial instrument capable of prosecuting individuals was still far off. As Pierre Hazan has outlined in his comprehensive account of the emergence of judicial mechanisms during the Bosnian war, European leaders feared that an international tribunal would

---

[45] Ó Tuathail, G. (1996). *Critical geopolitics*. London: Routledge.
[46] Andreas, The clandestine political economy, 32.
[47] See Owen, D. (1998). *Five wars in the former Yugoslavia*. Abu Dhabi: The Emirates Center for Strategic Studies and Research.

jeopardise chances of a negotiated peace.[48] In place of a tribunal, the Security Council agreed to a more limited commission to gather evidence of potential war crimes in October 1922. This body, known as the Commission of Experts Pursuant to Security Council 780 (abbreviated to 'the Commission of Experts'), was hampered from the outset by a lack of any allocated funds or resources. As Hazan notes, the Commission of Experts appeared to have been established as a public relations exercise – to demonstrate 'something was being done' – without the resources to harm the ongoing diplomatic effort in Bosnia. The commission rapporteur, Cherif Bassiouni, finally took the astonishing step of moving the Commission of Expert's activities from the (under-resourced) UN offices in Geneva to his university offices at DePaul University, Chicago, assuring computer access and establishing a secure archive of testimonies and observations.[49]

The case of the Commission of Experts serves as a precursor to the establishment of the ICTY. In 1993, the newly elected US President Bill Clinton viewed the establishment of an international tribunal as an alternative to his election campaign pledge to lift the arms embargo on the former Yugoslavia and carry out air strikes on Serb military positions. This new political will is supported by the then French foreign minister Roland Dumas, who since 1992 had mounted a personal campaign to establish a war crimes tribunal in the face of continuing reports from Bosnia of systematic rape, executions and the expulsion of civilians from their home.[50] Despite continuing reluctance from the United Kingdom, and concerns from China and Russia over precedent setting, the Security Council established the ICTY through Resolution 827 on 25 May 1993. In response to what it considered as 'grave breaches of the Geneva Conventions' the Resolution 827 tasked the tribunal with 'prosecuting persons responsible for serious violations of IHL committed in the territory of the former Yugoslavia' from January 1991 onwards.[51]

Reading the text of Resolution 827, the intention behind the court becomes clear: the preservation of international order.

---

[48] Hazan, P. (2004). *Justice in a time of war: The true story behind the International Criminal Tribunal for the Former Yugoslavia.* College Station: Texas A&M University Press.
[49] Ibid., 26–30.
[50] See ibid., pp. 34–37.
[51] Security Council Resolution 827, 25 May 1993.

> The Security Council ... [e]xpressing once again its grave alarm at continuing reports of widespread and flagrant violations of international humanitarian law occurring within the territory of the former Yugoslavia, and especially in the Republic of Bosnia and Herzegovina, including reports of mass killings, massive, organized and systematic detention and rape of women, and the continuance of the practice of 'ethnic cleansing', including for the acquisition and the holding of territory, [d]etermining that this situation continues to constitute a threat to international peace and security.[52]

The mandate of the ICTY states that it may claim 'primacy and may take over national investigations and proceedings at any stage if this proves to be in the interest of international justice'. The tribunal was comprised of three organs: a judiciary, initially consisting of 11 judges, though by 2008 they numbered 30; the Office of the Prosecutor, a position held by Richard Goldstone (1993–1995), Louise Arbour (1995–1999), Carla Del Ponte (1999–2008) and, since 2008, by Serge Brammertz; and the Registry, which provided administrative support.

The stated aim of the ICTY was always identify / prosecute / single out the principal actors responsible for the violence in BiH:

> The Council recognizes, as it has done on other occasions (for example in its resolution 1329 (2000) of 30 November 2000), that the ICTY should concentrate its work on the prosecution and trial of the civilian, military and paramilitary leaders suspected of being responsible for serious violations of international humanitarian law committed in the territory of the former Yugoslavia since 1991, rather than on minor actors.[53]

This limited remit carries a number of assumptions. The first is that the trials of high-ranking or prominent perpetrators of war crimes has a wider impact than a punitive function directed at an individual. The retributive process was imagined at the outset to communicate a broader message of the end of impunity for political and military elites in the prosecution of war. The second assumption is that the audience for the actions of the ICTY is located both within and beyond the borders of the former Yugoslav states. While, as Nettelfield suggests, the ICTY has clearly performed an important role within the borders of

---

[52] Ibid.
[53] Statement by the President of the Security Council S/PRST/2002/21, United Nations Security Council, 23 July 2002.

BiH in terms of 'norm change',[54] its impacts were blunted through the selective nature of indictments and the absence of a public outreach strategy until 1999, six years into its operation. In terms of a wider public, the ICTY served an experimental function for legal scholars across the globe: its innovation in international jurisprudence became a touchstone for work on the possibilities of international criminal justice.[55]

Taken together, the ICTY's formation and function, at least initially, reflected an attachment to humanitarian reason. It was designed as a mechanism of holding individuals to account for atrocities of such magnitude that they contravened international legal norms, as set out in the Geneva Conventions. Its legitimacy was founded in cosmopolitan accounts of law that assumed there were instances where the requirements of a common humanity were of greater significance than the legal sovereignty of individual states. Of course, compliance with the ICTY was enshrined in the Dayton General Framework Agreement for Peace (GFAP) signed in Paris in December 1995. But as the ICTY completed its indictment process and trials of key figures in the fragmentation of Yugoslavia the need to shift from a 'humanitarian' narrative of justice to an emphasis on the legitimacy of state sovereignty and the democratisation of judicial instruments grew. It is this reorientation towards the legal primacy of the state that occupies the remaining chapters of the book.

THE CREATION OF THE WAR CRIMES CHAMBER OF THE COURT OF BOSNIA AND HERZEGOVINA

On the 6 June 2002, the newly appointed replacement to Wolfgang Petritsch as High Representative, Paddy Ashdown, attended the inaugural session of the CBiH. To the assembled dignitaries and the newly appointed domestic and international judiciary, Ashdown outlined the

---

[54] Nettelfield, L. J. (2010). *Courting democracy in Bosnia and Herzegovina*. Cambridge: Cambridge University Press.
[55] See Engvall, L. (2007). The future of extended joint criminal enterprise: Will the ICTY's innovation meet the standards of the ICC? *Nordic Journal of International Law* 76(2/3): 241; Boas, G. (2000). Comparing the ICTY and the ICC: Some procedural and substantive issues. *Netherlands International Law Review* 47(3): 267–291.

significance of the inauguration of the Court to the establishment of the Bosnia and Herzegovinian state:

> [The inauguration] is about protecting the people of this country, protecting their rights and protecting their status as free citizens in a functioning democracy. This court enshrines a simple truth – that everyone is equal before the law. Justice is the foundation on which every society is built. Everything else we want to do here, from jobs to refugee returns to establishing a democratic system, depends on the rule of law.... A functioning judicial system is a key component of BiH's integration into European structures.[56]

From the outset the Court's creation has been about more than simply providing a new space to pursue legal redress. As indicated in Ashdown's comments, the Court has a symbolic function of constructing the internal and external legitimacy of BiH sovereignty. In internal terms, this has been a slow process involving the adoption of a new criminal procedure code in early 2003, based on US common law. This move aimed to transform prosecution and trial processes, in particular eliminating the need for an investigative judge, and introducing adversarial trial arrangements and introducing plea bargaining.[57] The commencement of trials at the Court required the training of domestic judiciary and the establishment of the State Investigation and Prosecution Agency (*Državna agencija za istrage i zaštitu* or SIPA). There was also the more straightforward need to locate a building that could house the trial processes and the necessary registry functions. The ultimate choice was to locate the building on the site of a former Yugoslav People's Army (Jugoslovenska narodna armija or JNA) barracks on Kraljice Jelene street, around five kilometres outside the centre of Sarajevo.

The slow and contested process by which the CBiH has come into existence illuminates the struggles to demonstrate the external legitimacy of BiH. At every stage, the creation of the court required international intervention, whether through: the drafting of laws; the use of

---

[56] Office of the High Representative (2002). *Remarks by the High Representative, Paddy Ashdown, at the inaugural session of the BiH State Court*, www.ohr.int/ohr-dept/presso/presssp/default.asp?content_id=8657 (accessed 12 November 2018).

[57] See Organisation for Security and Cooperation in Europe (2004). *OSCE Trial Monitoring Report*, www.oscebih.org/documents/osce_bih_doc_20101223105351111eng.pdf (accessed 11 March 2014).

executive powers to pass criminal procedure codes blocked by domestic legislators; the creation of a hybrid domestic and international judiciary; or raising capital for the court building through two donor conferences staged in The Hague (2003 and 2006), where governments pledged a total of more than €20 million. Of course, such impositions can lead to claims of the unwanted nature of the institutions or the anti-democratic characteristics of intervention.[58] But the court was also serving a wider international purpose as part of the completion mandate for the ICTY. From 2005 onwards the Court has accepted transferred cases from the ICTY while SIPA has also commenced investigations of newly uncovered crimes committed during the 1992–1995 conflict in BiH. The establishment of rule of law, and cooperation with the ICTY, is also an essential element of the Stabilisation and Association Agreement for negotiations over BiH's potential accession to the European Union. Recognition of BiH as a legitimate member of the international community required the demonstration a coherent, centralised and competent legal structure.

We can understand the production of a state legal system as a geopolitical practice because it is structured around a series of spatial imaginaries of the state. The first is the normative construction of the state as the locus of moral authority through which legal arbitration should be undertaken. This sense of the localisation of judicial processes reflects a response to what Neil Walker has referred to as the 'sovereignty surplus': where European citizens experience multiple layers of sovereign authority, entangling both state and European structures of governance.[59] The construction of the Court is – symbolically at least – a means through which the BiH state territoriality and sovereignty may be strengthened and asserted. The second aspect of such geopolitics of justice reflects the desire to perform a separation of responsibility between intervening agencies and the BiH state. In a language that tends to infantilise, the construction of the BiH legal system has been presented as the 'growing responsibility' of the BiH state for the crimes of its past and present.[60] The creation of a

---

[58] See, for example, Chandler, D. (1999). *Bosnia: Faking democracy after Dayton*. London: Pluto Press.

[59] Walker, N. (2010). Surface and depth: The EU's resilient sovereignty question. *University of Edinburgh School of Law Working Paper* 2010/10.

[60] Jansson, E. (2005). Risk of instability remains a factor, *The Financial Times*, 14 November.

new legal institution – like other aspects of state building – performs a sense of the democratisation of the new state coupled with the severing of responsibility of intervening actors.

But if the fraught processes of international state building after the Cold War have illustrated one persistent truth it is that there is a dissonance between the establishment of a new sovereign institution and its reception by the domestic population as a legitimate materialisation of the state. To understand the functioning of the Court we need to disentangle form and effect, to explore how the CBiH has been asserted and the sorts of contestation that have characterised its existence. These events speak not only of the challenge of assuming the construction of new state institutions necessarily leads to a strengthening of state sovereignty, but also point to the ways in which questions of trauma and victimhood are mobilised in the urban post-conflict landscape to assert alternative ideas of state legitimacy. This style of analysis carries the danger of viewing a straightforward geometry of power between the assertion of state sovereignty and more insurgent practices that seek to deliver its destabilisation.[61] This duality can naturalise a series of assumptions, for example that internationally conferred authority is more legitimate than other forms of practice or, alternatively, that domestically organised resistance to the Court carries with it an implicit democratic virtue. Of course, in practice neither is true because at every stage this form of scalar or normative politics is contested in practice.

Instead, we need to look to the forms of resources mobilised by agents to improvise the state, and from this certain assumptions about the nature of statehood and law come to the fore. To this end, we need to look beyond these broad (and broadly virtuous) accounts of the geopolitical implications of strengthening domestic legal systems and explore instead the effects of their creation and operation. Drawing analytical inspiration from Michael Dwyer's work on the varied conceptualisation of security in contemporary Laos,[62] we need to trace the *micro-geopolitics* of law. How particular outcomes reflect the wider assemblage of ideas, bodies and materials within which they are embedded. It is through these situated practices that we can begin to trace the

---

[61] Holston, J. (2008). *Insurgent citizenship disjunctions of democracy and modernity in Brazil*. Princeton, NJ: Princeton University Press.

[62] Dwyer, M. B. (2014). Micro-geopolitics: Capitalising security in Laos's golden quadrangle. *Geopolitics* 19(2): 377–405.

aesthetics and practices through which the adjudication of state legitimacy is traced and contested.

To understand the contestation over the CBiH and its particular micro-geopolitics we need to return to its performance and materiality, a specific focus of the following chapter. As Mulcahy has argued the architecture of court buildings represents more than simply the backdrop to legal processes. Their form and arrangement reflect relationships between authority and society.[63] Such attention to the physical manifestation of legal practice is particularly important where courts are used to consolidate and strengthen 'weak' states. A focus on materiality points to the inherent issue of visuality that underscores new judicial institutions and practices: it is not simply a case of ensuring that justice is done, but that it is *seen to be done*. Clarkson's (2014) account of the construction of the new South African Constitutional Court in Hillbrow, Johannesburg, highlights the significance of visibility. Identifying this location as a site where political prisoners were held during the Apartheid, she observes that in this act '[c]ertain events of the past *now* become the history of the constituted future, and the physical act of constructing a building itself lays the foundational stone of the constitution in both a literal and metaphoric sense'.[64] Demonstrating a political strategy of orientating citizenship around a shared future,[65] the South African example points to the power of reconfiguring the urban landscape to both commemorate and emphasise a decisive break with the past.

Similar themes of commemoration have encircled the establishment of the Court of Bosnia and Herzegovina, in particular through its building on Kraljice Jelene. The shift in context between the South African Constitutional Court and the CBiH is marked: the establishment of any state-level institution or competence in BiH has been strongly resisted by those who perceive such actions as eroding the constitutional arrangements established at the GFAP. In many ways the struggle over the legitimacy of the BiH state is materialised in the creation and workings of the Court. Perhaps most explicitly, political

---

[63] Mulcahy, L. (2010). *Legal architecture*. Abingdon: Routledge.
[64] Clarkson, C. (2014). *Drawing the line: Towards an aesthetics of transitional justice*. New York: Fordham University Press, p. 78.
[65] See Staeheli, L. A., & Hammett, D. (2010). Educating the new national citizen: Education, political subjectivity and divided societies. *Citizenship Studies* 14(6): 667–680.

leaders in the Republika Srpska, one of two substate political entities in Bosnia and Herzegovina formed at the GFAP, have viewed both the creation of state-level institutions or constitutional reform as direct threats to the autonomy their political entity. It is a measure of the confidence in this resistance that Milorad Dodik, first as prime minister of the RS and later as president, can mount a series of criticisms of the Court, infamously claiming in December 2008 that he would not allow 'Muslim judges' to preside over cases involving RS citizens:

> It is unacceptable for the RS that Muslim judges try us and throw out complaints that are legally founded. And we think that it is only because they are Muslims, Bosniaks and that they have a negative orientation towards the RS, and we see the conspiracy that has been created.
> (Milorad Dodik in B92, 2008)

This entwining of ethnic identity and legal bias reflects the deep entrenchment of what David Campbell,[66] drawing on Derrida,[67] has called the *ontopological* characteristics of Bosnia after the GFAP: where identity and territory are inextricably fused by nationalist politicians. In these terms the processes of legal arbitration is, like other elements of political choice, read off as a consequence of religious or ethnic characteristics.

Dodik's comments illuminate the 'herculean task'[68] of attempting to strengthen state sovereignty through the establishment of a transitional justice institution. The creation of the CBiH challenges ontopology through its territorial jurisdiction over the entire territory of BiH. But to do so, and in light of comments such as those raised by Dodik, it has involved a hybrid judiciary, comprising both domestic and international judges. Here then we see the paradox of using courts to build states: that they at once demand further incursions of external assistance to ensure the survival of an experimental legal instrument. In the case of the CBiH the mandate of the international judiciary has been repeatedly questioned by RS politicians who view their presence as a symbol of the neo-colonial character of the new Court. The

---

[66] Campbell, D. (1998). *National deconstruction: Violence, identity and justice in Bosnia*. Minneapolis: University of Minnesota Press.
[67] Derrida, J. (1994). *Specters of Marx: The state of the debt, the work of mourning and the new international*, trans. Peggy Kamuf. New York: Routledge.
[68] Human Rights Watch (2012). *Key lessons from Bosnia's war crimes prosecutions*, www.hrw.org/news/2012/03/12/bosnia-key-lessons-war-crimes-prosecutions (accessed 12 November 2018).

geopolitical imaginaries of separation and distance cultivated by devolving responsibility to BiH institutions is challenged and subverted through claims of international supervision.

But the lens of improvisation is designed to look at the intricacies through which law is performed rather than the more broad brush geometry of formal political posturing. The presence of international judges does not erase ethnic bias, but neither does a hybrid judiciary necessarily equate with entrenched international involvement. During the research, those working at the Court spoke of the challenge of judges coming together to work in the state Court, often in the shadow of animosity bred through the conflict of the 1990s. 'Everything at the Court is personal' one legal advisor to the CBiH stated during the research 'and most [judges] know each other from the pre-war system' (interview, Sarajevo, 10 December 2011). According to one legal NGO in Sarajevo the presence of the international judiciary was an important aspect of the functioning of the Court because the international judges often had experience of working in war crimes courts in other contexts (not least the ICTY or International Criminal Tribunal for Rwanda or ICTR). In this respect intervening authorities and Court officials have elevated the completion of trial processes above potential criticisms of international supervision. This does not stop resistance from BiH politicians to the presence of an international judiciary because in many ways this has become a proxy arena within which dissent against international involvement in BiH may be voiced.

CONCLUSION

> We are only too aware of the pernicious influence that indicted war criminals, like Mr Karadžić, are still able to exert over BiH's political environment. We know that peace cannot be described as fully entrenched until the perpetrators of these unspeakable crimes are finally brought to justice.[69]

Lord Paddy Ashdown, in a speech delivered at the United Nations in New York in August 2003, sets out a common refrain for the establishment of war crimes trials. By emphasising the need to end impunity, Ashdown publically imagines that the individual war criminal can stand as a proxy for the wider behaviour of groups and individuals both

---

[69] OHR (2018). Speech by High Representative for BiH Lord Paddy Ashdown to the United Nations, www.ohr.int/?p=47391&print=pdf (accessed 8 December 2018).

during conflict and after. The trial of the individual can thereby assist in the healing of a society divided by violence. This durable imagination frames transitional justice mechanisms as deliverers of humanitarian law. In this chapter I have sought to place this discourse of humanitarianism within a wider canvas of sources of legal legitimacy, particularly focusing on the significance of democratisation (will of the people) and the primacy of state sovereignty (the indivisibility of legal authority). The discussion has traced how the course of the emergence of transitional justice mechanisms in the former Yugoslavia, and BiH in particular, exhibits differing emphases on these accounts of the legitimacy of law. In the foundation of the ICTY we see concerns raised by members of the Security Council as to the precedent-setting possibilities of holding individuals accountable for actions during war and wider geopolitical tensions surrounding legal mechanisms at the international level. These deliberations exhibit a clear attachment to the primacy of state sovereignty in authority over law. But the formation of the ICTY, despite its contentious genesis, was framed in terms of the transcendent nature of international law, the significance of which was understood to eclipse that of individuals states. In the words of the first chief prosecutor to the ICTY, it was designed 'for humanity'.[70]

The establishment of the WCC reflects a more hybrid discursive framing. Unquestionably, a humanitarian justification endures, where the holding of individuals to account for atrocities enacted during war is a crucial part of the operation of the court. But this legal function is set within a wider set of political objectives, structured around handing back control of legal processes to BiH (democratisation) while unifying and strengthening the BiH state (enshrining state sovereignty). These differing objectives often sit in tension with one another, and – as we will see in later chapters – provide the basis for sustained contestation over the legal legitimacy of the court. To understand these processes we need to take a closer look at the materialisation of the court in Sarajevo, and how this materiality has shaped the public's perception of the court's impartiality.

[70] Goldstone, *For humanity*.

CHAPTER THREE

COURT MATERIALITY

INTRODUCTION

> *All of us working on the war crimes are under the scrutiny of the thousands of victims on different sides. Thus, we must always keep in mind Martin Luther King's words: 'Injustice anywhere is a threat to justice everywhere.' Those of you, working for the War Crimes Chamber in Sarajevo, will be monitored not only by the International Community, but even more so by your three peoples, two entities, your neighbours. The Court of BH must become a truly national court, which will mean a big step forward towards reconciliation. Enormous effort and crystal-clear fairness are needed to destroy suspicion, prejudice, lack of confidence. It is a great challenge, not a privilege. And in many ways your task will be more difficult, as you don't have the powers of the International Tribunal, however, your power and authority is even greater – as this is your country.*[1]

This excerpt, taken from the speech made by ICTY Prosecutor Carla Del Ponte at the inauguration of the WCC of the CBiH in Sarajevo in March 2005, emphasises the edge-making capacity of a domestic legal institution. In Del Ponte's evocative set of claims, the court's legitimacy

---

[1] Carla Del Ponte speaking at the inauguration of the War Crimes Chamber of the Court of Bosnia and Herzegovina, 9 March 2005, Sarajevo. ICTY (2018). Address of the Prosecutor at the Inauguration of the War Crimes Chamber of the Court of BH, www.icty.org/en/press/address-prosecutor-inauguration-war-crimes-chamber-court-bh (accessed 12 September 2018).

stems from its ownership: it is *of* rather than *for* BiH. In becoming a 'truly national court' it is imagined that its jurisdiction over the territory of the BiH state works to foster reconciliation and collective notions of justice. The edge of the BiH state becomes the container within which justice for war crimes is resolved through retributive mechanisms of law housed within the WCC. Recalling the discussions from the previous chapter, these claims perform discourses of democratisation and state sovereignty that enframe this institution of transitional justice: that its imagined implications extend beyond simply adjudicating on the guilt or innocence of war criminals into the enactment of the coherence of the BiH state.

'Localising' transitional justice is a powerful imaginary and it has been a key refrain within legal responses to mass violence over the past two decades.[2] One of focal points for scholarly studies of such processes has been the materiality of new legal institutions: how the process of localising law requires the fabrication of a new infrastructure and architecture of law. It is the purpose of this chapter to explore how these material considerations – such as the siting of war crimes courts – enter into the popular imagination of the legitimacy of the new court. Instead of seeing the establishment of a legal institution as the performance of a preexisting territorial entity, or its proximity to the people of BiH organically engendering popular legitimacy, in its materiality we see an array of struggles and contestations that reveal a more plural and dynamic reception of new judicial authority. In doing so we begin to see the fabrication of a new edge of law: the boundary that separates legal space from the non-legal, a necessary distinction that performs the elevation of legal deliberation from the everyday life.

This argument is made across three sections. In the first I examine the implications of a materialist approach to understandings of courts. I am particularly keen to think of the dynamic nature of court materiality, where an 'architectural' mindset is replaced by that of the building surveyor: recognising the transitory nature of any building or fabricated space. This necessitates a view of the court as an 'event' as opposed to a static site, where it 'is always being "made" and "unmade",

---

[2] See Shaw, R., Waldorf, L. & Hazan, P. (eds.). (2010). *Localizing transitional justice: Interventions and priorities after mass violence*. Palo Alto, CA: Stanford University Press.

always doing the work of holding together and pulling apart'.[3] This approach to understanding the material world calls into question one of the cherished imaginaries of a newly founded court, namely that it constitutes a break from the past and a blank canvas upon which a new legal system can be enacted. Of course, what we find in any court building, but the case of the WCC is particularly acute, are the legacies of the past incurring on public attitudes towards the court in the present. It is this past life of the court building that is examined in the second section of the chapter, where I trace the implications of the previous uses of the court on social attitudes towards its impartiality and legitimacy as a site of legal deliberation. In contrast to the international narratives – encapsulated in Del Ponte's speech that opened this chapter – where the novelty of the court is used as the grounds for a fresh start to judicial proceedings, the former uses of the building in which the WCC is housed means that it was, in many respects, created at a stage of maturity. This is not, then, a blank slate on which new legal practices may be played out, but instead a specific site where memories of previous events and uses incur on interpretations of the present.

The significance of the confluence of materiality and the passage of time is considered in the final section of the chapter, where the significance of more intimate and corporeal sites are considered in the production of the edge of law. This discussion considers how the materiality of the court spaces intersects with the embodied practice of the judicial system: performing trials, attending the public gallery and providing witness testimony. Focusing on embodiment places human agency within the web of materials and affects that constitute legal practices, illuminating how specific forms of comportment and behaviours come to be interpreted within the judgement of guilt or innocence. But perhaps most profoundly, the centrality of the human body as a vessel of testimony centres attention on the constraints of time on the possibility of achieving justice in BiH: as victims and witnesses grow older and the possibility of providing testimony diminishes, so too does the possibility of providing the evidential base to complete trials. The edge of law mutates and becomes a time horizon beyond which the resources to complete the legal process are no longer available. Thus, this chapter provides

---

[3] Jacobs, J. M. (2006). A geography of big things. *Cultural Geographies* 13(1): 1–27.

a vital introduction to later discussions of how the WCC has required forms of public outreach and engagement to build public support for the court, expedite the legal processes and trace possible sources of testimony.

COURT MATERIALITY

> *We inhabit a nomos - a normative universe. We constantly create and maintain a world of right and wrong, of lawful and unlawful, of valid and void.*[4]

To consider the materiality of the Court we must start by returning to the concept of the *nomos*. Introduced in the previous chapter, nomos has risen to prominence for its ability to orientate attention to the permeation of law through institutions, sites and landscapes. While Carl Schmitt[5] used the term to explain the early-twentieth century rise of Western-centric international law, Robert Cover sought to gesture to the moral frameworks through which law establishes its meaning and legitimacy. But this is not a dematerialised or universal notion and he therefore hints at structural qualities that shape the *nomos*, akin to laws found in the natural sciences. 'This *nomos*' he argues, 'is as much "our world" as is the physical universe of mass, energy, and momentum. Indeed, our apprehension of the structure of the normative world is no less fundamental than our appreciation of the structure of the physical world'.[6] In this account the *nomos* is set apart from the physical world, reproducing a fundamental division between human action and its environmental backdrop. This primordial separation has been contested in more recent accounts, for example Bartel et al., when considering law's materiality, suggest 'the physical realm, as manifest in various and highly specific geological, hydrological, atmospheric and climate conditions, determines the possibility and sustainability of laws and economies'.[7] But this can be read as a minimalist challenge to the

---

[4] P. 4 in Cover, R. M. (1983). Foreword: Nomos and narrative. *Harvard Law Review* 97: 4–68.
[5] Schmitt, C. (1950 [2003]). *The Nomos of the earth*. New York: Telos Press.
[6] Cover, Foreword, p. 5.
[7] P. 343 in Bartel, R., Graham, N., Jackson, S., Prior, J. H., Robinson, D., Sherval, M. & Williams, S. (2013). Legal geography: An Australian perspective. *Geographical Research* 51(4): 339–353.

separation of law and material environment because the notion of separate realms endures, the emphasis is simply shifted towards the structuring role of the physical environment on the production of law.

Others have mounted a more sustained challenge to separation between law and environment though retaining the rubric of the *nomos*. David Delaney[8] has provided a new vocabulary for understanding the relationship between law and space through his concept of the *nomosphere*, referring to 'the cultural – material environs that are constituted by the reciprocal materialization of the legal and the legal signification of the sociospatial'.[9] By foregrounding the production of spatiotemporal orders through enduring normative frameworks, the concept of the *nomosphere* has provoked work in as varied contexts as the moralities of market exchange in Morocco[10] and the production of licit narcotics in Tasmania.[11] In each of these works, reciprocation is key, gesturing at the mutual constitution of law and materiality. Delaney subsequently talks of *nomic settings* where particular constellations of statutes, rules and regulations interplay to constitute place.[12] In so doing he is returning to some of the more foundational understandings of the *nomos* as set out in the work of Schmitt who identifies the act of enclosure as a foundational legal moment, elevating 'land appropriation as the primeval act in founding law'.[13] This focus is perhaps no surprise and precedes the wide body of legal geographical work exploring property law, enclosure and the commons.[14] But what is crucial here

---

[8] See Delaney, D. (2004). Tracing displacements: Or evictions in the nomosphere. *Environment and Planning D: Society and Space* 22(6): 847–860; Delaney, D. (2010). *The spatial, the legal and the pragmatics of world-making: Nomospheric investigations.* Abingdon: Routledge; Delaney, D. (2014). At work in the nomosphere: The spatiolegal production of emotions at work, in Braverman, I., Blomley, N., Delaney, D. & Kedar, A. (eds.) *The expanding spaces of law: A timely legal geography.* Stanford, CA: Stanford University Press, pp. 239–262.

[9] Delaney, Tracing displacements, p. 858.

[10] Turner, B. (2013). Religious subtleties in disputing: Spatiotemporal inscriptions of faith in the nomosphere in rural Morocco, in von Benda-Beckmann, F., von Benda-Beckmann, K., Ramstedt, M. & Turner, B. (eds.) *Religion in dispute: Pervasiveness of religious normativity in disputing processes.* Basingstoke: Palgrave Macmillan, pp. 55–73.

[11] Williams, S. (2013). Licit narcotics production in Australia: Legal geographies nomospheric and topological. *Geographical Research* 51(4): 364–374.

[12] Delaney, At work in the nomosphere, p. 246.

[13] Schmitt, *The Nomos of the earth*, p. 45.

[14] Blomley, N. (2003). Law, property, and the geography of violence: The frontier, the survey, and the grid. *Annals of the Association of American Geographers* 93(1):

is the very physicality to the act of line drawing, not as an abstract concept that frames imaginations of inside and outside, but rather as a material process that embeds normative ideals of law and justice.

In her literary analysis of transitional justice, the legal philosopher Carrol Clarkson examines how the drawing of lines stabilises certain ideals of law, while also productive of specific *nomic settings* (though she does not use the term).[15] Clarkson interprets such practices, following Rancière, as *aesthetic acts*, 'configurations of experience that create new modes of sense perception and induce novel forms of political subjectivity'.[16] 'What interests me', Clarkson explains, 'is the context in which certain works, acts or encounters, by creating a new field of sensory perception, have the potential to bring about shifts in the way a community delineates itself in terms of what it *perceives* to be significant, or even noticeable at all'.[17] This interplay between visual practices and legal process has been explored in depth by the Forensic Architecture research group, exploring aesthetics as more than simply the visual qualities of the material world, to examine instead 'the sensory capacity of matter itself'.[18] Approaching aesthetics in these terms draws attention to the role of (amongst other things) colour, texture, screen resolution and graphic design in the presentation of courtroom evidence and the unfolding of law.

Beyond the presentation of evidence and the physicality of the legal process, the architecture of the court is itself an aesthetic act. Clarkson identifies the opening of the new South African in Hillbrow, Johannesburg, in March 2004 in these terms, placed on the site of the Old Fort where many of the 156 treason trialists had been held in 1956.[19] The construction of the court building and its function as a site of adjudication stabilised the new post-Apartheid administration, while commemorating injustices of the past. This symbolic function is consistent with a longer lineage of geographical and criminological

---

121–141; Jeffrey, A., McFarlane, C. & Vasudevan, A. (2012). Rethinking enclosure: Space, subjectivity and the commons. *Antipode* 44(4): 1247–1267.

[15] Clarkson, C. (2013). *Drawing the line: Toward an aesthetics of transitional justice*. Oxford: Oxford University Press.

[16] Rancière, J. (2004). *The politics of aesthetics: The distribution of the sensible*. London: Continuum, p. 9.

[17] Clarkson, *Drawing the line*, p. 3; emphasis in the original.

[18] P. 14 in Weizman, E. (2014). Introduction: Forensis, in Forensic Architecture (eds.), *Forensis*. Berlin: Sternberg Press, pp. 9–34.

[19] Clarkson, *Drawing the line*.

work that has explored the visual function of both court rooms and court architectures. One of the conclusions of this work is that judicial buildings have always been monumental enactments of authority, for example it is telling that the Stonehenge, the Neolithic monument in southern England, was known in Cornish dialect as *Merddin Embys*, signifying the 'fence of judgement'.[20] From these contemporary and historical examples underscore the significance of the visibility of the judicial spaces, cohering with the importance granted to justice being *seen* to be done in the operation of new legal systems.[21]

But in embracing this work we must be wary not to imagine visual prominence erases ambiguity. Novelists have been particularly attuned to the uncertain aesthetics of law, producing accounts that have illuminated the unease and social dislocation produced through contact with legal spaces. Kafka's *The Trial*,[22] perhaps the most celebrated example of this genre, traces the subjection of Josef K. to an inaccessible and uncertain legal authority to answer for unspecified crimes. Rather than a singular or comprehensible focus of authority, Kafka's account conjures an image of a legal order 'in which ignorance and confusion are pervasive, where law is unknowable but seemingly ubiquitous'.[23] This troubles a straightforward account of the monumental, or visual, basis of legal architecture, pointing to the fundamentally indecipherable and unseen qualities of authority. The writings of W. G. Sebald have done more than anyone to give voice to this sense of indecipherability, often drawing on the morphology of labyrinths to symbolise disorientation, loss and the inability to escape.[24] The figure of the labyrinth stalks Sebald's writing on legal space, for example

---

[20] Mulcahy, L. (2011). *Legal architecture: Justice, due process and the place of law*. Abingdon: Routledge, p. 15; see also Bellott, H. (1922). Some early courts and the English Bar. *Law Quarterly Review* 38: 168–184.

[21] Nagy, R. (2008). Transitional justice as global project: Critical reflections. *Third World Quarterly* 29(2): 275–289.

[22] Kafka, F. (2014 [1925]). *The Trial* (trans. David Wyllie). Dublin: Roads Publishing.

[23] P. 238 in Matthews, D. (2016). Book review: Robert P. Burns: Kafka's law: The trial and American criminal justice. *International Journal for the Semiotics of Law* 29: 237–241.

[24] See Baxter, J. (2013). Surrealist vertigo in Schwindel. Gefühle, in Baxter, J., Henitiuk, V. & Hutchinson, B. (eds.) *A literature of restitution: Critical essays on WG Sebald*. Oxford: Oxford University Press; Zilcosky, J. (2004). Sebald's uncanny travels: The impossibility of getting lost, in Long, J. J., & Whitehead, A. (eds.), *W. G. Sebald – A critical companion*. Seattle: University of Washington Press, pp. 102–120.

where he describes the Palais de Justice in Brussels, Belgium's primary court building, as 'a huge pile of over seven thousand cubic metres contain[ing] corridors and stairways leading nowhere, and doorless rooms and halls where no one would set foot, empty spaces surrounded by walls and representing the innermost secret of sanctioned authority'.[25] In this claustrophobic account, the reader is given the impression of a site of both monumental significance but also of bewildering proportions and design, both a visual spectacle but also an unseen, secret set of prerogatives.

Following Sebald it can be suggested that not all aesthetic acts carry consolidating power, not all communicate an unambiguous story of the social. Research conducted in Rwanda has illuminated the potentially divisive role of legal visibility in post-conflict environments. Barbara Oomen's study of the *Gacaca* courts in Rwanda has traced the ways in which they have been presented as a local, visible and, therefore, participatory form of post-genocide justice.[26] But Oomen's research highlights how these purportedly local courts have served to embed certain forms of internationally mediated justice and consolidate the power of particular local elites. 'Justice is presented as a neutral, technocratic and universalistic enterprise', Oomen writes, 'it is actually deeply enmeshed in local politics'.[27] The contestation over the siting and funding of Gacaca Courts underscores their centrality as *nomic settings*: establishing normative frameworks for social life.

These works provide an illustration of the role of the prominence of court buildings in shaping public perceptions of law. Alongside such contributions, the aesthetic and practical aspects of the internal organisation of the courts, their circulation spaces, security arrangements and layout have proved the site of sustained analysis by architects, criminologists and socio-legal studies scholars. Much of this work centres on technical questions of how the organisation of courtrooms can shape the outcome of trials, for example studying the impact of the securitisation of the defendant's dock on a jury's perception of guilt or innocence.[28] There have also been in-depth studies of the segregation of the

---

[25] Sebald, W. G. (2001). *Austerlitz*. London: Penguin Books, p. 39.
[26] Oomen, B. (2005). Donor-driven justice and its discontents: The case of Rwanda. *Development and Change* 36(5): 887–910.
[27] Ibid., p. 907.
[28] See Mulcahy, L. (2013). Putting the defendant in their place: Why do we still use the dock in criminal proceedings? *British Journal of Criminology* 53(6): 1139–1156;

courtroom and courthouse, to explore how participation and observation is enabled and constrained through factors such as seating design, the height of raised platforms and the sightlines from public galleries.[29] Perhaps unsurprisingly considering the theatrical nature of trials, others have been drawn to the dramaturgical language of Erving Goffman[30] to think through the 'front' and 'back' stage of court space, marking how judicial comportment and deliberation vary based on physical location.[31]

While it is difficult to neatly categorise the epistemological approach of these varied works, they share a concern for the role of space in constituting subjectivity. This focus has drawn upon the social theory of Michel Foucault, tracing the disciplinary function of court space as it organises bodies and marshals the conduct of participants.[32] Central to these mechanisms is the role of repetition of court room attributes in normalising judgement and stabilising legal identities within court spaces. Emblematic of this work is Linda Mulcahy's historical study of the function of architecture in the establishment of the English court system, illuminating the micro-geographies of court space and their function in constituting power relations and stabilising identity.[33] Mulcahy explores the exclusionary nature of court arrangements, observing that '[e]ach time a section of floor is raised, a barrier installed or a segregated circulation route added it has the potential to create insiders and outsiders; empowered and disempowered participants in a space ostensibly labelled "public" in which the intricacies of civil liberties and participatory democracy are played out'.[34]

Rossner, M. (2016). *In the dock: The placement of the accused at court and the right to a fair trial*. LSE Law – Policy Briefing Paper No. 18.

[29] See, for example, Rosenbloom, J. D. (1997). Social ideology as seen through courtroom and courthouse architecture. *Columbia-VLA Journal of Law and the Arts* 22: 463–524.

[30] Goffman, E. (1978). *The presentation of self in everyday life*. London: Harmondsworth.

[31] Portillo, S., Rudes, D. S., Viglione, J. & Nelson, M. (2013). Front-stage stars and backstage producers: The role of judges in problem-solving courts. *Victims and Offenders* 8(1): 1–22.

[32] Foucault, M. (1977). *Discipline and punish – The birth of the prison*. Trans. Alan Sheridan. London: Penguin.

[33] Mulcahy. L. (2011). *Legal architecture: Justice, due process and the place of law*. Abingdon: Routledge.

[34] Ibid., p. 1.

Adopting a Foucauldian approach facilitates an understanding of the dynamism of architecture, not as a static form but as a series of processes that enmesh the material, corporeal and affective. Reflecting this approach Jane M. Jacobs advocates a rubric of the architectural world that centres on *building events* where a building 'is always being "made" and "unmade", always doing the work of holding together and pulling apart'.[35] Taking this work seriously, we need to understand the *aesthetic act* not as a singular event and neither is the *nomic setting* a stable backdrop. Instead, courts are constantly being reconstituted through the life of the building, itself an assemblage of architectural form, bodies and things.[36] The work of Bruno Latour, and in specifically his study of the workings of the Conseil d'État,[37] has been at the forefront of a more materialist understanding of the working of the legal edifice. Reflecting an actor-network approach, Latour is interested in the mechanisms through which the coherence and stability of law is achieved, focusing in particular on the circulation of human and non-human actants within the court building. Following his earlier studies of the laboratory and the associated production of scientific knowledge, Latour is interested in the mechanisms through which legal rationality is separated and elevated from other forms of discourse through material and embodied practice. 'What makes a comparison between the world of science and law all the more interesting', Latour argues in an earlier essay, 'is that both domains emphasize the virtues of a disinterested and unprejudiced approach, based on distance and precision, and in both domains participants speak esoteric languages and reason in carefully cultivated styles'.[38] The task of the legal geographer is now to entwine this focus on the actor-networks of law with the materialist approach to the court as *building event*.

---

[35] P. 11 in Jacobs, J. M. (2006). A geography of big things. *Cultural Geographies* 13(1): 1–27; see also Weizman, Introduction, pp. 9–34 for an exploration of the continuous transformation of buildings.

[36] Dittmer, J. (2014). Geopolitical assemblages and complexity. *Progress in Human Geography* 38(3): 385–401.

[37] Latour, B. (2010). *The making of law: An ethnography of the Conseil d'État*. Cambridge: Polity.

[38] P. 73 in Latour, B. (2004). Scientific objects and legal objectivity, in Pottage, A., & Mundy, M. (eds.), *Law, anthropology, and the constitution of the social making persons and things*. Cambridge: Cambridge University Press, pp. 73–114.

THE WAR CRIMES CHAMBER

Through this history of monumental architecture of law in Western Europe we can discern two characteristics of court space, often operating in tension with one another. The first is the desire for public spectacle and openness, where courts architecturally signify a desire for participatory law. Examples abound, but Richard Rogers and Claude Bucher's design for the ECtHR provides something of an archetype, with its inclusion of a large plate glass entrance hall designed to materially perform a metaphor of transparency. This architectural facet is underscored in the significance of public galleries, television coverage or court artists, as mechanisms through which the spatial segregation of law from wider society may be disrupted. Such technologies, in turn, accentuate the underlying theatricality of the trial process; it is an event that constitutes individuals into specific roles, with various levels of agency as to the selection of script, costume or bodily disposition. The implications of such legal theatricality are scrutinised in Hannah Arendt's study of the trial of Nazi Bureaucrat Adolf Eichmann,[39] where she argues that the trial's theatricality distracted from its judicial function, in doing so conveying the sense that this was a trial for the wider crimes of the Holocaust rather than of a single individual.[40]

The second characteristic of court space is its segregation and specificity as a site of legal practice. At first glance this may appear in contrast to the argument of openness and theatricality, but they are, in practice, closely intertwined aspects of law's materiality. Formalist legal accounts stress the closed nature of legal rationality, envisaging a form of deliberation unsullied by social and political forces that foment outside its gates. This sense of separation is reflected in the lengths taken to designate court space as an alternative social sphere to the surrounding rooms or buildings. There is a geographical determinism framing individual locations within court space, most notably the judge's bench, the accused's dock, the benches for legal teams and the segregated public gallery. The significance of theatricality is clear:

---

[39] Arendt, H. (1963). *Eichmann in Jerusalem: A report on the banality of evil*. London: Penguin Books.

[40] See Felman, S. (2002). *The juridical unconscious trial and traumas in the twentieth century*. Cambridge, MA: Harvard University Press; Jeffrey, A., & Jakala, M. (2014). The hybrid legal geographies of a war crimes court. *Annals of the Association of American Geographers* 104(3): 652–667.

the audience is physically segregated from the unfolding legal drama, where the aesthetics of the action reflect state symbolism, legal tradition, judicial roles or trial function. As Blomley[41] makes clear in his study of the performative nature of property, such actions are not reflections of preexisting identities or relationships, instead their performance brings certain identities, hierarchies and relationship into existence.

Space, then, is not a neutral backdrop against which legal practices unfold; rather it is enrolled within the making of law. Again, the establishment of the CBiH illuminates the power of law's geography to shape public attitudes towards the possibilities for justice. In previous work I have discussed the contestation that surrounded the selection of the court building in Sarajevo,[42] but some elements of this dispute need updating. As mentioned in Chapter 2, the court is located around 5 km outside the centre of Sarajevo on Kraljice Jelene, a road that marks the former front line during the conflict in BiH. The building and surrounding complex had, during Yugoslav times, served as a JNA Barracks named Viktor Bubanj, after a Yugoslav-era military hero. During the conflict, the JNA left the barracks, and accounts vary as to whether they deserted the base as a strategic move (to consolidate JNA siege lines around Sarajevo) or they were forcibly expelled under enemy fire. The latter explanation was offered by Radovan Karadžić during trial testimony at the ICTY:

> In the afternoon they [the Mujahidin] would fire in bursts through the clinic's windows in the direction of the Viktor Bubanj barracks where a JNA unit was billeted. They also swore at the Serbs and announced that they would soon raze the Serb settlement of Nedzarici to the ground, and sow wheat where the Serb houses stood.
>
> (Radovan Karadžić, November 2012)

Subsequently the Viktor Bubanj barracks was renamed Ramiz Salcin, in honour of a Bosnian Government fighter who had died early in 1992, and used as an internment camp for prisoners of war. The nature of the activities that took place are disputed, some recollect a

---

[41] See Blomley, N. (2014). 'Making space for property.' *Annals of the Association of American Geographers* 104(6): 1291–1306.

[42] See Jeffrey, A. (2013). *The improvised state: Sovereignty, performance and agency in Dayton Bosnia.* Oxford: Wiley-Blackwell; Jeffrey, A., & Jakala, M. (2014). The hybrid legal geographies of a war crimes court. *Annals of the Association of American Geographers* 104(3): 652–667.

conventional prison environment where conditions were harsh but not illegal, while others, particularly those loyal to Serb causes, have attested that it was the site of war crimes. These accusations have led to the indictment in December 2012 of Besim Muderizović, Ramiz Avdović and Iulian-Nicolae Vintila by the prosecutor's office of Bosnia and Herzegovina of crimes against humanity, the indictment reads:

> they participated in establishing and maintaining a system of abuse of Serb civilians, by illegally incarcerating ethnic Serb civilians from the city of Sarajevo in the former military barrack 'Viktor Bubanj', where the detained civilians were subjected to intentional infliction of severe physical or mental pain or suffering (torture), violation of bodily integrity or health, and forced labor, which resulted in the death of eighteen prisoners. Thus, at least two hundred Serb civilians were captured in the former military barrack 'Viktor Bubanj' without being communicated the reason for capture, and without any criminal proceedings being initiated against the majority of them.
> (Special Prosecutor's Office, Sarajevo 12 December 2011)

Unsurprisingly this contested history of violence has shaped perceptions of the suitability of this location as a neutral site of legal arbitration. Where court locations have, in other transitional settings, been selected to spatially assert a shift in regime,[43] in the case of the CBiH the building has become a focal point for challenges to the possibility of transitional justice. For example, in 2003 the Savesa Logorasa RS (RS Association of Camp Detainees) organised a march on the CBiH to demand the inclusion of a plaque identifying the building as the site of a former death camp where '2000 Serb civilians were killed, assaulted or tortured'.[44] This performance before the world's media was clearly intended to challenge the neutrality of the new Court by emphasising its material basis as a site of Serb persecution. Emphasising the difference between Clarkson's case of the Constitutional Court in Hillbrow, Johannesburg, the location of the Court on the site of a former prison did not cultivate a sense of the unified BiH state, but was rather used as a symbolic resource that pointed to the imagined lack of neutrality in the new judicial system.

The visceral invocation of Serb victimhood at the Court site has led community associations to protest the absence of any form of

---

[43] See Clarkson, *Drawing the line*.
[44] Jeffrey, *The improvised state*, p. 142.

commemoration at the site. Even before it housed trial processes, public disputes erupted concerning the selection of the site, in particular from associations of camp detainees who has experienced either life in the Viktor Bubanj barracks or other camps across BiH.[45] In 2003, the *Saveza logoraša RS* (RS Association of Camp Detainees) organised a march on the CBiH site to protest about the absence of any commemoration to the site's former use and attempt to place a plaque on the building, marking the site as a former 'death camp' where '2000 Serb civilians were killed, assaulted or tortured'.[46] Using the same symbolic resource the domestic and international political elites used to commemorate the donation of furniture and materials for the court building, the plaque serves as a means through which materials may be enrolled into a politics of claiming space. Rather than commemorating generosity, in this case the desire is to materialise victimhood and stabilise moral claims with the urban landscape. As I discuss elsewhere,[47] the vice president of *Saveza logoraša RS*, Slavko Jović, drew a parallel between the desire amongst those loyal to Bosnijak causes for memorial at Srebrenica and the demands amongst pro-Serb groups for a plaque on the Court building.

While the presence of an international judiciary provoked accusations of international supervision, the claims of an engrained material bias through the selection of the building seeks to challenge the unification of the BiH state through the establishment of the Court. If claims of international supervision undermine a geopolitics of separation, the suggestion of a materially inscribed ethnic bias undermines a geopolitical strategy of spatial unification. The forms of resistance to the court are diverse, but they share a common aesthetic act: the projection of identity onto bodies (so-called Muslim judges) or materials (the imagined blood-stained walls) that limit the potential for the Court to be seen more broadly by the Bosnian public as an honest or universal site of arbitration. In this way we see the tensions of state

---

[45] For an account of the role of associations of camp detainees in trial processes see Delpla, I. (2007). 'In the midst of injustice: The ICTY from the perspective of some victim associations', in Bougarel, X., Helms, E. & Duijzings, G. (eds.), *The new Bosnian mosaic: Identities, memories and moral claims in a post-war society*. Aldershot: Ashgate, pp. 211–234.

[46] Superbosna (2003). Spomen ploča Srbima donešena i odnešena At. www.superbosna.com/vijesti/ostalo/spomen_plo%E8a_srbima_done%B9ena_i_odne%B9ena/ (accessed 8 December 2018).

[47] See Jeffrey, *The improvised state*.

improvisation – and the paradoxes of the Bosnian state – enacted in a single site. While the establishment of the Court is a performance of a unified BiH state, this could only be achieved through the retention of ethnically oriented BiH territories. Consequently, the enduring ontological context of post-GFAP BiH grants legitimacy to alternative, ethnically inscribed accounts of law and authority.

EMBODIED LAW

Focusing on the materiality of the court building reveals lines of contestation concerning the implications of its past for interpretations of its impartiality in the presence. But the materiality of the legal process did not end with the fabrication of the court building. The enactment of trials was necessarily a corporeal process that drew in a range of differently positioned bodies and inscribed upon them different roles within the legal proceedings (*inter alia* judiciary, accused, lawyers, witnesses and victims). In previous work, I have explored these enactments as a form of hybridity, emphasising how bodies and spaces are co-constituted through the legal process.[48] One of the key arguments within this work relates directly to the production of the edge of law: that exploring a legal process as a hybrid enterprise where bodies, materials and space are co-enacted illuminates the challenge of neatly delineating an edge separating legal deliberation from wider social contexts. This theoretical approach helps to illustrate how the arrangement of court space helps to constitute subjectivity, at times through very stark mechanisms – such as the securitised glass behind which the public gallery was located or the raised dais of the judicial bench – but also through more mundane arrangements such as the allocation of parallel benches where defendants would sit with their legal counsel, or the positioning of the digital visualiser recording each piece of submitted evidence.

But in a desire to thinking through the distributed nature of human agency within court space – between human and non-human actors and entwined in a set of material performances – we must be careful to retain a focus on embodied difference. The experience of monitoring trials provided repeated evidence of the gendered nature of power

---

[48] Jeffrey, A., & Jakala, M. (2014). The hybrid legal geographies of a war crimes court. *Annals of the Association of American Geographers* 104(3): 652–667; see also Whatmore, S. (2002). *Hybrid geographies: Natures cultures spaces*. London: Sage.

relations between differentially situated bodies within court space. We observed the enactment of forms of masculinity between defendants, as they greeted one another with familiarity and joviality, and publicly performed a sense of relaxation in court space, perhaps by reclining their chair, removing their translation headsets or laughing at a particular comment or set of circumstances. The nature of the trials at the WCC is that they are regularly held with multiple defendants, a mechanism to try and improve the efficiency of the court, but – in the cases observed – this led to a strengthening of solidarity and socialisation between defendants.

Such aspects of gendered performance were particularly acute in the experience of giving testimony, in particular during cases of war sexual violence where those giving testimony – in the cases covered by our research – were women and alleged perpetrators were men. The power asymmetry of the interrogations was acknowledged by the prosecutors, who felt concerned about the production of legal masculinities that thrived on the vulnerability of those testifying. During a public dialogue concerning trial practices in Tuzla, one prosecutor emphasised the incapacity of judges or prosecution teams to intervene and the potential for the cross-examination process to be wielded as a tool by defendants to unsettle the witness:

> we are talking about very vulnerable individuals. During the interrogations verbal offenses are being used to disturb an individual and neither we nor the judge nor the prosecutor can help.[49]

The frequency of these forms of intimidation under cross-examination led representatives of victims associations to suggest during the research that the legal process was protecting indicted defendants at the expense of victims and witnesses. One remarked:

> As for the treatment of the Prosecution towards victims, from my point of view, they are treated more like perpetrators and not like victims. Why? Why doesn't anybody do something to protect us, why doesn't a judge say: 'This cannot be done this way', but they let defence lawyers to interrogate us as we were the ones who were killing and not them. It sounds like we have done harm to them and not vice-versa. I have testified ... I have testified numerous times ... [and they were] showing me photos of the entire military squad, you can imagine how big a shock it was for me. One gets lost. As one lady said one gets silent. I didn't

[49] Interview with a Public Prosecutor, Tuzla, BiH, 19 April 2012.

know where I was. I do not remember where I was, what I was looking at in that moment, I was there, I was not here, I cannot describe to you that feeling.[50]

This account points to the unspeakable nature of the experience and the limits to language in conveying these embodied exchanges between defendant and victim/witness. This interpretation was further complicated by the suggestion by one BiH legal analyst that there were certain expectations of bodily comportment and behaviour for witnesses, and these contributed to the veracity of the testimony being recounted:

> It is not just expression it's the expectations as well, it's the way they [Judicial trial panel] stop or not, the questions they allow or not ... it's expressions, it's their expressions of faces.... I have a statement by one of the women who said that they didn't believe her [about being raped] until she started crying.[51]

These observations speak to the potential identification of expectations of bodily performance in the trial setting. Rather than adapting the court space or the trial procedure, some respondents, particular within the prosecution service, saw psychological preparation as the responsibility of the individual:

> That individual needs to come prepared ... and she should be informed that she will undergo some undesirable situations in the court room. The court cannot arrange it in the way which would suit the plaintiff, the victim. The way of interrogation and intonation is something which we cannot put up with easily.[52]

Later sessions in the same trial pointed to the forms of non-human agency that may be at work when considering the evidential processes within war crimes trials. In the following session of the same trial, the defence team offered a series of further submissions of material evidence, largely comprising a variety of identification cards that sought to illustrate their client's status as a prisoner of war. The document that elicited the most scrutiny was the fake military identification issued during the war in Bijeljina, BiH. A significant amount of time was spent examining the Bijeljina stamp dated 8 December 1994 to determine whether it was a real stamp from the war government. The

---

[50] Interview with a member of a Victims' Association, Tuzla, BiH, 19 April 2012.
[51] Ibid.
[52] Interview with a Public Prosecutor, Tuzla, BiH, 19 April 2012.

fragment of paper had a particular significance to the room, it was carefully considered by defence and prosecution lawyers, as each tried to gauge whether the stamp was genuine, carefully studying the faded and worn document. The deterioration was a product of the passage of time, it had been stored in the defendant's house and it had become bleached by the sun and crumpled against other papers. At the conclusion of the discussion the card was carefully placed on a scanner to be recorded electronically – frozen in time – and conveniently accessible for potential appeals. The incident once again underscored the significance of materials, but also pointed to the limits of human agency.[53] Each piece of evidence is itself decaying, slowly decomposing as it is exposed to atmosphere, buried in the soil or hidden in amongst mundane objects in potential defendants' homes.

CONCLUSION

> I think that a greater number of judges should be delegated exclusively to the Court for War Crimes because nature is not an ally in that case, many suspects are dying, many witnesses are dying, and in that respect court justice will not come to those it was intended to, but there is no political will. This situation suits everybody because it is being abused by politics. This suits politicians because they do not deal further with essential life questions.[54]

This chapter has examined the materiality of the WCC within the CBiH. The argument has drawn theoretical inspiration from work on both materiality to rethink the enactment of the court and to challenge an imagination of space as a neutral backdrop against which legal deliberations occur. The purpose of such a perspective extends beyond providing a more nuanced examination of legal processes; rather it is to unsettle the imagination of law and society as separate enterprises. The production of law is constituted through – and reliant upon – a wealth of purportedly non-legal actors, spaces and materials.[55] The ideal of separation – the performance of an edge of law – is structured around the imaginary of

---

[53] DeSilvey, C. (2006) Observed decay: telling stories with mutable things. *Journal of material Culture* 11 (3):318–338.
[54] Interview with human rights NGO member in Sarajevo, BiH, 24 April 2012.
[55] See McEvoy, K. (2007). Beyond legalism: Towards a thicker understanding of transitional justice. *Journal of Law and Society* 34: 411–440; Latour, B. (2010). *The making of law*. Cambridge: Polity Press.

legal exchanges as unsullied by wider social and political interests, and in the case of the CBiH through its representation by international agencies as an institution that is autonomous of international agendas with a jurisdiction over the entirety of BiH's territory. But as we have discussed, the nature of the CBiH's establishment, the constitution of its judiciary and even the selection of the building have challenged this account of purity and separation.

But exploration of the performance of law points to a more profound challenge to the fantasy of the birth of a new court than simply its imaginary separation from social life. Rather than understanding legal exchange as a textual or linguistic exercise, the chapter highlights the embodied and material events through which legal interactions have been performed. These exchanges pointed to the masculine bravado of the defence lawyer; the anxious and intimidated witness; and the crumpled and unclear identification card. They also illuminate the fallacy of novelty that encircles this institution. When seen through this lens the court is not 'new' at all. It is rather in a state of decay because – as the preceding quotation states – witnesses are dying, mass graves are decomposing and evidence is lost, faded and absent. As we have seen, law operates through the interaction of living and non-living beings, each subject to the corrosion of simply existing.[56] This is particularly acute in the case of transitional justice, where crimes are being addressed from previous political regimes sometimes years, if not decades, after the crimes are alleged to have taken place. The imaginary of a 'nascent' legal institution is permissive of a paternalistic approach by international agencies, mirroring similar processes of infantilism within post-colonial development programmes.[57] Presenting an institution as 'new' allows legacies, both material and ideological, to be sidelined in a desire to promote a multi-ethnic future, despite the ongoing antagonisms of the past.

Understanding the court as decaying has political consequences. The sluggish nature of war crimes trials was seen during the research to suit certain political parties in BiH who have mounted staunch attacks on the CBiH on the grounds of supposed bias towards those loyal to one

---

[56] DeSilvey, C. (2006) Observed decay: telling stories with mutable things. *Journal of material Culture* 11 (3):318–338.
[57] See, for example, Dogra, N. (2011). The mixed metaphor of 'Third World Woman': Gendered representations by international development NGOs. *Third World Quarterly* 32: 333–348.

ethnic cause or another.[58] The difference between the temporalities of law and politics have allowed politicians to present attempts at legal redress as ponderous, incompetent and biased. In addition, the concept of decay also foregrounds the wider limitations of using law as the central instrument of transitional justice after conflict. Where the Truth and Reconciliation Commission in South Africa combined legal redress with processes of truth telling and amnesty, the focus on retributive approaches in BiH has limited the possibilities of achieving a wider public archive of verdicts and testimony (previously conceived as a central outcome of transitional legal processes in BiH).[59] To advance the truth-telling aspects of the CBiH greater focus needs to be placed on the fragile and precarious nature of the legal process, not as a form of rationality that operates in isolation from wider social or material encumbrances, but rather a form of social process that is beholden to the spaces, materials and bodies of legal practice.

[58] For example see Nezavisne novine (2012). Dodik: Sud odlučio o Srebrenici pod pritiskom stranaca, www.nezavisne.com/novosti/bih/Dodik-Apelacioni-sud-odlucio-o-Srebrenici-pod-pritiskom-stranaca-171147.html (accessed 3 December 2018).
[59] See Campbell, D. (1998). *National deconstruction: Violence, identity, and justice in Bosnia*. Minneapolis: University of Minnesota Press.

PART II
POLITICS AT THE EDGE OF LAW

CHAPTER FOUR

PUBLIC OUTREACH

INTRODUCTION

In this chapter I explore how the edge of law has been constituted and transgressed in the operation of the WCC. This requires an expanded legal geography of the court's activities, to trace how the fulfilment of trials at the court has required the enrolment of civil society organisations to both communicate the legitimacy of the new legal institution and to assist with the practical activity of supplying witnesses and material evidence. Theoretically, this contributes to work that has sought to decentre legal processes within the operation of transitional justice, to think through the wider array of social actors that are complicit and necessary in successfully operating processes of transitional justice. While legal practices are rightly key elements of transitional justice responses, these operate through and summon into existence a series of non-legal spaces and actors.

This argument is made in response to a growing sense in affiliated disciplines, particularly criminology, that the study of transitional justice has been characterised by a dominance of 'legalism'.[1] This term is used to indicate the privileging of legal institutions within attempts to foster transitional justice and the allied dominance of the perspectives of lawyers and judges within scholarly and policy debates. In intellectual terms, legalism can be understood as a process that seeks to separate

---

[1] McEvoy, K. (2007). Beyond legalism: Towards a thicker understanding of transitional justice. *Journal of Law and Society* 34: 411–440.

law from other social sciences; most notably politics.[2] I will argue that a legalistic understanding of transitional justice elevates the significance of certain spaces and spatial practices (e.g., courts and legal processes) over the wider institutional and political setting in which they operate (including, though not restricted to, human rights NGOs, political parties and state agencies). Consequently, this chapter seeks to destabilise a legalistic understanding of transitional justice and highlight the spatial practices of non-legal institutions and individuals.

To illustrate this argument, the chapter draws on empirical material relating mechanisms enacted by the WCC designed to build links with victims of, and witnesses to, the war crimes committed during the 1992–1995 conflict. This draws attention to an array of practices that are often labelled as 'public outreach', the mechanisms used by a legal institution to communicate its activities to a wider public and foster engagement with trial justice.[3] As discussed in Chapter 2, since 2005 the WCC has been granted jurisdiction over intermediate and lower-ranking war crimes cases.[4] In an attempt to build links with communities in BiH the Court established, in 2006, a Court Support Network (CSN) comprising five NGOs located in towns across the country. This chapter assesses the establishment of this outreach initiative and the new spatialities of justice that it has created. The activities of the CSN point to the importance of non-legal agencies to the completion of legal processes. In addition, the qualitative responses of the NGO members point to innovative configurations of space, law and justice that operate outside of the formal legal processes. These situated knowledges challenge a narrow legalistic understanding of transitional justice and illustrate the production of new imaginaries of justice and the future. In disciplinary terms this argument contributes to the work of legal geographers in challenging the conception of law operating outside or 'above' the society it serves. In ethical and political terms,

---

[2] Shklar, J. N. (1986). *Legalism: law, morals, and political trials*. London: Harvard University Press.
[3] Lambourne, W. (2009). Transitional justice and peacebuilding after mass violence. *International Journal of Transitional Justice* 3(1): 28–48.
[4] As discussed in Chapter 2 a central component of the completion strategy of the ICTY comprises the transfer of cases against intermediate and lower-level accused to competent national jurisdictions in BiH, Croatia and Serbia. While sensitive cases will remain under the jurisdiction of the WCC, other war crimes cases in BiH are expected to be devolved to courts in the Republika Srpska and the Muslim-Croat Federation.

the empirical material illustrates the importance of non-legal actors and spaces in generating deliberative notions of just outcomes following conflict.

As set out in Chapter 1, the empirical material is drawn from qualitative research conducted during residential fieldwork in the Bosnian towns of Sarajevo, Mostar and Bijeljina in January 2007 and October 2009, building on a long-term research engagement examining the nature of international intervention in BiH since 1999. Taking seriously Megoran's call for greater emphasis within political geographic inquiry on 'people's experience and everyday understandings of the phenomena under question',[5] this approach seeks to explore the mundane and prosaic operation of new legal mechanisms in BiH as they shape, and are shaped by, the civil society organisations under examination. The research visits involved 75 semi-structured interviews with representatives from the Court (in particular the Court Public Information and Outreach division), from wider judicial bodies such as the ICTY liaison team in Sarajevo, with other international organisations such as the Office of the High Representative (OHR), United Nations Development Programme (UNDP) and the European Commission, and with NGOs both within and beyond the CSN. In addition, the research involved translating and reviewing institutional literature from the Court, the ICTY and the NGO community.

The first section of the chapter outlines how geographers have explored the relationship between law and space, work that provides critical insights to the production of legal knowledge and its ability to produce spatial outcomes. The second section outlines the history of transitional justice, focusing in particular on its operation through temporal and spatial distance. In the third section, I outline a critical geopolitics of justice in BiH, exploring in particular how the international response to the Bosnian war has shaped the possibilities and format of subsequent judicial interventions. The fourth section examines the establishment of the CBiH, drawing on the wider context of the international response to the war in Bosnia and Herzegovina. The fifth section draws on the empirical material to illustrate the role played by NGOs in supporting the work of the WCC, focusing in particular on the 'invited' and 'invented' spaces of justice that have been produced.

---

[5] P. 622 in Megoran, N. (2006). For ethnography in political geography: Experiencing and re-imagining Ferghana Valley boundary closures *Political Geography* 25: 622–640.

RETURNING TO THE EDGE OF LAW

The rubric of 'public outreach' highlights the manifestation of the edge of law, where the need for deliberate practices of communication perform an expected disconnect between the operation of a legal process and its host society. To understand these communicative practices – these attempts to transcend the edge of law – we need to revisit work that has sought to trace how the operation of law is productive of ideas of space. In the previous chapter we engaged with Delaney's notion of the *nomosphere*,[6] highlighting how law and space is an immanent and dynamic co-production. One of the implications of such a perspective is the requirement to examine the substance of legal practices as they unfold in specific geographical contexts, with the capacity to produce spatial arrangements and erase or exclude others. One of the key objects of concern for the study of the WCC is the relationship between law and state spatiality, where a legal process is imagined strengthening the coherence of a post-conflict state. As Delaney identifies, the conventional distinction between 'domestic' and 'international' law renders state sovereignty at the heart of understandings of legal spatiality.[7] In a sense, the centrality of the state points to a wider 'territorial trap' in legal studies, whereby state territoriality is presented as a preexisting spatial framework within and between which legal obligations and rights operate in a systematic fashion.[8] This straightforward understanding of the spatiality of law has been challenged by geographers who have sought to explore the productive capacity of legal discourses to produce spatial arrangements.

Consequently, scholars have drawn inspiration from this understanding of law as a performance of, and through, space. For example, Sallie Marston examines the spatial effects of legal judgements on the participation of a gay, lesbian and bisexual group in the St. Patrick's Day parade in Boston, Massachusetts.[9] Marston explores how the legal

---

[6] Delaney, D. (2010). *The spatial, the legal and the pragmatics of world-making: Nomospheric investigations.* Routledge-Cavendish.

[7] Delaney, D. (2001). Introduction: Globalization and law, in Blomley, N., Delaney, D. & Ford, R. T. (eds.), *The legal geographies reader: Law, power and space.* Oxford: Blackwell, pp. 252–255.

[8] Agnew, J. (1994). The territorial trap: The geographical assumptions of international relation theory. *Review of International Political Economy* 1: 53–80.

[9] Marston, S. (2004). Space, culture, state: Uneven developments in political geography. *Political Geography* 23: 1–16.

processes 'fixed' certain understandings of society, space and culture. Significantly, these were not neutral definitions of these concepts, but were rather served to promote understandings of society that excluded groups that did not conform to hegemonic expectations. By tracing the path of legislation through the US State and Supreme courts, Marston highlights the way in which legal judgements hinged on a particular understanding of society and space that held them as distinct spheres, rather than as 'mutually constitutive processes'.[10] Marston argues that this separation had profound consequences for how culture was understood as a commodity that belongs to one group rather than 'something that is constantly negotiated and transformed through the public give and take of changing ideas and meaning systems in a changing world'.[11] Within this account legal decisions are not technical adjudications on an external reality but are rather incursions of power that categorise the social world to endorse dominant conceptualisations of identity and belonging.

As discussed in the previous chapter, recently scholars have turned to the materiality of legal practices to confront the perception of law as 'a universal abstraction, set apart from the messy realities of local particularities'.[12] This work has illuminated the spaces through which legal authority is produced, for example through court rooms, government departments and international bureaucracies.[13] By employing ethnographic methodologies to study the materials and contexts of lawmaking, scholars have highlighted the role of everyday bureaucratic processes in shaping legal outcomes, challenging the notion of a clear separation between law and society. In addition to troubling the purity of legal knowledge, these insights highlight the enrolment of spatial abstraction in producing legal authority, from the micro-geographies of the body and the court room, through to the separation of legal buildings from surrounding infrastructures.

The experiential and material attributes of the state-law relationship prompts a concern with the production of legal knowledge and its

---

[10] Ibid., p. 11.
[11] Ibid., p. 14.
[12] Blomley, N. (2008). Making space for law, in Cox, K., Low, M. & Robinson, J. (eds.), *The Sage handbook of political geography*. London: Sage, p. 161.
[13] See Gregory, D. (2007). Vanishing points, in Gregory, D., & Pred, A. (eds.), *Violent geographies fear, terror and political violence*. New York: Routledge; Latour, B. (2010). *The making of law*. Cambridge: Polity Press.

ability to bring certain subjectivities and spaces into being. One of the key insights shared by these strands of work is the recognition that the operation of law exceeds the arenas conventionally set out for the performance of legal dramas. Just as scholars have sought to question the rigid distinction between state and society, the mutual co-constitution of law and society can, therefore, be traced through social practices and routines. Following the work of law-in-society and critical legal studies scholars, I would argue that law is a socially embedded process of knowledge production that enrols individuals and institutions beyond the confines of law courts and judicial pronouncements. This approach highlights the governmental nature of legal discourses, where spaces and subjects are labelled and organised through the practice of law. But this framework also focuses attention on the necessity of understanding the ways in which purportedly 'non-legal' actors and institutions are drawn into the practice of law.

This focus on the substance of law orientates attention to the nature of human agency within legal processes. As the scholarship in legal and political geography has primed us to expect, individuals are not benign recipients of legal discourses but actively constitute and resist these discourses through their everyday lives. To conceptualise this notion of agency I will draw on Miraftab and Wills's account of activism against water and electricity privatisation in the Western Cape in South Africa.[14] This research stratifies citizenship into 'invited' and 'invented' practices, illuminating a distinction between formal ('invited') notions of neoliberal citizenship centred on voting rights and the consumption of private services, and more improvised ('invented') understandings of citizenship focusing on human rights and equality. This vocabulary has spatial implications. In material terms this work illuminates the 'invented' spaces through which struggles over citizenship were performed: the street, the home and the infrastructure of the city. In more imaginative terms, this work demonstrates the ways in which 'invented' citizenship relied on forms of solidarity that operate across a series of spatial scales within and beyond the state: from the neighbourhood, to the city and through to transnational ties with other activist groups.

The use of legal instruments to implement transitional justice in BiH can be analysed through this distinction between 'invited' and

---

[14] Miraftab, F., & Wills, S. (2005). Insurgency and spaces of active citizenship. *Journal of Planning Education and Research* 25: 200–217; see also Cornwall, A. (2002). Locating citizen participation. *IDS Bulletin* 33: i–x.

'invented' practices. This is not to reify these as either fixed or mutually exclusive domains, rather making the distinction between invited and invented spaces of justice illustrates the connections between formal legal practices and the agency of individuals and groups within and beyond BiH. In doing so, this approach illustrates the ways in which formal sites of justice are simultaneously sustained and challenged through invented practices embedded in civil society, while illustrating the plural spatiality of transitional justice beyond state territoriality. Applying this mode of spatial inquiry to the case of transitional justice requires an exploration of the particular nature of such legal initiatives and their emergence over the past century.

THE DISTANCE OF TRANSITIONAL JUSTICE

The UN Security Council define transitional justice as the 'full range of processes and mechanism's associated with a society's attempts to come to terms with a legacy of past abuses, in order to ensure accountability, serve justice and achieve reconciliation'.[15] While this definition is by no means uncontested,[16] it serves as a starting point for an analysis of the ways in which transitional justice operates through distance. This distance can be articulated in three ways.

First, transitional justice operates across a temporal shift, namely that the crimes and the judicial response are occurring at different times, under purportedly different regimes. Consequently, written into varying definitions of the concept of transitional justice is a sense of the passage of time, setting a distance between crime and punishment. In early attempts to establish instruments of transitional justice, this distancing opened legal questions as to the possibility of trying individuals for crimes committed under different legal rule sets. Specifically, the Nuremburg Trials at the end of World War II were criticised at the time for instituting *ex post facto* law, and challenging the fundamental legal principle of *nullum crimen sine lege, nulla poena sine lege* (no crime without a law, no punishment without a law).[17] Despite the

---

[15] UN Security Council (2004). *The rule of law and transitional justice in conflict and post-conflict societies*. New York: United Nations, pp. 1–24.
[16] For example, see Teitel, R. (2003). Transitional justice genealogy. *Harvard Human Rights Journal* 69: 69–94.
[17] Kerr, R., & Mobekk, E. (2007). *Peace and justice seeking accountability after war*. Cambridge: Polity Press, p. 20.

codification of war crimes in the Geneva Conventions in 1949, the challenge of trying individuals under new legal and political circumstances remains. The significance of shifting political contexts was illustrated in Radovan Karadžić's pre-trial defence at the ICTY in 2009, where he argued that he had secured immunity from prosecution from the US chief peace negotiator during the Bosnian War, Richard Holbrooke. While refuted by Holbrooke[18] – though seemingly confirmed by recent anonymous US State Department accounts[19] – this attempt to challenge the jurisdiction of the court illustrates the space opened for contestation through the time delay between crime and trial. In addition to the changing political and legal context, the temporal shift also poses logistical problems for the operation of transitional justice. There are clear challenges to conducting trials after the crimes are alleged to take place, for example the mortality of witnesses, victims and offender as well as the degradation of material evidence.

Secondly, the institutions of transitional justice are often spatially removed from the context within which the crimes took place. Sriram and Ross describe this as the 'externalisation of justice', where 'trials and legal processes occur far from the locus of the crime'.[20] This is most evident in the cases of the tribunals for the conflicts Yugoslavia and the International Criminal Court (ICC), which are both currently based in The Hague in the Netherlands. But even where domestic tribunals or court facilities are used, their sites are often separated from the geographical context of the crimes and victim communities, either through their location in the capital city or through security measures separating the courts from surrounding infrastructures. The *Gacaca* courts in Rwanda, which have attempted to institute more traditional dispute-resolution mechanisms, offer an example of a more socially embedded legal process.[21] But even in these attempts, the justice process is

---

[18] See Holbrooke, R. (2008). *The face of evil.* London: The Guardian.
[19] See Klemenčić, M. (2009). The international community and the FRY/Belligerents 1989–1997, in Ingrao, C., & Emmert, T. (eds.), *Confronting the Yugoslav controversies: A scholar's initiative.* Washington, DC: US Institute for Peace Press, pp. 152–199.
[20] Sriram, C., & Ross, A. (2007). Geographies of crime and justice: Contemporary transitional justice and the creation of 'zones of impunity'. *The International Journal of Transitional Justice* 1: 25–65.
[21] Clark, P. (2007). Hybridity, holism and 'traditional' justice: The case of the Gacaca community courts in post-genocide Rwanda. *George Washington International Law Review* 39: 765–838.

confronting a social and demographic context that has radically changed through the conflict and post-conflict periods. In cases such as the former Yugoslavia, the displacement and migration of victim communities means that courts often have to face the logistical challenge of gaining testimony from witnesses and victims distributed across the globe. But even where refugees have returned, internal displacements and demographic changes can pose a challenge to the operation of justice. The Rwandan programme of *Imidugudu* ('villagisation'), undertaken since 1997, provides an example of the role of government-sponsored social engineering creating new spatial challenges to the operation of transitional justice, where former social ties are disrupted and potential trial participants redistributed across the territory of the state.[22]

Attempts have been made to address the temporal and spatial separation of legal mechanisms of transitional justice from the societies and contexts within which the crimes took place. Notable examples include the establishment of the Truth and Reconciliation Commission (TRC) in South Africa to confront the crimes of the apartheid or the hybrid international/local courts established in Timor-Leste and Cambodia. But these institutional responses do not detract from a third form of distancing: the use of law. While institutional forms of transitional justice have varied over the last century, they have been structured around the use of law as a mechanism through which justice may be sought. This approach has prioritised the establishment of new judicial institutions and the design of new legal and criminal codes through which crimes may be prosecuted. This is necessarily a practice of distancing, where contestation is removed from its social context and evaluated court rooms and legal chambers.

The reliance of legal authority on a degree of separation from 'local particularities'[23] has engendered a policy response by international organisations, such as the United Nations, which have adopted programmes to widen 'access to justice' (UNDP 2010). These large-scale policy formulations have cultivated civil society responses seeking to build connections between court processes and

---

[22] Van Leeuwen, M. (2001). Rwanda's Imidugudu programme and earlier experiences with villagisation and resettlement in East Africa. *The Journal of Modern African Studies* 39(4): 623–644.

[23] Blomley, N. (2008). Making space for law, in Cox, K., Low, M. & Robinson, J. (eds.), *The Sage handbook of political geography*. London: Sage, pp. 155–168.

community groups.[24] In the following sections, the chapter examines how widening access to transitional justice trials in BiH has not only assisted in the formal legal process but also has brought new spaces of justice into being through education programmes, transnational connections and innovative forms of political participation. These constitute invented rather than invited spaces of law, where civil society organisations bring into existence new deliberative forms of justice.

CRITICAL GEOPOLITICS OF JUSTICE

The distancing of transitional justice has been a particular issue in the case of the international response to the fragmentation of Yugoslavia and, in particular, the war in BiH between 1992 and 1995. The abstraction of judicial instruments from the context of the crimes, both spatially and temporally, has increased the necessity for forms of public outreach to generate understanding of, and cooperation with, the institutions of transitional justice. Exploring this process requires a consideration of the history of international involvement in addressing the violence of the Bosnian War. But in doing so it is important to avoid presenting a neat historical narrative of the international response to the conflict because these protean historical and geographical events are only intelligible through their complexity and specificity.

To challenge dominant narratives as essential truths, scholars have drawn on post-structural political theory to present a critical geopolitics of the conflict, which illustrates the competing and coexisting discourses that framed the military and political strategies during the conflict and post-conflict periods.[25] As Merje Kuus points out, discourses do not 'cause' a particular judicial outcome, but rather 'frame political debate in such a way as to make certain policies seem reasonable and feasible while marginalizing other policy options as

---

[24] See Hodžić, R. (2010). Living the legacy of mass atrocities: Victims' perspectives on war crimes trials. *Journal of International Criminal Justice* 8: 113–136.

[25] Campbell, D. (1998). *National deconstruction: Violence, identity and justice in Bosnia*. Minneapolis: University of Minnesota Press; Jeffrey, A. (2013). *The improvised state: Sovereignty, performance and agency in Dayton Bosnia*. Oxford: Wiley-Blackwell; Ó Tuathail, G. (1996). *Critical geopolitics*. London: Routledge; Ó Tuathail, G. (2002). Theorizing practical geopolitical reasoning: The case of the United States' response to the war in Bosnia. *Political Geography* 21: 601–628.

unreasonable and unfeasible'.[26] By exploring these intertwining discourses we begin to see how the separation of transitional justice mechanisms from Bosnian society was a necessary part of the operation of intervention.

The first discursive frame is that of national security. The initial political and military confrontations in BiH in 1992 were framed by nationalist leaders (both within BiH and in other former Yugoslav republics) in terms of competing understandings of national security, structured around mutual fear of minority status in new state territorialities. Political groups representing Bosnian Muslims (or Bosniaks) and Croats feared Serb political dominance in what remained of the Yugoslav state (following the secession of Croatia and Slovenia in 1991). In contrast, Serb nationalist political parties, in particular the *Srpska demokratska stranka* (SDS) led by Radovan Karadžić, feared minority status in an independent BiH. These fears fuelled antagonistic political rhetoric that transformed into violence following the Bosnian government's declaration of independence in April 1992.[27] Over the following months, Serb military and paramilitary forces, supported by well-armed Yugoslav People's Army (JNA), attempted to create an ethnically homogenous territory within BiH, called the Republika Srpska (or RS).[28] This action involved the expulsion or execution of non-Serb populations, the besieging of key cities such as Sarajevo and Goražde, and the holding of prisoner populations in a series of camps in Prijedor, Brčko and Bijeljina, amongst others.[29] Similar atrocities, if on a smaller scale, were committed by groups claiming to represent Bosniak or Croat national interests, in particular in the southern Bosnian towns of Konjic, Mostar and Čelebići.

The second discursive frame was humanitarianism. Western political elites portrayed the violence as a humanitarian disaster,[30] focusing attention on the plight of Bosnian citizenry in particular in the besieged streets of Sarajevo. This biopolitical label drew attention to the

---

[26] Kuus, M. (2007). *Geopolitics reframed: Security and identity in Europe's eastern enlargement*. New York and Houndsmills: Palgrave Macmillan, p. 10.
[27] Silber, L., & Little, A. (1996). *The death of Yugoslavia*. London: Penguin.
[28] Kadrić, J. (1998). *Brcko: Genocide and testimony*. Sarajevo: Institute for the Research of Crimes Against Humanity and International Law.
[29] Dahlman, C., & Ó Tuathail, G. (2005). Broken Bosnia: The localized geopolitics of displacement and return in two Bosnian places. *Annals of the Association of American Geographers* 95: 644–662.
[30] Ó Tuathail, Theorizing practical geopolitical reasoning, 601–628.

outcome of violence and the failure of the state to perform its function of protecting its citizenry, but it simultaneously erased a conception of victim and perpetrator. Presenting the conflict in these terms allowed for an institutional response that focuses on the distribution of aid and promotion of NGOs. The humanitarian label was sustained through explanations by politicians in the United States and the United Kingdom that the violence was a consequence of 'ancient ethnic hatreds' or 'primordial evil', labels that present conflict as biologically predetermined and an essential part of a Balkan temperament rather than as a political manoeuvre. The outcome of this primordial understanding of the violence was an attempt to identify a division of Bosnian territory that would appease all warring parties.[31] In doing so, we can see how the rubric of humanitarianism only sustained the discursive framing of the conflict in terms of national security.

Alongside the entwined discourses of national security and humanitarianism there circulated a third discursive frame of the Bosnian War: accountability. The images of war crimes broadcast through international media networks, in particular the pictures of emaciated Bosniak men behind barbed wire at the Omarska prison camp in 1992, jarred with discourses of national security or humanitarianism. The organic narrative of violence encapsulated by a humanitarian interpretation of the conflict was challenged by the outpouring of public and political fury provoked by reports of war crimes and displaced people. As Ó Tuathail notes, allegations of genocide in Europe raised the spectre of the impotence of Western Allies in the face of the Holocaust in World War II and the subsequent commitment to 'never again' stand by while atrocities on such scale were committed.[32] As a response to these apparent violations of the Geneva Conventions in October 1992 the UN Security Council established a commission of experts to investigate alleged war crimes in BiH. The findings of this commission led to pressure within the United Nations to establish a tribunal to hold individuals to account for the acts against civilians in BiH. The material outcome of these pressures was the establishment by the UN Security Council of the International Criminal Tribunal for the Former Yugoslavia (ICTY) through Resolution 827 on 25 May 1993. The resolution tasked the

---

[31] Campbell, D. (1998). *National deconstruction: Violence, identity, and justice in Bosnia.* Minneapolis: University of Minnesota Press.
[32] Ó Tuathail, *Critical geopolitics.*

tribunal with 'prosecuting persons responsible for serious violations of international humanitarian law committed in the territory of the former Yugoslavia' from January 1991 onwards.[33]

As Hazan has illustrated, this institutional response was shaped by the dominant discourse of the conflict of national security.[34] The initial work of the tribunal was hampered by poor resourcing and internal disputes between the panel of international judges and the first chief prosecutor, Richard Goldstone. A particular criticism levelled by the jurists was the extremely slow pace of initial indictments and the focus placed by Goldstone on lower-level military officers rather than targeting wartime leaders. In this respect, Hazan suggests that Goldstone was performing a political function for Western leaders by intimidating the leadership of warring parties, but 'stopping short of indicting them'.[35] In addition, local and national courts and prosecution offices across the territory of the former Yugoslavia began conducting war crimes cases and compiling lists of alleged perpetrators. As Mallinder notes, minority groups perceived these practices as reflecting the political interests of the demographic majority in a particular locality.[36] In February 1996 the Bosnian government formally agreed to halt the arrest of individuals who has been indicted by the ICTY, in a set of procedures known as the 'Rules of the Road'.

The discourse of national security was further emboldened through the internationally brokered resolution to the violence in BiH. As the work of Campbell has demonstrated,[37] the Dayton Peace Accords (DPA) in 1995 emphasised a commitment to ethnically defined territories, albeit with the paradoxical guarantee of the right of return for refugees and internally displaced people. While this outcome reproduces a discourse of national security, it could be argued that concerns over accountability acted as a backdrop to Dayton negotiations, in particular since Radovan Karadžić and Bosnian Serb Army General

---

[33] UN Security Council Resolution 827, 25 May 1993.
[34] Hazan, P. (2004). *Justice in a time of war: The true story behind the international criminal tribunal for the former Yugoslavia.* College Station: Texas A&M University Press.
[35] Ibid., p. 61.
[36] Mallinder, L. (2009). *Retribution, restitution and reconciliation: Limited amnesty in Bosnia-Herzegovina.* Master's thesis, Queen's University Belfast.
[37] Campbell, D. (1998). *National deconstruction: Violence, identity and justice in Bosnia.* Minneapolis: University of Minnesota Press.

Ratko Mladić were indicted for a second time during the negotiation process[38] and compliance with the ICTY was written in to Annex 6 (Chapter 3) of the resulting Peace Accords. But despite these moves, in the immediate post-conflict period the momentum for the judicial response to the violence was lost, reflected in the shift to language of democratisation, in particular prioritising democratic elections that strengthened nationalist political parties[39] and the weak terms of engagement for the NATO implementation force (I-For), which acted as a barrier to the arrest of indicted individuals.[40]

This outcome ensured that the judicial instruments designed to hold war criminals to account were located at a distance to the localities at which the crimes took place. The devolved nature of the Bosnian state, and the subsequent strength of the entity-level governments, resulted in political stagnation in creating a single legal entity capable of performing war crimes trials in BiH.[41] The powers of the international community have been concentrated in the OHR, and singularly in the figure of the High Representative, an appointee of the Peace Implementation Council (PIC). Since 1997 the High Representative has held Bonn Powers, named after the PIC conference at which they were authorised, which grant executive and legislative powers over the Bosnian state in the name of implementing the Dayton Agreement. In the face of 'centrifugal forces', the OHR has used Bonn Powers to make basic reforms to elements of the education system, the divided military and stagnating system of government.[42] A critical study of the geopolitical framing of the war in BiH can, therefore, draw a connection between the international endorsement of discourses of national security, and the resultant fragmented state dependent upon international supervision with strong executive and legislative powers.

---

[38] Goldstone, For humanity, pp. 107–108.
[39] See Donais, T. (2000). Division and democracy: Bosnia's post-Dayton elections, in Spencer, M. (ed.), The lessons of Yugoslavia. London: JAI Elsevier Science, pp. 229–258.
[40] The first arrest by the NATO-led multinational force in Bosnia (then S-For) was Milan Kovacević on 10 July 1997.
[41] See Jeffrey, A. (2009). Justice incomplete: Radovan Karadžić, the ICTY and the spaces of international law. Environment and Planning D: Society and Space 27: 387–402.
[42] International Crisis Group (2007). Ensuring Bosnia's Future: A New International Engagement Strategy. International Crisis Group, Sarajevo/Brussels.

THE WAR CRIMES CHAMBER

One of the key impositions made by then High Representative Lord Paddy Ashdown on 3 July 2002 was to impose The Law on the CBiH, legislation that established for the first time the possibility of a state level court in BiH. This was realised in March 2005 through a joint initiative between the ICTY and OHR established the WCC of the CBiH. This organisation, operating within the Criminal Division of the CBiH, accepted transferred cases from the ICTY in addition to commencing new prosecutions and investigations.

There are a number of important facets to the WCC. First, from the outset this body has been supported by international personnel within both the Prosecutor's Office and Judiciary. This involvement is unpopular with domestic political parties, in particular within the RS, and in October 2009 the Bosnian government ordered for international participation to cease, though was overruled by the High Representative. Second, the trials take place within the CBiH building, funded by the European Union and the government of Japan, and containing eight court rooms each constructed and equipped through funding from multilateral and bilateral sources. Figure 4.1 shows Courtroom 6, a high-security facility funded by the Belgian government and used in high-profile war crimes cases.

Through analysis of the discursive framing of the violence in BiH we can discern three reasons for the necessity of a public outreach initiative involving NGOs in fostering understanding in the work of the WCC. First, the WCC is a new institutional response to the violence of the conflict and, consequently, it may be unfamiliar to communities in BiH. Certainly the PIOS official suggested that there is a longer legacy of perceiving courts as removed from wider society in the former Yugoslavia:

> The idea was that people felt more comfortable contacting an NGO than contacting a court, people were concerned about contacting courts, they were not seen as accessible, this was a legacy of the Yugoslav past where courts were always seen as up here [gestures with her hands]. So people didn't want to contact the court.[43]

Second, the origins of the WCC in OHR decision-making and the subsequent involvement of an international judiciary has led to the

---
[43] PIOS Official, Sarajevo, 8 October 2009.

Figure 4.1 Courtroom 6, Court of Bosnia and Herzegovina (Photo: author's own)

Court being seen as international imposition by some segments of the Bosnian public. This is often not meant as a criticism; indeed many of the NGO officials I interviewed for this research saw the retention of an international judiciary as crucial to the continued functioning of the court. However, the international presence was identified by both the Bosnian Court official and the ICTY Liaison Officer as a key reason to promote public outreach to build community trust in the judicial process. Finally, the establishment of the WCC was strongly opposed by nationalist politicians in BiH, in particular Milorad Dodik's *Savez nezavisnih socijaldemokrata* (SNSD) party in the RS. This domestic hostility to the WCC, coupled with the novelty of this institutional form and the perception of international imposition, strengthened attempts within the court to establish some form of public outreach initiative.[44] This came to fruition in 2005 with the creation of PIOS as part of the CBiH, and specifically with attempts to create links with

[44] ICTY Liaison Officer and co-instigator of the CSN, Sarajevo, 9 October 2009.

Bosnian NGOs working in the fields of human rights, education and reconciliation.

INVITED AND INVENTED SPACES OF JUSTICE

The Court Support Network (CSN) was established by PIOS in 2005. Its mission was 'to integrate the mission of the Court into the wider Bosnian community',[45] an objective that one of the instigators described as 'more than PR'.[46] The Court approached five human rights NGOs located in the Bosnian towns of Sarajevo (Žene ženama), Mostar (Centri civilnih inicijativa or CCI), Prijedor (Izvor), Bijeljina (Helsinški komitet) and Tuzla (Forum građana). The idea was to reach a wide geographical spread and through these organisations establish a sustainable network which would spread information about the Court, and in particular the WCC.[47]

The original CSN programme was funded by the Court for six months and provided resources to each NGO to dedicate two staff to work on networking activities. One of the key objectives behind the CSN was for the organisations involved to develop their own network, and thus the reach of the court would extend into Bosnian communities through the operation of civil society groups. After the end of the first phase of funding this had not been achieved and one of the officials involved remarked that the lack of follow-up funding was a reflection of changing priorities in PIOS away from outreach work and towards public and media relations.[48] But despite the weakening of the formal network approach, the participant NGOs have continued to work with the Court (and in particular the WCC) and have remained in loose affiliation while the concept of the CSN remains a core part of the Court's public relations materials. As part of this research project I examined the activities in detail of two of the organisations within the CSN: CCI in southern town of Mostar and Helsinški komitet in the northern town of Bijeljina. Through the interviews with these organisations, and studying their promotional and policy documentation, ambiguities emerge as to the position and nature of their activities. While providing logistical assistance to the trial process, these

---

[45] Ibid.
[46] Ibid.
[47] PIOS Official, Sarajevo, 8 October 2009.
[48] ICTY Liaison Officer and co-instigator of the CSN, Sarajevo, 9 October 2009.

organisations also offer space for critique and rejection of the mechanisms of transitional justice initiated in BiH since the end of the war. To illustrate these diverse functions I am drawing on the framework introduced by Miraftab and Wills (2005) to group them under the headings 'invited' and 'invented' spaces of justice. As discussed earlier in the chapter, these labels provide a sense of the agency of the CSN institutions as they operated both within and beyond the roles prescribed by PIOS and the WCC. Consistent with the main argument of the chapter, these functions illustrate the significance of non-legal institutions and practices in shaping the legal process and offering alternative spaces of transitional justice. I will explore each in turn.

Invited Spaces
'The Court Support Network was meant to be for all the [Bosnian] public' related an official from the CCI, 'but it was mostly used by potential witnesses'.[49] This comment encapsulates what was perceived by both those managing and participating in the CSN: that its primary focus was on encouraging and supporting witnesses of war crimes to come forward and testify at the WCC. Part of this function was logistical, providing the Court and, in particular, the prosecutor's office with assistance in getting in touch with witnesses, assisting with transportation arrangements and keeping contacts open between witnesses and court officials. But this narrow interpretation of the role of the CSN overlooks the ways in which these apparently mundane practices are reshaped by the political and economic geographies of post-Dayton BiH. In particular two challenges confronted the CSN organisations: the prioritisation of social and economic considerations over participation in the court and the stigmatisation of participation by sections of the community that resist the establishment of a state court and/or institutions of transitional justice.

In the first case the representative from CCI was explicit that participation in trial processes was a low priority for those struggling to survive in the tough economic conditions of contemporary BiH where GDP per capita in 2009 was only $7,764:[50]

---

[49] Member of Centre for Civil Initiative Official, Mostar, 12 October 2009.
[50] UNDP (2009). Human Development Report Bosnia and Herzegovina. United Nations Development Programme, Sarajevo.

So our idea was that if you have some basic problems, like of you cannot feed your children how can you decide to go to the court of BiH and be a witness, I mean this is not a priority in your life.[51]

To confront this issue the organisation sought to provide a broad approach to witness support that understood the importance of economic, social and psychological factors in shaping decision-making processes. One activity undertaken by CCI was informing witnesses of their potential eligibility to receive a small state pension on behalf of deceased relatives who were recognised as Civil Victim of War.[52] The representative explained the struggle in convincing people that they were eligible for this money:

> When we told them you have a right to this money, they would say 'no, who is going to give us money?' You know, people didn't trust anything. Even if you explain to them the law and their rights, they are sceptical about many things.[53]

These quotations illustrate the disjuncture between the existence of certain legal or judicial rights, and their adoption by potential witnesses. The simple invitation to participate – whether in the WCC process or through the civil victim status – was insufficient to ensure involvement. By exploring the individual motivations for individual participation and coupling this with psychological barriers to trust in authority structures, the CSN was able to foster participation. The CSN were adept at presenting the activities of the WCC as embedded in the social context of BiH post-Dayton .

This point was further enforced through the interview comments regarding the wider Bosnian political landscape and its effect on participation rates. The interviewees spoke of the significant role played by the dominance of nationalist political parties in shaping participation in the WCC. In particular they pointed to the role of mythical tales of heroic wartime leaders in shaping public opinion. To one extent, this reflects the sustained primacy of discourses of national security in

---

[51] Ibid.
[52] The legislation differs in the RS and Federation, but both offer pensions for victims of war that suffer '60% or more' physical disability including death or disappearance (see FBiH Law on Principles of Social Protection, Protection of Civil Victims of War and Protection of Families with Children, article 54 Official Gazette of the FBiH no. 36/99 and The Law on Protection of Civil Victims of War , article 2 Official Gazette of RS, no. 25/93).
[53] Member of Centre for Civil Initiative Official, Mostar, 12 October 2009.

shaping domestic politics in BiH over the last 15 years. But the interviews suggested that this was also reflective of the distanced nature of transitional justice over this period. The absence of an ICTY-led public outreach initiative until 1999 was blamed by a representative from *Helsinški komitet* for providing the space for the political manipulation of transitional justice in BiH:

> it was a basic mistake they [the ICTY] made in the beginning. The ICTY was established in 1993 but the outreach office of the ICTY was established in 1999. These six years were used by political leaders in the region to use cases in front of the ICTY for their political agendas.[54]

The perceived failure of the ICTY to reach out to potential witnesses in the past, therefore, reverberated into the present through the unfavourable political contexts for participation in the WCC. The CSN NGOs sought to break down this animosity by introducing schemes that foster trust in the WCC, and these initiatives involved a range of economic, psychological and political strategies. For example, CCI teamed up with a mental health NGO to provide psychological support for potential witnesses that faced the dual challenge of revisiting past traumas while risking being labelled a traitor by segments of their community on account of their participation with the WCC.

In sum, the trial assistance offered by the CSN was crucial to the operation of war crimes trials at the WCC in Sarajevo. By embedding the trial process in the economic and social context in contemporary BiH, the NGOs were able to foster participation in the legal process. Contrary to abstracting law from society, this work involved the careful grounding of these processes in the communities and localities within which the crimes took place and in which victims and witnesses continue to seek redress.

Invented Spaces
In addition to the work supporting the trial process, the CSN organisations have been performing a broader role outside the operation of the WCC since 2005. Through a range of workshops, seminars and cultural events, the NGOs were seeking to foster public debate concerning the nature of transitional justice in BiH. These actions were 'invented' as they demonstrated the ability of these organisations to operate outside the legal process and summon into existence new

[54] Member of Helsinški komitet, Bijeljina, 18 October 2009.

spaces of deliberation over the nature of transitional justice in BiH. These practices illustrated a more nuanced spatiality of justice in Bosnia. Perhaps most explicitly they bring into view the range of physical spaces that are drawn upon as part of the judicial process. Coffee shops, homes, university campuses and individual human bodies are brought into the practice of transitional justice through these improvised activities. But they also illustrate the enrolment of a range of imaginative geographies that are enrolled into the practice of transitional justice, such as universal human rights, cosmopolitan senses of belonging and nostalgia for Yugoslav solidarity. While these activities often supported the approach of the WCC they also included opportunities for critique and the hope for alternative judicial arrangements in the future. By their disparate and, at times, improvised nature these activities defy easy categorisation, but to illustrate aspects of their effects I will examine two processes: community workshops and university education.

First, the NGOs sought to localise the legal process by organising workshops involving victim groups, legal representatives and NGO staff within the communities in which the crimes took place. Such events involved prosecutors talking through the evidence as it was presented and jurists explaining the sentence (if passed) and fielding questions concerning the trial process. The interactive component of the event posed logistical problems for the NGOs because there was often high demand amongst victim groups to attend and there was resistance from NGO staff to turn people away. The success of this format has seen it adopted by the ICTY, which has recently organised similar workshops in BiH to explain case decisions. Of course, such events are not simply a transfer from legal experts to local communities. The NGO representatives discussed how new prosecutions had occurred after victim groups had approached prosecutors, emboldened by hearing about successful prosecutions in other cases.

While the trial workshops required considerable involvement of the WCC and prosecutor's office, the NGOs stressed the forms of local knowledge and contacts required to organise such events. Through family connections, personal experiences and professional relationships, the NGOs had developed networks with war crime victims that were vital in securing their participation in the workshops. These connections allowed the NGOs to bring together antagonistic victim groups into single-site workshops:

But the biggest issue is actually the preparation work. It is a much bigger issue to get in the same place people from different ethnic communities who are perceived as victims. For example you have to spend three days drinking *rakija* [plum brandy] with [name] if you want him to come. Or in some villages you have to convince [name] to come to the Čelebići case. It just needs time. And in some cases they have the experience other from other NGOs who come and say 'we need three victims to talk about something', but that is not how it works, they are not on standby.[55]

This comment encapsulates the forms of knowledge brought into the process of transitional justice by the CSN NGOs. It also demonstrates the ways in which the space of transitional justice extended beyond the hired workshop venue, and brings into view the *rakija* stall, the *kafana* (coffee shop) and the homes of victims. But this account illustrates more than the micro-geographies through which public outreach operates; it also reflects a different conception of the figure of the individual within judicial programmes. The reference to 'not being on standby' illustrates the ways in which participation was conceived by the Helsinški komitet as a human process of negotiation that required established bonds and trust rather than a mechanistic process of participation in a formal legal process.

The NGOs stressed that the localisation of judicial processes was more than a 'communicative' strategy; it sought to shift the focus of transitional justice from perpetrators onto victims. The retributive judicial approach employed by both the ICTY and the WCC has, they argued, orientated attention on those who committed crimes as opposed to those who had been victims. This situation has been exacerbated by the close allegiance between media outlets and nationalist political parties, a relationship that the NGOs felt had promoted the heroism of wartime leaders and served to question the veracity of reports of mass atrocities during the war. One case that was repeatedly cited during the research process was that of Radovan Stanković. Stanković was a fighter in the Bosnian Serb Army who was sentenced in March 2007 to 20 years of imprisonment for the crimes of systematic rape and imprisonment of women in what was termed *Karamanova kuća* (Karaman's house) in Foča municipality during 1992. But in May 2007 Stanković escaped from prison because he was sent to serve his

---

[55] Ibid.; the names of two prominent victims have been removed to protect anonymity.

sentence in Foča, a place where he had previously claimed that it would be easy to escape on the basis of his friends and contacts.[56] This case illustrates the weaknesses in the Bosnian prison system; where despite plans there is no state-level prison (penal governance is devolved to the two substate entities, the RS and Federation of Bosnia and Herzegovina). But more significantly, subsequently Stanković has refuted the charges through communication with RS newspapers. The effect of these processes was explained by the representative from *Helsinški komitet*:

In the RS there was no public space given to the presentation of facts. There is enough space given for Stanković to send letters from wherever he lives now, explaining that this is an attack on the Serb people and he is not guilty, and they gave him two pages in the newspapers. But no one is giving space to those who suffered. To the girl who is now 26 years old, or 27, and she is more dead than alive because she was kept for three months in Karaman's House and was systematically raped by more than 20 soldiers.

The Stanković case provides an acute example of the coupling of judicial failure and the capture of news media by the interests of hardline nationalist political parties. The response of the NGOs has been to provide spaces such as the workshops through which victims may meet and challenge the formal judicial structures through debate and questions. Part of this process relates to a desire to reshape the 'invited' spaces of justice through changes in the penal strategy, providing greater clarity in sentencing decisions and improving specific aspects of access to the judicial process. But more significantly, these activities also illustrate the way in which the CSN envisages a different form of justice that shifts attention away from retribution and orientates attention on restorative notions of deliberation and reconciliation. One of the key points made by each of the NGOs is that the workshops must be attended by representatives from each of the parties in the conflict, and mix civilians with veterans. As the representative from CCI emphasised, 'we have all been victims in some part of our lives'. This was in part a reference to her own personal experience, but also drew attention to a key point: that the CSN was attempting to reconceptualise justice as a shared experience rather than a legal process.

---

[56] See Balkan Transitional Justice (2010). Search for Convicted Criminal Stanković Continues, http://archive.balkaninsight.com/en/article/search-for-convicted-criminal-stankovic-continues/1458/228 (accessed 6 June 2019).

The second set of activities that brought into existence invented spaces of justice related to education. All the CSN NGOs have strong education components within their portfolio of activities. For *Helsinški komitet* this involved university-level education in transitional justice, exercised through a series of different channels. First, the organisation has sought to introduce the specifics of the WCC into law degrees across the RS:

> We made an announcement through law students in the RS, so I did several groups throughout the year bringing them to the court, to talk to the president of the court, the main prosecutor, to see a trial and how it is organised and to see the court, witness preparation and protection and to talk to other NGOs who are working with victims. And we had more than 3000 students pass this.[57]

As stated earlier in the discussion, there is considerable political animosity towards the WCC in the RS so these activities mark a considerable achievement in sharing information concerning the legal processes in BiH. But to build on this success the organisation developed a second approach to university-level education: designing a module on transitional justice and human rights to be run in the University of Bijeljina. During the interview, the NGO official said with a smile that they had described the module as concerning 'intercultural understanding and non-violent communication'[58] as this was unlikely to raise objections from university administrators, in a way that mentioning the WCC or transitional justice might. This initiative began with 83 students in October 2009 but there are hopes to expand:

> We are starting with the Bijeljina Faculty, then Mostar is going to start Eastern Sarajevo, Pale they are going to start next year and then Sarajevo is going to start next year.... On the other side we are currently working on making a group of professors from law schools from five different universities, political science departments, the journalism departments, and social sciences and we are going to work with them for one year to make it possible to see how much of transitional justice they can actually put in a formal education frame, what they would need, on what they could agree, and how to teach it.

This focus on university education illustrates the significant emphasis placed on setting the terms of public debate concerning transitional

---

[57] Ibid.
[58] Ibid.

PUBLIC OUTREACH

justice. One of the repeated concerns of NGOs members both within and beyond the CSN was the media presentation of transitional justice as 'simply' the actions of the ICTY and WCC, rather than discussing the nature and implications of different approaches to justice after war. In the absence of a unified commemoration of the conflict and the associated fragmented historical narratives of the past, these approaches placed the WCC in a historical and theoretical context. This approach sought to shift attention away from the particulars of the BiH context and think through more cosmopolitan understandings of justice and rights. This 'invented' space moves beyond the physical realm of the campus and seminar room, to confront the imaginative geographies enrolled in processes of transitional justice.

Drawing the distinction between invited and invented spaces of justice illuminates the role played by the CSN in the operation of transitional justice in BiH. While these accounts provide a vivid illustration of the importance of civil society actors in facilitating the trial process, they also demonstrate how these organisations conceive of justice in radically different ways to those offered through the formal legal institutions. This does not mean law is marginalised, the NGOs considered its operation vital to generating a sense of accountability amongst victim population. Instead, the legal process was presented as a starting point that provoked public debate and the potential to bring victim groups together to discuss common concerns. Through the legal process, the CSN was able to create a series of spaces of justice as a more deliberative practice.

CONCLUSIONS

Towards the end of the fieldwork process I had arranged a meeting with the programme manager of UNDP BiH's Access to Justice programme at their head office in Sarajevo. This initiative provides assistance to the CBiH through training of the judiciary, capacity-building Bosnian state agencies and providing material support for the court (such as office furniture and IT equipment). After we had introduced ourselves, I explained the purpose of my research and my interest in the WCC's outreach projects. 'Ah,' replied the programme manager, '*you* are interested in questions of "soft" justice, *we* are currently interested in questions of "hard" justice.'[59] The programme manager's use of this

---

[59] Programme Manager of UNDP Access to Justice BiH, Sarajevo, 15 October 2009.

distinction was a surprise considering the UNDP's commitment to fostering civil society engagement with processes of transitional justice in BiH.[60] But in doing so, the UNDP official was deploying well-established categories demarcating legal from non-legal approaches. But these labels do not simply describe judicial practice but also structure regimes of thought on transitional justice. The distinction of 'hard' and 'soft' justice supports the conception that there is a possibility of separating these two arenas, where the 'hard' legal processes operate in isolation from the 'soft' social, political and spatial settings within which they are embedded. This separation is reflected in the wider scholarly study of transitional justice that has explored the nature of legal processes at the expense of either wider non-legal activities or the constructed nature of the legal/non-legal binary.

This chapter has offered a corrective by examining the contribution of a geographical analysis on the study of transitional justice in BiH. There are two specific outcomes from this argument. Firstly, the study of the critical geopolitics of the conflict and post-conflict periods illuminates the spacing of transitional justice in BiH. The presentation of the violence by wartime leaders as a necessity to ensure national security, and the validation of these imaginaries at the Dayton Peace Accords, ensured that legal processes of justice remained remote from the locations where the crimes took place. This distance was reflected through the physical location of the ICTY at The Hague and the executive control over the process by international supervisory agencies in Bosnia (most notably the OHR). But perhaps most profoundly, this distance is reflected in the prominence given to legal processes as the primary implement of justice. This form of judicial response has set the tone for the nature of post-conflict justice in BiH, specifically focusing on a retributive programme that seeks to hold war criminals to account, rather than a restorative process that seeks to establish shared truths and build trust between antagonistic groups.

As a second geographical lens this chapter has examined how the political and scholarly focus on legal processes has marginalised a series of non-legal spaces, actors and practices. Through the examination of the prosaic operation of the CSN a more complex spatiality of transitional justice emerged. Using the analytical distinction developed by Miraftab and Wills (2005), these were explored through the framework

[60] UNDP (2009). Transitional Justices Guidebook for Bosnia and Herzegovina. United Nations Development Programme, Sarajevo.

of 'invited' and 'invented' spaces of justice. This brought to the fore the centrality of CSN organisations in facilitating the work of the WCC by supporting witness testimony and establishing contact with victims. But the work of the CSN extended beyond these instrumental practices because they were using their contacts with victim groups to establish practices of justice that were operated beyond the formal legal process. These activities work through a series of geographies: such as the coffee shop, the seminar room, the campus and the human body. But inventing such improvised spaces of deliberation over justice required conveying normative arguments for the kinds of transnational solidarity and rights that were at the heart of transitional justice programmes. In this sense, invented spaces of justice sought to look beyond the BiH state territory and foster conceptions of common humanity and transnational belonging. In contrast to the retributive mode of formal judicial practices, the improvised activities were often structured around deliberation and confrontation. This more agonistic approach provided space for victims to offer critiques of the formal trial processes and sought to embed legal mechanisms in the context of wider scholarly and policy reflection on the nature of justice.

CHAPTER FIVE

LAW AND CITIZENSHIP

INTRODUCTION

On 6 June 2002 the then High Representative of Bosnia and Herzegovina (BiH), Lord Paddy Ashdown, attended the inaugural session of the Court of Bosnia and Herzegovina (CBiH) and addressed the assembled local and international dignitaries. Reflecting his responsibility for implementing the 1995 General Framework Agreement for Peace (GFAP) and the legislative powers of the Office of the High Representative (OHR), Ashdown had recently imposed the creation of the CBiH in the face of domestic political opposition. In doing so, the legal territory of BiH was unified for the first time since the end of the 1992–1995 conflict, establishing a jurisdiction 'above' that of the two substate entities – the Federation of Bosnia and Herzegovina (FBiH) and the Republika Srpska (RS). Ashdown described the impacts of a unified court in terms of fostering liberal democratic citizenship:

> [The court] is about protecting the people of this country, protecting their rights and protecting their status as free citizens in a functioning democracy. This court enshrines a simple truth – that everyone is equal before the law. Justice is the foundation on which every society is built. Everything else we want to do here, from jobs to refugee returns to establishing a democratic system, depends on the rule of law.[1]

---

[1] Office of the High Representative, Remarks by the High Representative, Paddy Ashdown, at the inaugural session of the BiH State Court (2002), www.ohr.int/ ohr-dept/presso/presssp/default.asp?content_id=8657 (accessed 18 November 2018).

Just more than 10 years later in a conference room in central Sarajevo, on 20 September 2012, a workshop took place to discuss the findings from research exploring the implementation of the CBiH. In front of assembled court officials, members of international organisations, human rights non-governmental organisations (NGOs) and academics, Amina, the president of a prominent association of women victims of war, explained the challenges that members of her association faced pursuing justice through the CBiH. Challenging the sense of universal liberal democratic citizenship envisaged a decade earlier, Amina shook with anger and held pictures of prominent alleged war criminals from the Visegrad area of eastern BiH:

> Since I was a victim and witness at The Hague Tribunal and Court of BiH, I have heard it all and I was aware of it. I feel sorry to say that victims are fed up with all sorts of projects, all kinds of conclusions and reports and nothing has been completed by now.... Twenty one years have passed since the war started. Victims are dying every day and they will not live long enough to see justice.
> (Sarajevo Workshop, 20 September 2012)

The chapter starts with these two moments in the creation and operation of a state-level court to point to some of the fundamental tensions within understandings of the geographies of citizenship. As much of the scholarship in this field has pointed out, citizenship is a contested term that orientates attention on both forms of political collectivity and individual political practices.[2] Starting from this distinction between the collective and the individual we can begin to trace a series of tensions that inhabit the concept of citizenship, between citizenship as a form of governmental technique that seeks to order and classify a population and as a set of individual behaviours that seek to intervene and shape the nature of communities and practices of rule.[3] This distinction between a governmentally inscribed form of citizenship and a set of political practices is reflected in the conceptual separation between liberal democratic citizenship and civic republican citizenship. Where liberal democratic citizenship emphasises

---

[2] Desforges, L., Jones, R. & Woods, M. (2005). New geographies of citizenship. *Citizenship Studies* 9(5): 439–451; Staeheli, L. A. (2011). Political geography: Where's citizenship? *Progress in Human Geography* 35(3): 393–400.

[3] Staeheli, L. A., Ehrkamp, P., Leitner, H. & Nagel, C. R. (2012). Dreaming the ordinary daily life and the complex geographies of citizenship. *Progress in Human Geography* 36(5): 628–644.

the constitution of certain universal rights that derive from membership of a political community (usually a state), civic republican citizenship emphasises the duties of the individual in serving and constituting such a political community. In Ashdown's framework, the establishment of the Court consolidates liberal democratic citizenship in BiH, a territory partitioned down ethnic lines after the GFAP.[4] Capturing the celebratory spirit of early works on the expansion of liberal democratic citizenship;[5] the court was imagined by Ashdown to play a significant part in unifying the state and cultivating a sense of the universal rights and duties that comprised BiH citizenship.

In contrast to Ashdown's expectation of universalism, Amina's response a decade later speaks of the uneven nature of access to the legal process. In Amina's view, the lack of legal support, the exclusion of women from decision-making bodies and the absence of victim's voice from the judicial process were all playing a role in marginalising individuals on the basis of wealth, gender or geographical location.[6] In doing so, this statement echoes the work of critical scholars who have pointed to the multiple scales of exclusion and marginalisation that are often masked by the purported universalism of liberal democratic citizenship. For example, Painter and Philo argue that it is through the demarcation of 'insiders' and 'outsiders' that liberal citizenship asserts its right to rule.[7] One of the key messages of this work has been that forms of exclusion take many forms, from the securitisation of borders and tightening of immigration controls,[8] to socially and culturally inscribed mechanisms of exclusion based on gender,[9]

---

[4] See Campbell, D. (1998). *National deconstruction: Violence, identity and justice in Bosnia*. Minneapolis: University of Minnesota Press; Toal, G., & Dahlman, C. T. (2011). *Bosnia remade: Ethnic cleansing and its reversal*. Oxford: Oxford University Press.

[5] Marshall, T. H. (1950). *Citizenship and social class*. Cambridge: Cambridge University Press.

[6] Sarajevo Workshop, 20 September 2012.

[7] Painter, J., & Philo, C. (1995). Spaces of citizenship: An introduction. *Political Geography* 14: 107–120; see also Isin, E. F. (2002). *Being political geneaologies of citizenship*. Minneapolis: University of Minnesota Press.

[8] See Leitner, H., & Strunk, C. (2014). Spaces of immigrant advocacy and liberal democratic citizenship. *Annals of the Association of American Geographers* 104(2): 348–356; Sparke, M. B. (2006). A neoliberal nexus: Economy, security and the biopolitics of citizenship on the border. *Political Geography* 25: 151–180.

[9] Goldring, L. (2001). The gender and geography of citizenship in Mexico-US transnational spaces. *Identities Global Studies in Culture and Power* 7(4): 501–537.

class,[10] sexuality,[11] disability[12] and race.[13] The co-presence of so many strands of potential exclusion has led scholars to rely upon a distinction between de facto and de jure citizenship to highlight the distinction between the conferment of citizenship rights and the possibility of practicing or accessing such.[14]

But in making this point I need to be careful to avoid the construction of a rigid distinction between inclusion and exclusion. Much of the scholarship critiquing a liberal democratic understanding of citizenship has done so to highlight the alternative citizenship practices that may be masked by focusing solely on the allocation of formal political rights. In this sense, Amina's statement must be coupled with her position within a civil society organisation mobilising to enact change: her association is actively demanding its legal rights and setting about to voice concerns. This form of active citizenship can be interpreted in two ways. In the first it reflects a move towards a model of civil republican citizenship, rejecting the atomised individualism of the liberal democratic model and emphasising a sense of collective politics required to lay claims to rights.[15] This expectation of civic collective action has been a feature of international intervention in developmental and post-conflict environments,[16] and not least in BiH.[17] As a second interpretation Amina's actions could be understood as a form

---

[10] Pykett, J. (2009). Making citizens in the classroom: An urban geography of citizenship education? *Urban Studies* 46(4): 803–823.

[11] Bell, D. (1995). Pleasure and danger: The paradoxical spaces of sexual citizenship. *Political Geography* 14(2): 139–153; Binnie, J., & Valentine, G. (1999). Geographies of sexuality: A review of progress. *Progress in Human Geography* 23(2): 175–187; Hubbard, P. (2001). Sex zones: Intimacy, citizenship and public space. *Sexualities* 4(1): 51–71.

[12] Valentine, G., & Skelton, T. (2007). The right to be heard: Citizenship and language. *Political Geography* 26: 121–140.

[13] Kofman, E. (1995). Citizenship for some but not for others: Spaces of citizenship in contemporary Europe. *Political Geography* 14(2): 121–137.

[14] See, for example, Valentine & Skelton, The right to be heard, 121–140.

[15] P. 32 in Lister, R. (1997). Citizenship: Towards a feminist synthesis. *Feminist Review* 57: 28–48.

[16] Mohan, G. (2002). The disappointments of civil society: The politics of NGO intervention in northern Ghana. *Political Geography* 21(1): 125–154.

[17] Belloni, R. (2001). Civil society and peacebuilding in Bosnia and Herzegovina. *Journal of Peace Research* 38: 163–180; Fagan, A. (2005). Civil society in Bosnia ten years after Dayton. *International Peacekeeping* 12: 406–419; Jeffrey, A. (2007). The geopolitical framing of localized struggles: NGOs in Bosnia and Herzegovina. *Development and Change* 38(2): 251–274.

of activist citizenship, a more radical form of insurgent citizenship that seeks to transform the existing political system and enact new forms of rights.[18] Such actions may not be directed solely against the state, but instead confront the multiple scales – from the city to international organisations – from which perceived injustices stem.[19]

This chapter explores these tensions between the expectations of liberal democratic citizenship and its practice through the establishment of the WCC at the CBiH. By tracing the relationship between the governmental intervention, and in particular the establishment of a new legal institution, and subsequent practices of citizenship we are keen to pursue in empirical detail the notion of citizenship as a 'dynamic concept in which process and outcome stand in a dialectical relationship to each other'.[20] Rather than reifying a straightforward geometry between state-sanctioned notions of liberal democratic citizenship and the more activist practices found within civil society, the evidence from the establishment of the court points to a plural story, where individuals are using informal spaces and practices to seek to access rights that they believe to be the responsibility of the BiH state. Part articulated through a nostalgia for Socialist modernity and part through a weariness of a dysfunctional post-conflict state, these claims for state-based rights view war crimes trials as necessary for achieving justice but insufficient to strengthen the capacity of the state.

This focus on process and outcome of citizenship is conducted through a study of the use of law to consolidate the state. By exploring the forms of international intervention in BiH since 2002 the chapter argues that there is a central tension between the function of law (to arbitrate on crime) and the desire to consolidate the state (to reconcile different stories of the past and visions of the future). To make this argument, I will draw on qualitative data gathered over 12 months of

---

[18] Holston, J. (2008). *Insurgent citizenship disjunctions of democracy and modernity in Brazil*. Princeton, NJ: Princeton University Press; Leitner, H., & Strunk, C. (2014). Spaces of immigrant advocacy and liberal democratic citizenship. *Annals of the Association of American Geographers* 104(2): 348–356.

[19] See, for example, Jeffrey, A., Staeheli, L. A., Buire, C. & Čelebičić, V. (2018). Drinking coffee, rehearsing civility, making subjects. *Political Geography* 67: 125–134; Miraftab, F., & Wills, S. (2005). Insurgency and spaces of active citizenship the story of Western Cape anti-eviction campaign in South Africa. *Journal of Planning Education and Research* 25(2): 200–217.

[20] P. 355 in Lister, R. (1997). Citizenship: Towards a feminist synthesis. *Feminist Review* 57: 28–48.

residential fieldwork in BiH conducted between July 2011 and August 2012. The research design was informed by studies of citizenship that have sought to study both the contexts and practices through which concepts of citizenship are articulated and challenged.[21] This approach gleaned information about both concerning elite discourse and what Desforges et al. term 'actual existing citizenship'.[22] The research involved more than 60 interviews with court officials, members of human rights NGOs, members of international organisations, embassy officials and representatives within Bosnian victims' associations. The research also involved participant observation of outreach programmes led by the CBiH, the International Criminal Tribunal for the former Yugoslavia (ICTY), Swiss organisation Track Impunity Always (TRIAL) and Medica Zenica. Finally, the research involved monitoring war crimes trials at the CBiH and, where possible, tracking a trial from indictment through to verdict. In this chapter I will use this material to examine the establishment of the CBiH, focusing on the mechanisms used by court officials and international agencies to build the legitimacy of these new legal orders and institutions.[23]

As we have seen in previous chapters, a specific start date for the Court cannot be discerned, it rather faded into existence through a series of new laws and initiatives. Most notably in 2002 the OHR imposed a law on the CBiH, and a year later imposed a new Criminal Procedure Code in 2003 based on US common law. These moves aimed to transform prosecution and trial processes, in particular eliminating the need for an investigative judge and introducing adversarial trial arrangements and plea bargaining.[24] The commencement of trials at the Court required the training (or retraining) of the domestic judiciary and the establishment of the State Investigation and

---

[21] See, for example, Isin, E. F., & Nielsen, G. M. (eds.). (2013). *Acts of citizenship*. London: Zed Books Ltd; McNamara, R. S. N., & Morse, S. (2004). Voices from the aid 'chain': The personal dynamics of care. *Social and Cultural Geography* 5(2): 253–270; Mohan, G. (2002). The disappointments of civil society: The politics of NGO intervention in northern Ghana. *Political Geography* 21(1): 125–154.

[22] P. 448 in Desforges, L., Jones, R. & Woods, M. (2005). New geographies of citizenship. *Citizenship Studies* 9(5): 439–451.

[23] In this chapter we have used pseudonyms for research participants with the exception of respondents who have given permission for their names to be used.

[24] See discussion in Chapter 7, in addition to Organisation for Security and Cooperation in Europe, OSCE Trial Monitoring Report (2004), www.oscebih.org/documents/osce_bih_doc_20101223105351111eng.pdf (accessed 18 November 2018).

Prosecution Agency (Državna agencija za istrage i zaštitu or SIPA). The creation of the Court served a dual function: first, it was tasked with consolidating a legal system that, since the GFAP, had been highly fragmented. As has been well documented,[25] the GFAP retained the borders of the BiH state but devolved substantial powers to the two substate political 'entities' the Republika Srpska (RS) and the Federation of Bosnia and Herzegovina, and later to a special district around the northern town of Brčko. In the absence of a state court, trials were conducted at the entity level or below using the 1976 Criminal Code of the former Socialist Federal Republic of Yugoslavia. The second objective of the Court was to serve as part of the completion mandate for ICTY. As discussed in Chapter 2, since 1993 war crimes cases had been held at the ICTY at The Hague under the mandate provided by UN Security Council Resolution 808. International officials viewed the CBiH as an institution that could initially handle transferred cases from the ICTY while employing its own investigative and prosecutorial competences to indict and try those suspected of war crimes in BiH.

The dual function of the CBiH is reflected in aspects of its structure. The Court's trial activities are divided into three sections: war crimes cases, organised crime and other criminal cases in BiH that are not covered by municipal courts. Between 2005 and 2011, 13 war crimes cases were transferred from the ICTY to the CBiH, while more than 50 further war crimes trials were being heard by the Court.[26] Located in a refurbished Yugoslav People's Army (Jugoslovenska narodna armija or JNA) barracks on Kraljice Jelene street, the Court building was completed in 2006 using funds from the European Community and the government of Japan, with bilateral donations paying for the refurbishment of individual courtrooms. Since its creation it has been a 'hybrid' court, drawing its judiciary from both domestic and international

---

[25] See Campbell, D. (1998). *National deconstruction: Violence, identity and justice in Bosnia*. Minneapolis: University of Minnesota Press; Campbell, D. (1999). Apartheid cartography: The political anthropology and spatial effects of international diplomacy in Bosnia. *Political Geography* 18: 395–435; Helms, E., Bougarel, X. & Duijzings, G. (eds.). (2007). *The new Bosnian mosaic*. London: Routledge; Jeffrey, A. (2013). *The improvised state: Sovereignty, performance and agency in Dayton Bosnia*. Oxford: Wiley-Blackwell; Toal, G., & Dahlman, C. T. (2011). *Bosnia remade: Ethnic cleansing and its reversal*. Oxford: Oxford University Press.

[26] TRIAL (2018). The War Crimes Chamber of the CBiH, www.trial-ch.org/en/resources/tribunals/hybrid-tribunals/war-crimes-chamber-in-bosnia-herzegovina.html (accessed 18 November 2018).

sources. The enrolment of international judges has become a focal point for critique by domestic politicians keen to portray this legal enterprise as anti-democratic and internationally imposed.

The establishment of the CBiH, therefore, provides a valuable insight into the creation of a new state-level institution in a country that has been highly devolved in the post-GFAP period. The CBiH illustrates the paradoxes of internationally sponsored state building, in particular using externally conferred powers to strengthen the internal sovereignty of a post-conflict state.[27] Consequently, the establishment of the Court has required a range of initiatives aimed at communicating its legitimacy to a wider Bosnian public. Collectively referred to as 'public outreach', these processes have enrolled civil society organisations as partners in conveying the aims and activities of the CBiH across BiH territory. Tracing the nature and outcomes of these activities provides an opportunity to explore these more 'prosaic'[28] and 'improvised'[29] mechanisms through which legal legitimacy is conveyed. While the notion of establishing legal jurisdiction is suggestive of an abstract and instrumental process, studying the establishment of the Court allows an exploration of how performances of law unfold in actual places and are carried into existence by individual bodies.[30] Legal places are as mutable and dynamic as any other and the establishment of jurisdiction requires the constant production of particular subjectivities and specific geographical imaginaries. We are not arguing here simply of the complexity of varied contrasting imaginations of law and state that circulate in post-conflict BiH. Rather, we are suggesting that attempts to establish liberal democratic citizenship rights through the creation of the CBiH are productive of alternative understandings of justice and differing interpretations of responsibilities of the state. This line of critical legal geography begins to challenge the singularity of jurisdiction, illuminating instead the uneven nature of individual submissions to new legal orders and the creation of alternative legal geographies that bolster particular claims to state sovereignty.

---

[27] See Chapter 2, and the discussion in Elden, S. (2009). *Territory and terror the spatial extent of sovereignty*. Minneapolis: University of Minnesota Press.
[28] Painter, J. (2006). Prosaic geographies of stateness. *Political Geography* 25: 752–774.
[29] Jeffrey, A. (2013). *The improvised state: Sovereignty, performance and agency in Dayton Bosnia*. Oxford: Wiley-Blackwell.
[30] See discussion of this imagination of performed and embodied space in Massey, D. (2004). Geographies of responsibility. *Geografiska Annaler B* 86: 5–18.

The chapter is divided into the following four sections. In the first I examine the primacy given to law and legality within international interventions in both developmental and post-conflict settings. The increased use of law has a distinctly uneven spatiality, where it is often justified through global or universal assertions of humanitarian law, though territorialised within states and directed towards fostering liberal democratic citizenship. The second section focuses on the experience of BiH and examines how the CBiH attempted to convey its legitimacy following its creation in 2002, a process that involved constituting a Bosnian public as a site of intervention. The imagined qualities of such a public shaped the practices of outreach performed by the Court. The distance between these expectations and their realisation through the public outreach process is examined in the third section. This discussion points to the competing spaces of citizenship enacted through public outreach, as alternative ideas of the locus of justice are mobilised alongside support for the BiH state. The chapter concludes by reflecting on the geographies of law, where the imagined sense of universal jurisdiction is undermined by social concerns of the forms of barrier that prevent access to justice.

INTERVENTION, RIGHTS AND CITIZENSHIP

International intervention in state sovereignty produces a set of complex citizenship effects. Scholars from a range of disciplines have traced how foreign policy elites, in particular – though not exclusively – in North America and Western Europe, have justified military and developmental interventions on the basis of the concept of protecting rights, and in particular in the notion of humanitarianism.[31] The 1999 NATO intervention in Kosovo has become an archetype of such discursive framing,[32] though similar humanitarian refrains have been articulated in the recent interventions in Afghanistan, Iraq and Libya.[33] Rooted

---

[31] See Fassin, D. (2012). *Humanitarian reason: A moral history of the present*. Berkeley: University of California Press; Rieff, D. (2003). *A bed for the night: Humanitarianism in crisis*. London: Vintage; Weizman, E. (2012). *The least of all possible evils: Humanitarian violence from Arendt to Gaza*. London: Verso Books.

[32] Chomsky, N. (1999). *The new military humanism: Lessons from Kosovo*. London: Pluto Press.

[33] Gregory, D. (2004). *The colonial present: Afghanistan, Palestine, Iraq*. Malden, MA: Blackwell; Ingram, A., & Dodds, K. (2016). *Spaces of security and insecurity: Geographies of the war on terror*. London: Routledge.

institutionally in the United Nations' 1995 initiative 'Responsibility to Protect', these actions base their legitimacy on the need to intervene where states are failing to protect the humanitarian needs of their citizenry. While these actions have received considerable scholarly scrutiny, there is an allied set of legal manoeuvres that have only recently begun to garner geographical attention. Perhaps the central schism of intervention relates to the spatiality of legal decision-making, where claims to legality and illegality are flexibly appropriated and/or projected in line with particular political causes. At once, certain performances of the state are emboldened and reinforced while other state practices or state-like territories are declared illegal.[34]

The institutionalisation of transitional justice has consistently exhibited a tension between the desires of state building and the transnational impulses of humanitarian law. Reviewing twentieth-century legal innovations, advocates suggest the tribunals following World War II in Germany and Japan introduced a sense of accountability into armed conflict; grand claims that were suggestive of an emergent global jurisdiction.[35] This seemingly universal objective was further strengthened by the subsequent agreement of the fourth Geneva Convention (1949) relating to the humanitarian treatment of civilians during war. Of course, critics both at the time and since have argued that the application of such purportedly universal legal norms was partial, noting in particular that Allied aerial bombardments of both Germany and Japan were not classified as war crimes.[36] These examples illustrate a number of axes in tension between the state and imagined universalism, enabling victors to claim legal supremacy through the application of humanitarian law while also establishing a new narrative of German statehood as responsibility was projected on a narrow section of the political and military elite.

As scholars across criminology, socio-legal studies and geography have noted, such tensions between particularist state interests and

---

[34] See Jeffrey, A. (2009). Containers of fate: Labelling states in the 'war on terror', in Dodds, K., & Ingram, A. (eds.), *Spaces of security and insecurity: Geographies of the war on terror*. Aldershot: Ashgate, pp. 43–64; McConnell, F. (2009). De facto, displaced, tacit: The sovereign articulations of the Tibetan government-in-exile. *Political Geography* 28: 343–352.

[35] Goldstone, R. (2000). *For humanity reflections of a war crimes investigator*. New Haven, CT: Yale University Press.

[36] Grayling, A. C. (2006). *Among the dead cities: Was the Allied bombing of civilians in WWII a necessity or a crime?* London: Bloomsbury Publishing.

universal humanitarian law have been exacerbated in recent years.[37] The emergence of new institutions of transitional justice in the early 1990s reflected a desire amongst UN Security Council members to end impunity for crimes committed during war. The first institutional responses to this objective were the ICTY (established in 1993 by UN Security Council Resolution 827) and the International Criminal Tribunal for Rwanda (ICTR) (established in 1994 through UN Security Council Resolution 955). Both initially located in The Hague, these institutions focused on high-ranking officials in the genocides and violence that had occurred in the remains of Yugoslavia (1992–1999) and Rwanda (1994). This model of transitional justice severed the pursuit of justice from the geographical contexts within which the crimes took place and appears to circumscribe state sovereignty in the name of a more universal conception of rights and responsibilities.

But alongside these institutional practices can be traced a wider deployment of legal language, practices and justifications for relationships both between and within states. Oomen has defined this shift as the 'judicialization of international relations' recognising 'an increased emphasis on the law (in particular human rights) and legal institutions in nations' dealing with one another'.[38] Thus international humanitarian law is not simply the legal backdrop that legitimises military action; law has become a focal point for subsequent attempts to consolidate states and foster economic development. Over the past two decades we can trace a general reformulation of international development objectives towards the promotion of the rule of law, through assistance to human rights NGOs, writing laws and building courts.[39] For example, the UN Development Programme (UNDP) has developed a global set of programmes entitled 'Access to Justice and the Rule of Law', arguing that these two poles can 'spur economic growth and help to create a safe and secure environment for recovery in the aftermath of conflict or disaster'.[40]

---

[37] Fassin, D. (2012). *Humanitarian reason: A moral history of the present*. Berkeley: University of California Press; McEvoy, K. (2007). Beyond legalism: Towards a thicker understanding of transitional justice. *Journal of Law and Society* 34: 411–440.
[38] P. 890 in Oomen, B. (2005). Donor-driven justice and its discontents: The case of Rwanda. *Development and Change* 36: 887–910.
[39] See Waldorf, L. (2018). Legal empowerment and horizontal inequalities after conflict. *The Journal of Development Studies* 1–19.
[40] UN Development Programme (2013). Access to justice and rule of law, www.undp.org/content/undp/en/home/ourwork/democraticgovernance/focus_areas/focus_justice_law/ (accessed 11 November 2018).

Confirming this significance, UNDP's January 2013 policy brief seeks to integrate rule of law into the post-2015 Development Framework, successor to the Millennium Development Goals. Where policies of 'good governance' have long emphasised the significance of democratic institutions to notions of progress, these approaches specifically connect intervention with the legal configuration of rights and responsibilities. Perhaps one of the most explicit consequences of this shift is the expansion of programmes of transitional justice beyond post-conflict settings to becoming a blanket term relating to the protection of rights in circumstances of changing political authority.[41]

An examination of the creation of a new state court therefore sits at the interface of socio-legal studies and political geography. Critical legal scholars are keen to disrupt a sense of international humanitarian law as a disembodied set of ideals, exploring instead its implementation within actual existing sites, from courtrooms to human bodies.[42] Advocating more situated and embodied accounts, scholars have investigated the role of individual comportment, assertions of masculinity and the body as a site of violence (and, consequently, a repository of evidence) within the practice of law.[43] This re-materialised sense of legal practice intersects with critical and feminist political geography that has sought to examine the plural positions of those producing – and subject to – forms of legal or political intervention.[44] The spatial imaginaries of legal intervention suggest the cultivation of global forms of solidarity nested within the spatiality of the state, where, in contrast, the lived experience of state-building is replete with contradictory forms of solidarity and belonging, including intersecting ethnic, urban,

---

[41] UN Security Council (2004). *The rule of law and transitional justice in conflict and post-conflict societies.* New York: United Nations, pp. 1–24.

[42] See, for example, Hyde, A. (1997). *Bodies of law.* Princeton, NJ: Princeton University Press; Latour, B. (2010). *The making of law.* Cambridge: Polity Press.

[43] Clarkson, C. (2014). *Drawing the line: Toward an aesthetics of transitional justice.* New York: Fordham University Press; Felman, S. (2002). *The juridical unconscious trial and traumas in the twentieth century.* Cambridge, MA: Harvard University Press; Mulcahy, L. (2010). *Legal architecture: Justice, due process and the place of law.* Chicago: Routledge.

[44] Blomley, N. (2008). Making space for law, in Cox, K., Low, M. & Robinson, J. (eds.), *The Sage handbook of political geography.* London: Sage, pp. 155–168; Kuus, M. (2013). *Geopolitics and expertise: Knowledge and authority in European diplomacy.* Oxford: John Wiley & Sons; Staeheli, L., & Nagel, C. R. (2013). Whose awakening is it? Youth and the geopolitics of civic engagement in the 'Arab Awakening'. *European Urban and Regional Studies* 20(1): 115–119.

familial or state-based identities. Therefore, a study of social responses to the establishment of the CBiH provides a critique of the classical geopolitical image of intervention as necessarily strengthening forms of state citizenship, and instead highlights the plural forms of citizenship practice that co-exist in these moments of political transformation.

CONSTITUTING THE PUBLIC

The first step in creating a public communication strategy from a legal, political or scientific entity is to discern the characteristics of the 'public'.[45] There is a primary distancing involved in this process, whereby the institution is rendered as a specialist communicating outwards to the public.[46] While this reproduces a rather transactional understanding of public outreach, the form and purpose of this communication reveals much about the Court's understanding of the characteristics of the BiH public. Attempts to establish a programme of public outreach at the CBiH exhibit the tripartite challenges of creating a new state-level legal institution in a partitioned post-conflict environment: conveying legitimacy across a fragmented political landscape, translating new legal processes into an intelligible format for those under its jurisdiction and using human rights NGOs as mediating associations. In these terms, outreach concerns three interventions: projecting universal law across BiH territory, communicating rights and fostering civil society.

The first challenge, that of communicating law across a politically fragmented territory, is a necessity in a political environment where the CBiH is viewed with suspicion. In particular, political elites see the creation of a Court at the state level undermining the authority of the Republika Srpska and the FBiH. The partitioning of state competences between the two entities has provided the context for the emergence of 'ethnocratic' rule at the local level, where ethnically aligned political actors dominate local government and corporate life. This entwining of ethnic identity, economic primacy and territorial control has proved extremely durable over the 20 years since the end

---

[45] Barry, A. (2013). *Material politics: Disputes along the pipeline*. Oxford: John Wiley & Sons.

[46] Lambourne, W. (2012). Outreach, inreach and civil society participation in transitional justice, in Palmer, N., Clark, P. & Granville, D. (eds.), *Critical perspectives in transitional justice*. Cambridge: Intersentia, pp. 235–261.

of the conflict.[47] Neither attempts to renegotiate the constitution nor conditionality related to European Union accession have produced significant alterations to GFAP territoriality. As discussed in Chapter 2, it is in this context of solidified ethnocratic rule that political elites, particularly in the RS, have sought to present the Court as an ethnically aligned and/or neo-colonial enterprise.

In this respect, public outreach is an adversarial practice, seeking to challenge existing discourses of justice that emphasise division in post-conflict BiH. These characteristics of outreach were emphasised in the 2011 Medium Term Institutional Development Plan for the Court of the Prosecutor's Office of BiH:

> Public perceptions of the work of [the court and prosecutor's office] is distorted by misunderstandings of their fundamental role and by political rhetorical attacks on the institutions ... efforts should be made to encourage the delivery of public information through the media with the assistance of donors.
>
> (CBiH, 2011)

But over the course of the interviews with donors and international elites, interpretations of outreach extended beyond countering divisive discourses of BiH citizenship. In addition, individuals were keen to present the Court as an institution through which a cohesive vision of BiH may be communicated:

> [The Court is] an important institution for Bosnia and Herzegovina, we want to support it as much as we can. It is important we send the message that state institutions function, and particularly state institutions that are supporting the rule of law ... I would say that the future of this country depends on a functioning state court.
> (Interview with European Ambassador, 29 November 2011, Sarajevo)

The second interpretation of the necessity for public outreach did not relate directly to the spatial cohesion of BiH, but rather to the need to communicate the form and characteristics of Court processes, both in terms of the adoption of US common law and the increased role of the Court in war crimes trials. As Almira, a member of a legal advocacy NGO in the northern town of Bijeljina, remarked:

---

[47] Toal, G., & Dahlman, C. T. (2011). *Bosnia remade: Ethnic cleansing and its reversal.* Oxford: Oxford University Press.

This is a new institute, a new legal institute for the Bosnian society. We need to have it explained, victims need to have it explained ... what kind of facts are established, and how we are using the facts? This is something we do not understand each other very well ... and they think that their job has been done by the sentence.... It's not. It's definitely not. It's just the start of the work within the process of confronting what happened to us, and this constantly here and this is now something we are not saying publicly.

(Interview, 10 May 2012, Bijeljina)

Here, the novelty of legal proceedings is related to the need to extend forms of communication beyond law, using the legal process as a means through which individual and collective rights may be publicly discussed. In doing so, the NGO representative is extending the remit of outreach, arguing that the prosecution of law creates the moral responsibility to open public dialogue concerning justice.

This approach to the need to create new communicative strategies reflects broader concerns over the weakness of media activities in BiH, cited by interview respondents as a consequence of the commercialisation of media outlets and a legacy of Socialist Yugoslavia. In terms of commercialisation, Zoran, who works as a journalist in a news agency in Sarajevo suggested that 'the effect of the commercialization of the new radio stations and the development of new media has actually led to the decrease in the quality of journalism. So it's really a disaster if a trial starts in front of the Balkan judiciary and the public has no insight' (interview, 20 March 2012, Sarajevo). This comment seems to reflect Taylor and Kent's finding that the abrupt end of state-controlled media has led to a plethora of politically funded news outlets without a strong commitment to investigative or independent journalism.[48] In terms of the past, interview respondents viewed the reticence of legal officials to undertake outreach activities as a reflection of the Socialist past, where the 'freedom of the press' remained within the confines and limits of the party, leaving no space for subversion of the system.[49] In these terms, the notion that the court system – as well as judicial

---

[48] Taylor, M., & Kent, M. L. (2000). Media transitions in Bosnia from propagandistic past to uncertain future. *International Communication Gazette* 62(5): 355–378.

[49] Baltic, N. (2007). Theory and practice of human and minority rights under the Yugoslav communist system, www.eurac.edu/en/research/institutes/imr/Documents/ReportontheTheoryandPracticeofHumanRightsandMinorityRightsundertheYugoslavCommunistS.pdf (accessed 20 November 2018).

representatives – engaged with the media and, ultimately, the public would carry the supposed risk of subverting the system. This latter interpretation calls to mind the imagined purity of law as separated from the 'messy realities of local particularities'.[50]

The imagined purity of law is also a feature of the third challenge of creating a process of public outreach. Citing a concern that Courts are perceived to be aloof and unapproachable (CBiH public outreach official, 8 October 2009), from their outset in 2006 public outreach programmes conducted by the CBiH have worked through civil society organisations. Reflecting the normative placement of civil society as key agents in democratising post-conflict states,[51] human rights NGOs and, to a lesser extent, victims' associations have been at the centre of mechanisms used by the Court to communicate with the BiH public. In 2006 the Court established a 'Court Support Network' (CSN) to create an infrastructure through which Court activities and objectives could be conveyed to the BiH public. The CSN was formed of four NGOs and a victims' association located across BiH: the Sarajevo-based Žene ženama, Mostar-based Centri Civilnih Inicijativa (CCI), Prijedor-based victim association Udruženje Prijedorčanki Izvor (IZVOR), Tuzla-based Forum Građana Tuzle and Bijeljina-based Helsinki Komitet. These NGOs and victims' association were selected by the CBiH based on their experience with issues of human rights and reconciliation within BiH. The idea was for organisations to become hubs within their communities and draw upon both their local networks and knowledge to weave an intricate system of exchange between networks, hubs and Court. Provisional funding was provided for the members for the first six months allowing for each member to hire two members of staff to the activities of the CSN. The activities undertaken included a hotline to the Court which members of the public could phone and ask questions concerning the work of the CBiH, a programme of Court visits aimed at bringing victims to the Court, the formation of connections with local media and a series of events in which Court representatives spoke with communities affected by atrocities. After the initial six months of funding a letter was provided to

---

[50] Blomley, Making space for law, p. 161.
[51] See Belloni, R. (2001). Civil society and peacebuilding in Bosnia and Herzegovina. *Journal of Peace Research* 38: 163–180; Fagan, Civil society in Bosnia ten years after Dayton, 406–419; Jeffrey, A. (2007). The geopolitical framing of localized struggles: NGOs in Bosnia and Herzegovina. *Development and Change* 38(2): 251–274.

each CSN member by the CBiH to be used to find alternative funding to continue CSN activities.

The conclusion of the CSN as a formal infrastructure connected to the Court has not limited the activities of the NGOs that were involved, or reduced the level of cooperation between these organisations. For example, Izvor in Prijedor continues to seek out funding to continue activities that directly link the victim community in Prijedor and surrounding areas with the Court. They continue to provide an information hotline for victims to ask questions regarding the war crimes process, transportation for witnesses to and from the local courts as well as to the CBiH and transportation for victims and families to the reading of verdicts at the CBiH, and have also organised self-help groups for members. In 2012, they launched a campaign to commemorate the genocide that took place in the Prijedor region in 1992. This campaign included an international book launch commemorating missing persons from the region as well as memorials at Omarska and Keraterm and the launch of the global *Stop* Genocide Denial Campaign. Another former CSN member organisation, Helsinki Komitet, has continued to develop outreach initiatives that have included a series of television debates, human rights summer schools for youth from across the former Yugoslavia as well as developing a transitional justice course for university students in BiH. In addition, over the course of the research period a series of Public Dialogues on Sexual Violence took place in locations across BiH, hosted by the women's organisation Medica Zenica, the Swiss organisation Track Impunity Always (TRIAL), the ICTY Outreach Programme in BiH and the BiH Office of UN Women.

The practice of public outreach has therefore sought to constitute a BiH public into which interventions may be made and undertaken activities designed to foster understanding of, and engagement with, the work of the CBiH. These practices have made a series of assumptions concerning the spatiality, competences and associative life of BiH and, consequently, have constructed practices of outreach that seek to provide correctives through civil society organisations. The following section examines how these interpretations of public outreach were received, adopted or challenged by those targeted by its activity. From early in the research period it became clear that these responses do not seek to foment an alternative imaginary of citizenship than that articulated within processes of outreach. Instead, organisations and individuals lamented the widening gap between the expectations of legal processes and the activities of the Court. There was a recurrent sense of the failure of the state to secure the rights that were not only imagined by NGO members to derive from state but were also part of the claims made for the establishment of the CBiH.

SPACES OF CITIZENSHIP

While communicating universal legal rights across BiH territory was a key motivation for the establishment of the CBiH, the operation of public outreach activities pointed to a more complex spatiality. For some of those involved the selection of a dispersed set of associations within the CSN reified the localised geography of the post-conflict state, where organisations could build significant local networks in isolation from wider public outreach activities. For example Sanela, the Director of an NGO working with victims of sexual violence in the central Bosnian town of Zenica, used a public forum on the nature of legal support for survivors of wartime rape to discuss the creation of a legal support network in their town. She articulated a key problem of accountability that stemmed from this localised practice of outreach:

> Seventeen representatives have signed up for this network [in Zenica] and we have many details to speak about, steps, problems, difficulties we are facing as working group, and in fact the biggest problem in the beginning was that everybody wanted to transfer their responsibilities and jurisdictions to somebody else and not to undertake it with his institutions.
> (Submission to Tuzla public dialogue, 19 April 2012)

The sense of competing or alternative jurisdictions is key, and not merely reflective of the competing layers of judicial responsibility in contemporary BiH. The existence of the OHR's executive and legislative powers over the state since 1997 have normalised a sense that competing sovereignties coexist in any given BiH locality. Toal and Dahlman document in detail the interplay between international agencies and local officials in municipalities across BiH, where the transfer of responsibility for decision-making was a common tactic amongst political elites when faced with unpopular choices.[52] In the case of the Zenica NGO, the challenge of the local is the existence of

---

[52] Toal, G., & Dahlman, C. T. (2011). *Bosnia remade: Ethnic cleansing and its reversal.* Oxford: Oxford University Press.

other scales of legal practice, in terms of the state-level CBiH but also within European judicial institutions, such as the European Court of Human Rights (ECtHR). As we will see in Chapter 7, this latter jurisdiction is open to both victims of war crimes seeking compensation but also, as in the 2008 case *Maktouf and Damjanović vs. Bosnia and Herzegovina*, for convicted war criminals to query the legitimacy of their trial.[53]

Others involved in the network saw the localised nature of the outreach process as a virtue, a means through which durable coalitions may be forged. This position recalls critical scholarship that has focused on local spaces as site through which individuals may become 'subjects rather than objects' of citizenship.[54] This was particularly significant in BiH, where the plurality of different levels of accountability rendered the local more significant as a tangible space of support and collective action. These accounts emphasised the desirability of avoiding state-level political institutions and, instead, prioritising the initiative and capacities of individuals involved. For example, Dragomir, a member of a Sarajevo-based international missing persons NGO, rejected the claim that localisation was undermining state-based practices:

> you have to have personal will and local will, you know, to start something which, in so many other communities in Bosnia, has not been the case, and I think the example in Prijedor shows you how, even with the lack of some state level political will, you can, as I call it, localise transitional justice in your own area if possible.
> (Interview, Sarajevo, October 28 2012)

This focus on self-provisioning reproduces a sense of the active or insurgent transitional citizen, seeking to produce networks of support

---

[53] In this case discussed in Chapter 7 where two applicants brought a case to the ECHR on account of the CBiH convicting and sentencing them under the 2003 Criminal Code of Bosnia and Herzegovina. They complained that 'the failure of the State Court to apply the 1976 Criminal Code of the former Socialist Federal Republic of Yugoslavia ("the former SFRY"), which had been applicable at the time of the commission of the war crimes, had amounted to a violation of the rule of non-retroactivity of punishments' (ECHR, 2008). In July 2013 the ECHR found in the complainants favour, arguing that the retroactive use of the 2003 Criminal Code of Bosnia and Herzegovina violated their rights as they would expect a more lenient sentence if the 1976 Criminal Code of the former SFRY had been used.
[54] P. 32 in Lister, R. (1997). Citizenship: Towards a feminist synthesis. *Feminist Review* 57: 28–48.

and justice outwith the formal legal process.[55] Reflecting the wider expectations for civil society within public outreach processes, this comment suggests that the existence and vibrancy of associative life can compensate for failings within formal political or legal institutions.

While the virtues of localised practices were lauded by some, a far larger number of organisations and individuals lamented the devolving of responsibility for witness support – and in particular psychosocial care – to human rights NGOs. In this optic, civil society had neither the appropriate skills nor sufficient funding to meet the needs of individuals coming into contact with the transitional justice process. The reliance on a small number of NGOs had the consequence of very uneven forms of support across BiH, in particular in situations in which displaced persons had returned to areas where they were an ethnic minority. One member of an NGO in the northwestern Bosnian town of Ključ stated at a public outreach event in Prijedor that he was concerned about the uneven nature of support for victims across BiH:

> We do not have a universal approach to all the victims. Our witnesses and our victims are always being distinguished territorially, nationally and politically and even religiously. What is missing is universality to the approach, I do not know why; maybe because non-governmental organizations often imitate political elites . . . not all of them but some of them. The problem of victims of rape, wartime victims and witnesses of war crimes is too deep for the non-governmental sector to deal with it exclusively.
>
> (Submission to public dialogue, 23 May 2012, Prijedor)

What is striking in this excerpt is the invocation of the concept of the 'universal'. It illustrates a commonly held belief amongst respondents that the problem was not the absence of tailored support, but rather the lack of a commonly experienced access to legal information, the prosecutor's office or details of trial processes and outcomes. NGOs regularly referred to the BiH state as 'weak' or 'abnormal' because it was perceived to be unable to adequately cope with the volume of war crimes cases or the social obligations that stemmed from these legal activities. Civil society organisations did not consider themselves as a suitable replacement, largely because these organisations often

---

[55] Jones, B., Jeffrey, A. & Jakala, M. (2013). The 'transitional citizen': Civil society, political agency and hopes for transitional justice in Bosnia-Herzegovina, in Simić, O., & Volčić, Z. (eds.), *Transitional justice and civil society in the Balkans*. New York: Springer Publishing, pp. 87–104.

projected particular ethno-national interests.[56] In these terms, the informality of civil society as harbingers of legal information was a problem in constituting a sense of a coherent BiH state. When a representative from the Mostar CSN organisation exclaimed that she shouldn't be doing this job, 'it is the job of the Ministry of Justice' (interview, 12 October 2009), she was inferring that it was not the provisioning of the individual but the responsibilities of the state that were emphasised by civil society respondents. As an interesting consequence of this perception of the absentee state, one legal advocacy NGO was concerned about taking a case to the ECHR because this projected a sense of the weakness of BiH to manage its own legal affairs, exclaiming that she 'did not want give the idea that the state could not organise reparations for victims of war' (interview, 4 November 2011).

If the practice of public outreach highlighted a nested set of local and state-level spaces of citizenship action, it also illustrated the challenge of using public outreach to contribute to understandings of citizenship rights. The key issue here related to the legalistic nature of the transitional justice process in BiH: legal practices and the attitudes of jurists had been prioritised over alternative forms of restorative or reconciliatory justice.[57] Dragomir, a representative from an international missing persons NGO, viewed this as a form of legal isolation: 'it's almost like their legal function takes place in some kind of vacuum, it doesn't happen within a broader society, where there are people with, you know, wants, needs, emotions' (interview, 28 October 2011, Sarajevo). The prioritisation of legalism is encapsulated by the prominence given to transparency within the outreach process, where the possibility of viewing the legal process or accessing legal documentation is understood by Court officials as the optimal expression of public engagement. But as Dragomir suggests, this disembodies the outreach process as each viewer is assumed to be able to assume a similar vantage point. Consequently, the imaginary of transparency underplays the forms of

---

[56] For a detailed discussion of such of the politics of victims associations in BiH see Delpla, I. (2007). In the midst of injustice: The ICTY from the perspective of some victim associations, in Bougarel, X., Helms E. & Duijzings, G. (eds.), *The new Bosnian mosaic: Identities, memories and moral claims in a post-war society*. Aldershot: Ashgate, pp. 211–234.

[57] See McEvoy, K. (2007). Beyond legalism: Towards a thicker understanding of transitional justice. *Journal of Law and Society* 34: 411–440; Oomen, B. (2005). Donor-driven justice and its discontents: The case of Rwanda. *Development and Change* 36: 887–910.

constructed invisibility, where the public is unable to either access or comprehend legal processes and decisions. For Gordana, a member of a Sarajevo-based human rights NGO, the emphasis on legal specialism shaped the possibility of communication with the public:

> [t]he Court keeps the ideology that only a person with educational background in a legal field can be managing this job [of public outreach]. That is a cardinal mistake because legal staff do not know how to communicate legal decisions with the local community and that is where the problem of communication has been created which, again, is not a financial or ethical issue but something that could be resolved through dialogue.
> (Submission to Sarajevo workshop, 20 September 2012)

Gordana's account betrays an alternative communicative strategy, not centred around transparency but rather on dialogue. This sense of the unidirectional nature of outreach processes was amplified when the demographic of those targeted by the outreach process was also considered. Gordana's colleague, Vesna, was animated in her frustration with a process that assumed certain competences and facilities were available to those seeking information concerning legal processes:

> We are not realizing at all what the target group of the people we are referring to is and in which way we have to communicate with our target group, which is primarily victims. And if you are not able to explain to the victim what the adjudication is, what is the decision of the Court what is the point in sending that announcement?... I cannot tell to my grandmother to go on Internet and download the adjudication if she is interested in it.
> (Submission to Sarajevo workshop, 20 September 2012)

Through these accounts of transparency and transactional forms of communication we return to the issue of universalism. While civil society organisations lamented the absence of universal access to support and legal advice, they simultaneously critiqued an approach that treated victims and witnesses as disembodied, without 'wants, needs, emotions', and lacking standard access to channels of communication. This challenges a virtuous imaginary of law as a technical practice that somehow operates outside particularistic politics. Such an image of technocratic intervention is familiar to those who have studied the past 20 years of internationally led state building practices in BiH, stalked as they have been by a desire to emphasise the moral equivalency between ethnic groups, as if this marks the route to reconciliation.[58] In similar terms, the enrolment of civil society is based on their positioning as intermediaries between the Court and the public, an abstract form of social placement that both denies the variations in actual existing organisations and underplays the role of such organisations as dissenting voices from the GFAP state.

The central tension, then, is between a legalistic understanding of citizenship that is structured around the visibility of law, and the lived experience of partial support, slow trial processes and the absence of information. Within this argument are a complex set of normative positions at work relating to the appropriate spatial framework for citizenship, reflecting what Staeheli has referred to as the 'co-presence of forces that reinforce states and challenge them'.[59] The critique of state level law by civil society agencies was not made, in the main, in an attempt to cultivate 'localised' alternatives. Instead, they undertook local practices that emphasised the embodied and situated nature of the justice process, but wished to see greater centralisation of legal services and universal forms of support. Here, then, we see the difference between the localisation of responsibility, as has characterised the public outreach process, and the embedding of a universal form of provision that is attentive to local sites, spaces and bodies.

CONCLUSION

> Bosnia is an absolute leader when it comes to statistics in war crimes processing. But, what does it mean for an individual victim? What do these statistics mean for a person who was raped and held for, let's say, five months, as a sex slave, for instance, or another person who just can't find his or her father, who just disappeared and they just found one bone, you know, and they can't find anything else, and this person still thinks where are the, you know, the other parts of the body, and so on. So what do these statistics mean after all? They don't mean a thing, you know, and that's what's bothering me, this, yeah, between the institutional approach and this individual perspective, and these two are so far away from each other.
>
> (Interview with Dragomir, member of missing persons NGO, 28 October 2011, Sarajevo)

---

[58] See Simms, B. (2002). *Unfinest hour: Britain and the destruction of Bosnia*. London: Penguin UK.
[59] P. 394 in Staeheli, L. A. (2011). Political geography: Where's citizenship? *Progress in Human Geography* 35(3): 393–400.

This chapter has examined the plural spaces of citizenship imagined and enacted within a transitional justice programme, where a court is used to assist in the consolidation of a post-conflict state. In the wake of failed constitutional negotiations to revise the BiH constitution and the increasing solidification of the GFAP internal boundaries, the CBiH has been lauded as a means through which a liberal democratic citizenship could be fostered at a state level. At the same time, international elites have presented the 'localisation' of war crimes trials as part of the completion mandate of the ICTY, while also emphasising the opportunity to democratise the war crimes process, foster participation and spread understanding of the crimes of the past. As exhibited in the preceding comment from Dragomir, it is this entwining of legal and political objectives that has raised expectations concerning the potential impacts of the Court. In one interview a respondent from a Tuzla-based community group described this as the difference between 'court justice' and 'historic justice' (interview, 24 April 2012). In the absence of more reconciliatory or restorative forms of justice, the use of trial processes has been viewed as insufficient for victims and witnesses, many of whom have yet to see culprits brought to justice. Even where trials have occurred, victims lamented the ability for perpetrators to claim innocence, even when a guilty verdict has been made (and in some cases for sentenced individuals to take their trial to review within the ECHR).[60]

Thus the key tension exhibited in the qualitative data related to the relationship between legal mechanisms and the constitution of liberal democratic citizenship. In justifying the establishment of the court as a step towards state consolidation, intervening agencies were reflecting a common post–Cold War policy prescription of viewing states as the containers through which human rights obligations are legally guaranteed. In this sense, the state remains a privileged scale, where the language of aspatial humanitarianism is materialised within state territoriality. This observation contributes to critical scholarship that has argued that such statism reproduces classical geopolitical scripts emphasising the territorialisation of responsibility, as state-building seeks to place a boundary around the deviance of state failure, terrorism or conflict. But perhaps more explicitly, it draws a clear line between

---

[60] See European Court of Human Rights (2013). Annual report 2013, www.echr.coe.int/Documents/Annual_report_2013_prov_ENG.pdf (accessed 11 November 2018).

the projection of universal jurisdiction over territory and the consequent creation of rights-based citizenship amongst the BiH population.

The first challenge to this rather technocratic understanding of the constitution of citizenship came through the necessity for public outreach schemes. Such practices are expanding across legal instruments that understand the legitimacy of their authority is an accomplishment rather than a pre-given condition.[61] These processes cast light on the irony of claims of the separation of legal rationality from wider social contexts, recognising instead that the achievement of law requires the consent and participation of non-legal actors (not least in terms of providing testimony and coming forward with allegations of criminal acts). This latter point is particularly pertinent within war crimes trials where the evidential base rests heavily on witness testimony in the absence of documentary or material evidence.

There is a paradox, then, between the desire to 'localise' war crimes trials through the construction of a state court and the necessity of public outreach processes designed to cultivate participation and engagement with the Court. While one views 'the local' as the BiH state (in contrast to the ICTY's operation at a transnational scale), the other localises through the creation of a network of civil society organisations. The attitudes of those involved in this process suggest a sense of unease about the use of this scalar rhetoric to justify forms of intervention. In particular, respondents exhibited nostalgia for a form of modernity where the state played a key role in provisioning rights, even when they were members of NGOs and civil society organisations that were involved in encouraging participation in the Court's activities. In these terms, locality is not understood as the site of more virtuous or authentic politics, but the contested site of struggles over territory, identity and justice.

In making this argument I am not dismissing civil society in BiH or elsewhere as a significant site for the securing of rights. Rather I am pointing to the need to understand civil society as a diverse, situated and embodied set of actors that are neither an extension of – nor straightforwardly in antagonism with – the state. This was neither a story of acquiescence or insurgency, but instead involved forms of strategic action and mobilisation that sought to draw on different spatial scales to embolden the work of their organisation. This

---

[61] See, for example, ibid.

observation supports the need to engage in actual existing practices of law and citizenship in their plurality, often pursuing seemingly divergent political agendas. This argument orientates attention to the ways individuals and associations interpret and challenge the constructions of law. This sense of the exasperated audience permeates accounts of the 2014 popular protests across BiH. Where BiH citizens have taken to the streets to demand more effective and equal forms of state government, their manifestation has been through the creation of citizen councils, or *plenums*, at the local level.[62] Underlining one of the key findings in this research, these mobilisations point to the hybridity of spaces of citizenship, where the 'local' is not claimed exclusively as a site for local transformation but as a means through which to stabilise and strengthen the state.

---

[62] Štiks, I., & Horvat, S. (2014). The new Balkan revolts: From protests to plenums, and beyond, *openDemocracy*, www.opendemocracy.net/can-europe-make-it/igor-%C5%A1tiks-sre%C4%87ko-horvat/new-balkan-revolts-from-protests-to-plenums-and-beyond (accessed 20 November 2018). Riding, J. (2018). A new regional geography of a revolution: Bosnia's plenum movement. *Territory, Politics, Governance* 6(1): 16–41.

PART III

CONTESTING THE EDGE OF LAW

CHAPTER SIX

RULES OF LAW

INTRODUCTION

> Lawyers, but also social scientists, have suffered from a chronic inability to see that the legal reality of the modern state is not all that of the tidy, consistent, organised ideal so nicely captured in the identification of 'law' and 'legal system', but that legal reality is a rather unsystematic collage of inconsistent and overlapping parts, lending itself to no legal interpretation, morally and aesthetically offensive to the eye of the liberal idealist, and almost incomprehensible in its complexity to the would-be empirical student.[1]

There have been a number of moments in this book where the inconsistent and overlapping aspects of the legal system in BiH have been evident. The establishment of the WCC in the CBiH – despite the state-building rhetoric that surrounded its formation – has produced a series of struggles over the appropriate form and purpose of law. The requirement to enrol civil society actors, the focus of Chapters 4 and 5, has illuminated the plural spaces both formal and informal, in which transitional justice has been enacted. One aspect of this process that has, so far, received less attention is the legal code that underpins the production of the WCC. One of the reasons for delaying this discussion is that it requires a consideration of the future enactment of transitional justice both in BiH and elsewhere. Across these final two chapters I am

---

[1] P. 4 in Griffiths, J. (1986). What is legal pluralism? *The Journal of Legal Pluralism and Unofficial Law* 18(24): 1–55.

seeking to examine the implications of the institutions and laws enacted in BiH for both interventions in other post-conflict scenarios and the ambiguous role of law in consolidating states.

In this chapter the ambiguities of law are considered through the existence of competing loci of legal authority in BiH, both within and beyond the boundaries of the state. While the focus of the discussion thus far has been the WCC of the CBiH, there are, in practice, a number of different legal authorities that individuals may enrol to lay claim to their rights or challenge the decisions made in state courts. Such legal pluralism has been the focus of sustained interest in legal, criminological and socio-legal scholarship over the past 30 years, reflecting a recognition of the presence of different normative regimes produced through discourses of human rights, the violence of colonial encounters and/or the interventions made in the name of post-conflict or developmental objectives.[2] One of the key areas of deliberation emerging from this work is the problem of comparison: in particular whether the evocation of legal pluralism renders very different normative regimes as similarly 'law'. In short, does the very notion of 'legal pluralism' obscure 'the fundamental differences in form, structure and sanctioning potential or effective sanctioning between state law and other normative orders'.[3]

Tensions surrounding differences in potential or effective sanctioning lie at the heart of the plural legal systems. When BiH joined the Council of Europe in April 2002 it fell under the jurisdiction of the European Court of Human Rights (ECtHR), thereby allowing individual applicants within BiH to bring forward cases where their human rights – as set out in the ECHR – were breached by the actions of the state. There have subsequently been a series of high-profile cases where individuals have challenged rulings or constitutional norms in BiH on the grounds of the state's commitments to the ECHR. The most prominent example of such cases is that of *Sejdić and Finci v. Bosnia and Herzegovina*, brought by Dervo Sejdić and Jakob Finci in 2006 to challenge the structure of the BiH Constitution established within the General Framework Agreement for Peace (GFAP). Specifically, this case sought to overturn the rule whereby the rotating presidency of the

---

[2] See, ibid.; Merry, S. E. (1988). Legal pluralism. *Law and Society Review* 22: 869; von Benda-Beckmann, F. (2002). Who's afraid of legal pluralism? *The Journal of Legal Pluralism and Unofficial Law* 34(47): 37–82.

[3] von Benda-Beckmann, Who's afraid of legal pluralism?, p. 37.

House of Peoples (the upper house within the BiH state) was open to only ethnic Bosniaks, Bosnian Serbs and Bosnian Croats. As Roma and Jewish, Sejdić or Finci asserted that this was a discriminatory aspect of the law and thereby contravened their human rights. In December 2009, the ECtHR came to a judgement in their favour and stipulated that the discrimination on the grounds of ethnic difference found in the BiH Constitution was not compatible with the duties of being a signatory to the ECHR. Interestingly, the judgement views the necessity of the ethnic balance within the BiH House of Peoples as an immediate post-conflict concern, vital to the restoration of peace between ethnically aligned parties. It also recognises that Roma and Jewish groups were not represented at the peace negotiations, thereby their significance to the successful operation of the post-conflict state is understated in the Dayton Constitution. However, it is with the increasingly international nature of the BiH state, and in particular membership of multilateral agencies, that new obligations to conform to international legal norms becomes a responsibility of the state:

> [B]y becoming a member of the Council of Europe in 2002 and by ratifying the Convention and the Protocols thereto without reservations, the respondent State has voluntarily agreed to meet the relevant standards. It has specifically undertaken to 'review within one year, with the assistance of the European Commission for Democracy through Law (Venice Commission), the electoral legislation in the light of Council of Europe standards, and to revise it where necessary'. Likewise, by ratifying a Stabilisation and Association Agreement with the European Union in 2008, the respondent State committed itself to 'amend[ing] electoral legislation regarding members of the Bosnia and Herzegovina Presidency and House of Peoples delegates to ensure full compliance with the European Convention on Human Rights and the Council of Europe post-accession commitments' within one to two years.[4]

Despite compliance with the *Sejdić and Finci v. Bosnia and Herzegovina* ruling as a condition of progress in European Stabilisation and Accession talks, little has been done to revise the constitution to meet the demands of the judgement.[5] This lack of progress points to the

---

[4] See Case of Sejdić and Finci v. Bosnia and Herzegovina (Applications nos. 27996/06 and 34836/06), https://hudoc.echr.coe.int/app/conversion/pdf/?library=eCHR&id=001-96491& (accessed 12 November 2018).
[5] Brljavac, B. (2017). Barrier to the EU membership: The institutional discrimination of minority groups in Bosnia and Herzegovina. *Geografia-Malaysian Journal of Society*

challenge of straightforward comparisons between legal regimes with different powers of sanction. Where the state may exert forms of punishment on non-compliance with law, within the realm of human rights the forms of sanction available to the courts are necessarily limited.

The tensions between these two bodies of judicial redress point to different conceptualisations of the spatiality of law, and thereby different understandings of the edge. As we have seen in preceding chapters, the establishment of the WWC was enframed in a discourse of localisation and the strengthening of BiH state sovereignty. The territoriality of the BiH state is thereby consolidated through the launching of new criminal procedure code and the delegation of authority for war crimes trials transferred from The Hague to the WCC and affiliated agencies in Sarajevo. The closer integration to the multilateral agencies of Europe, in particular the Council of Europe and the European Union, present a different spatial imaginary, where the territory of BiH is incorporated into the homogenised legal space of Europe. This is not an imaginary of localisation but one of collaboration. As opposed to law bound to the territoriality of the state, in this framework normative claims stem from shared humanity.[6] To understand the tensions within this legal pluralism the first task is to trace the production of ideas of transnational commonality within the legal system.

INTERNATIONAL HUMAN RIGHTS LAW AS A LEGAL COMMONS

The imagination of human rights law as a form of commons challenges a spatial conception of law – prominent in other chapters of this book – where the state is imagined as a pre-given container to the exercise of law. But there are a number of immediate tensions involved in any attempt to entwine law and the commons. In many respects, the terms work in opposition to each other, for where law operates as a tool of, first, imperialism and, second, capitalism, it is central to set of processes that have divided, converted and undermined various forms of public

---

and Space 8(1): 30–37; Katz, V. (2018). The position of national minorities in Bosnia and Hercegovina before and after the breakup of Jugoslavia. *Studia Środkowoeuropejskie i Bałkanistyczne 2017* (Tom XXVI): 193–204.

[6] McMurtry, J. (2011). Human rights versus corporate rights: Life value, the civil commons and social justice. *Studies in Social Justice* 5(1): 11–61.

life.[7] But if work exploring the commons has conventionally centred on the relationship between humans and environmental resource allocation,[8] law has also been a fundamental framework through which claims to just access and allocation have been made. The central function of law, as Hyde sets out, is to provide a 'totalizing vocabulary'[9] through which people can conceptualise their rights in a standardised fashion. While Hyde goes on to question and subvert this sense of totalization, this discourse of universalism, where law is imagined as immutable over time (as a rule of law) and over space (as a jurisdiction), has proved central to the assertion of legal legitimacy.[10] On the surface, this deviates some distance from a Marxist-inspired notion of the commons as the antithesis of capitalist enclosure, a situation wherein regimes of private property and individual obligation to the state crowd out other forms or spaces of common ownership and control.[11] But in this understanding of law there is also a minimalist interpretation of a legal commons centring on the experience of being bound to a common set of *rules*. Such rules nevertheless set to work on different spatial scales, so whilst law becomes the underpinning of certain *state*-conferred citizenship rights, it is also the means through which *global* commons (whether territorial or rights based) may be protected.

This tension at the heart of law – between a repressive function of control and an emancipatory force of protecting rights and incursions – can be traced historically, as in the pioneering work of E. P. Thompson,

---

[7] Blomley, Nicholas (2008). Making space for law, in *The Sage handbook of political geography*, Cox, K., Low, M. & Robinson, J. (eds.). London: Sage, pp. 155–168; Comaroff, J., & Comaroff, J. (2006). Law and disorder in the postcolony: An introduction, in *Law and disorder in the postcolony*, Comaroff, J., & Comaroff, J. (eds.). Chicago: University of Chicago Press, pp. 1–56; Jeffrey, A., McFarlane, C. & Vasudevan, A. (eds.) (2012). Rethinking enclosure: Space, subjectivity and the commons. *Antipode* 44(4): 1247–1267.

[8] See Bakker, K. (2007). The 'commons' versus the 'commodity': Alter-globalization, anti-privatization and the human right to water in the Global South. *Antipode* 39 (3): 430–455.

[9] Hyde, A. (1997). *Bodies of law*. Princeton, NJ: Princeton University Press, p. 48.

[10] Valverde, M. (2009). Jurisdiction and scale: Legal technicalities as resources for theory. *Social and Legal Studies* 18(2): 139–157.

[11] See Blomley, N. (2003). Law, property, and the geography of violence: The frontier, the survey, and the grid. *Annals of the Association of American Geographers* 93(1): 121–141; Blomley, N. (2015). The ties that blind: Making fee simple in the British Columbia treaty process. *Transactions of the Institute of British Geographers* 40(2): 168–179.

which attests both to the savagery of law (particularly in its criminalisation of 'commoning') and to its radical potential.[12] The establishment of common law in Europe in the twelfth and thirteenth centuries points to this duality. As responsibility for the adjudication of law shifted from local county courts to more centralised royal authority, so the more arbitrary elements of ecclesiastical jurisdiction were removed in favour of a standardised jury system. The perceived virtues of this system are clear: the delivery of justice becomes (more) consistent and the arbitration of guilt or innocence is the responsibility of fellow citizens. But as Blomley notes,[13] the exercise of law always involves the exercise of violence (whether actual or implied, physical or symbolic) and the establishment of common law in England was a means through which new forms of monarchic power could be exercised in the nascent polity, a process that led to the enclosure of common lands and the assertion of class-based hierarchies. Comaroff and Comaroff trace similar tensions between the supposed standardisation of law and the entrenchment of practices of dispossession within – and beyond – postcolonial states.[14] There are, then, both interpretive and normative problems. The standardisation of law, the regulation of legal practice and the participation of citizens in arbitration all gesture at a legal system that displays elements of a communal enterprise. The rule of law may thus point to a sense of a 'legal commons'. But at the same time, the exercise of law always unfolds within established power hierarchies and inevitably asserts the legitimacy of ruling elites.[15] In this sense the creation of the legal system may be at the same time a repressive process that reproduces existing patterns of authority.

This dialectic of democratic and repressive functions has also been traced through the spatial attributes of lawmaking, trial justice and recent work on 'lawfare'.[16] Any legal system requires a sense of the spatial limits of jurisdiction, thus suggesting a uniform plane within which certain bodies

---

[12] Thompson, E. P. (1975). *Whigs and hunters: The origins of the Black Act*. New York: Pantheon.
[13] Blomley, Law, property, and the geography of violence, pp. 121–141.
[14] Comaroff & Comaroff, Law and disorder in the postcolony.
[15] Jones, C. A. (2016). Lawfare and the juridification of late modern war. *Progress in Human Geography* 40(2): 221–239.
[16] Delaney, D. (2015). Legal geography I: Constitutivities, complexities, and contingencies, *Progress in Human Geography* 39(1): 96–102; Jones, Lawfare and the juridification of late modern war, 221–239; Gregory, D. (2010). War and peace. *Transactions of the Institute of British Geographers* 35(2): 154–186.

and objects are subject to a specific legal regime.[17] This simple framework is, however, troubled by the more intricate geographies through which law achieves its authority. The enactment of law depends upon the division and bounding of space, the careful surveying of territories and bodies within a legal system and internal spatial divisions to demarcate different property or rights claims.[18] Such analysis prompts reflections on the specific – and asymmetric – geopolitical histories of law, in particular illuminating the colonial legacies that are masked by attempts to convey the neutrality and universalism of international law.[19] But alongside such spatial practices sits the enactment of law, a set of performances that have – since the classical regimes of Greek and Roman law – sought to use space as a means through which the legitimacy of legal deliberation may be conveyed. As discussed in Chapter 3, from the public agora through to Richard Rogers's ECtHR building, legal practices have been imagined as public practices that adjudicate on behalf of – and in sight of – a particular collective. In both senses, law emerges less as an abstract articulation of a particular social order and more as a set of grounded and unfolding practices that are continually asserted and reworked.

This tension between spatial enclosure and legal universalism may be traced through recent legal innovations which established institutions to try individuals for breaches of international humanitarian law (IHL). This body of law refers to instances where the norms of war, as laid out in the 1949 Geneva Conventions, are violated.[20] The geography of IHL has attracted less scholarly interest than other aspects of law. In part, this reflects the primacy of state-based legal systems and the lack of clear institutionalisation of international legal practices.[21] As I have

---

[17] Valverde, M. (2009). Jurisdiction and scale: Legal technicalities as resources for theory. *Social & Legal Studies* 18(2): 139–157.
[18] See Chapter 1 and also Braverman, I., Blomley, N., Delaney, D. & Kedar, A. (eds.). (2014). *The expanding spaces of law: A timely legal geography*. Palo Alto, CA: Stanford University Press; Philippopoulos-Mihalopoulos, A. (2014). *Spatial justice: Body, lawscape, atmosphere*. Abingdon and New York: Routledge.
[19] Anghie, A. (2007). *Imperialism, sovereignty and the making of international law*. Cambridge: Cambridge University Press; Jones, C. A. (2016). Lawfare and the juridification of late modern war. *Progress in Human Geography* 40(2): 221–239.
[20] O'Brien, J. (1993). The international tribunal for violations of international humanitarian law in the former Yugoslavia. *American Journal of International Law* 639–659.
[21] Pearson, Z. (2008). Spaces of international law. *Griffith Law Review* 17: 489–514; Silbey, S. (1997). Presidential address: 'Let them eat cake': Globalization, postmodern colonialism, and the possibilities of justice. *Law and Society Review* 207–235.

explored in earlier chapters of this book, the study of international law has often been caught in a 'territorial trap', whereby spatial intricacies are aggregated to competing state interests within the international system.[22] But the purpose of this chapter is not simply to add spatial nuance to critical understandings of international law. Rather, I am seeking to focus on one particular element of the international legal system: whether we can see in the operation of IHL the basis for a revived notion of the *commons*. In doing so, the very conceptualisation of the commons comes into renewed focus. In spatial terms, the invocation of IHL is suggestive of a *planetary* sense of rights conferred by our common species membership, coupled with novel coalitions that operate transnationally to agitate for legal redress where violations of IHL have taken place. But the implications of law cannot be contained within the operation of international jurisprudence.[23] The institutionalisation of IHL has also orientated attention to the role and significance of testimony, and in particular to the extent to which it is possible to bear witness to traumatic events and forge connections between violence in disparate parts of the planet. Finally, the operation of law, its materiality, performance and outcomes, has required new mobilisations, in terms of both expert interpretation of evidence and the enrolment of purportedly non-legal actors into juridical processes. These actions have blurred the distinction between law and non-law, where pressure is exerted through new transnational coalitions of knowledge production and innovative forms of civic action outside the legal arena. Certainly, this formulation is at some remove from more materialist understandings of the commons, but the argument instead orientates attention to what is held *in common* through the operation of law, and the resources this provides for challenging violations of human rights.

The possibility of a legal commons, then, rests on an appreciation of the fragility and excesses of law – viewing law as a precarious achievement and one whose social effects always extend beyond the juridical. This argument builds on previous work, with Colin McFarlane and

---

[22] Agnew, J. (1994). The territorial trap: The geographical assumptions of international relation theory. *Review of International Political Economy* 1(1): 53–80.

[23] Boyle, M., & Kobayashi, A. (2015). In the face of epistemic injustices? On the meaning of people-led war crimes tribunals. *Environment and Planning D: Society and Space* 33(4): 697–713.

Alex Vasudevan,[24] in which the relationship between enclosure and the commons (or 'commoning') were understood to operate in a dialectic, arguing that a resurgent form of neoliberal geopolitics is producing possibilities for new forms of collective practice. If law is understood as a form of enclosure on more open-ended and socially mediated forms of conflict resolution, so we simultaneously see potential for progressive interventions that widen access to rights and foster new forms of justice. To trace these processes, we need to reflect on primary questions relating to the competing origins of law in any given setting, in particular whether law is a product of the pronouncements of a sovereign or, in contrast, it stems from the moral impulses of the human soul.

COMPETING ORIGINS OF LAW

1st Gent. An ancient land in ancient oracles
Is called 'law-thirsty': all struggle there
Was after order and a perfect rule.
Pray, where lie such lands now?. . .
2nd Gent. Why, where they lay of old – in human souls.[25]

When confronted with a concept as polyvalent and indistinct as law, it comes as no surprise that scholars have committed considerable attention to tracing its origins. There is a sense that returning to primary questions may help unpick some of the sustained ambiguities in the operation of law. Repeating the practice of Peter Fitzpatrick in *Modernism and the Grounds of Law*, I open this section with an epigraph from George Eliot's Middlemarch. Though Fitzpatrick does not comment on its content, the exchange encapsulates some of the obscurity of the origins of law, as the (seemingly unachieved) lawfulness imagined by the 1st Gent meets both its realisation and impossibility in the 2nd Gent's suggestion that the 'law thirsty lands' now reside in the human soul. As literary scholar Rosalind Morris has remarked, it remains unclear from Eliot's text 'whether the ancient land finally achieved a state of lawfulness (and entered its own modernity) or whether it

---

[24] Jeffrey, A., McFarlane, C. & Vasudevan, A. (2012). Rethinking enclosure: Space, subjectivity and the commons. *Antipode* 44(4): 1247–1267.
[25] Eliot, G. (1965). *Middlemarch*. London: Penguin, p. 98, cited in Fitzpatrick, P. (2001). *Modernism and the grounds of law*. Cambridge: Cambridge University Press, p. 11.

matured into the realization that perfect rule is unattainable'.[26] This sets the scene for a more general philosophical reflection on the basis of legal systems. Are they a reflection of particular aspects of human characteristics or a product of particular historical and developmental circumstances? Fitzpatrick explores the most prominent example of the former argument, exploring the implications of Sigmund Freud's assertion that law was a product of psychosexual development, and in particular a reflection of the primary parricide committed by two sons against their father. This act becomes an origin myth that sustains a series of social taboos, constituting an origin of law. In contrast, and reflected in Eliot's exchange, others have traced the establishment of legal systems as products of wider social and political transformations, marking out key polities (the Roman Empire and the seventeenth-century establishment of nation-states, for example) or signal moments (the Holocaust or 9/11) as particular foundation points for legal innovation.[27] These debates seem to orientate around a beguilingly simple question: Does the impulse towards legal codification come from within (the human soul or human psychosexual development) or from without (through the regulation of action to support a particular claim to authority, the rule of law)?

While I am not going to dwell for too long on this question, it is worth at least attempting to transcend the binary logic that it produces. As both legal scholars and social theorists have argued, the rigidity of such a binary between the internal and external dynamics of law is an artifice: it is the internalisation of particular legal norms that secures their legitimacy.[28] It is this point regarding the personality of law that Stuart Elden takes up in relation to the rediscovery of Roman Law in eleventh- and twelfth-century Europe.[29] While the larger body of this

---

[26] P. 388 in Morris, R. C. (2011). In the name of trauma: Notes on testimony, truth telling and the secret of literature in South Africa. *Comparative Literature Studies* 48 (3): 388–416.

[27] See Elden, S. (2013). *The birth of territory*. Chicago: University of Chicago Press; Felman, S. (2002). *The juridical unconscious: Trials and traumas in the twentieth century*. Cambridge, MA: Harvard University Press; Gregory, D. (2007). Vanishing points, in Gregory, D., & Pred, A. (eds.). *Violent geographies fear, terror and political violence*. New York: Routledge, pp. 205–236.

[28] Bourdieu, P. (1987). The force of law: Toward a sociology of the juridical field. *Hastings Law Journal* 38(5): 814–853; Felman, S. (2002). *The juridical unconscious: Trials and traumas in the twentieth century*. Cambridge, MA: Harvard University Press.

[29] Elden, S. (2013). *The birth of territory*. Chicago: University of Chicago Press.

study examines the territorial implications of this rejuvenation, Elden makes two interlinked points that will be important for my subsequent argument. The first is the role of scholarly and legal authorities (in Elden's work *the Glossators* and *the Commentators*) in interpreting Roman law for a new social context. Rather than simply applying the *Corpus Juris Civilis*, Emperor Justinian's sixth-century body of Roman legal doctrine, the law required careful annotation to navigate conflicts between competing jurisdictions. The second point regards the pervasive nature of Roman jurisprudence in the social contexts in which it was being rediscovered; Elden mentions in passing the adoption of Roman legal terminology in the Vulgate Latin translation of the Bible.[30] Familiarity with Roman legal relations and language allows a social precedence for the recodification of Roman law in the medieval period. There are, then, contingent historical events that shape the imposition of Roman law, but also a human population that is familiar with such jurisprudence through religious practice.

In the context of transitional justice this question of the origin of law is particularly acute. The cherished continuity that underpins the principle of *stare decisis*[31] within the rule of law is challenged by the shift in political authority.[32] Hence the concept of trials for crimes committed under a previous regime undermines the principle that individuals are subject to the law of the time. But in the case of war crimes or crimes against humanity, it can be argued that these constitute special circumstances where IHL, as codified in the 1949 Fourth Geneva Convention, has been broken. The schism between a positivist and more critical form of legal scholarship is illuminated in debates concerning this legal shift, evident in particular when it was applied to the trials of Nazi officials and their collaborators at Nuremburg in the aftermath of World War II.[33] Legal positivists, such as H. L. A. Hart,[34] argued for the strict application of prior rule of law – regardless of supposed immorality. While, in this view, the integrity of law stands above the moral deliberations of society, moral philosophers, such as

---

[30] Ibid., p. 215.
[31] 'To stand by things decided', a principal that emphasises the centrality of legal precedent to the operation of law.
[32] Teitel, R. G. (2000). *Transitional justice*. Oxford: Oxford University Press.
[33] Ibid., pp. 12–13.
[34] Hart, H. L. A. (1958). Positivism and the separation of law and morals. *Harvard Law Review* 71: 593–629.

Lon Fuller, argued that there is a key distinction between procedural and substantive justice;[35] procedures could be retrospectively changed to serve the higher purpose of justice. But, of course, the question of who defines 'substantive justice' remains. For example, in other cases of legal transitions – particularly in the post-colonial world – the invocation of the superiority of humanitarian law has led to the denigration of local legal systems and the adoption of Western codifications of law.[36]

COMPETING LEGAL CODES

Such scholarly debates concerning the origins and purpose of law are reflected in legal disputes over the legitimacy and operation of transitional justice. In practice, the moral coordinates of transitions from conflict to peace are rarely as clear-cut as the case of the transition from Nazism to the fragile and divided post-conflict German state. In the case of BiH, the co-presence of multiple legal codes and overlapping jurisdictions has challenged the very possibility of transitional justice. The earlier chapters of this book have traced the institutional shift from the ICTY, which since 1993 had held jurisdiction over grave breaches of the Geneva Conventions, violations of the laws or customs of war, genocide, and crimes against humanity committed during the fragmentation of Yugoslavia 1992–1995.[37] Since 2005, and reflecting the need for the ICTY to complete its mandate, increasing responsibility for prosecutions in these areas has been transferred to the CBiH in Sarajevo. But this institutional story is underpinned by changes in the legal codes within BiH. To accommodate the shifting responsibility from the Hague to Sarajevo the OHR, the leading international agency responsible for implementing 1995's Dayton GFAP, imposed a new Criminal Code of BiH 2003 (CCBiH), with the crucial insertion of a chapter relating to crimes against humanity and values protected by international law.[38]

[35] Fuller, L. L. (1958). Positivism and fidelity to law: A reply to Professor Hart. *Harvard Law Review 71*: 630–672.
[36] Comaroff & Comaroff, Law and disorder in the postcolony.
[37] See Nettelfield, L. J. (2010). *Courting democracy in Bosnia and Herzegovina*. Cambridge: Cambridge University Press.
[38] See Office of the High Representative (2003). Criminal Code of Bosnia and Herzegovina 'Official Gazette' of Bosnia and Herzegovina, 3/03, www.ohr.int/ohr-dept/legal/oth-legist/doc/criminal-code-of-bih.doc (accessed 17 December 2018).

From the outset, the creation of the new criminal code was presented by international officials as both a political and legal innovation. In political terms, the creation of a single territorial jurisdiction provided a mechanism for consolidating the devolved BiH state, framing the rule of law as a(?) precursor to other forms of state consolidation. CBiH was something of a rarity: a functioning state-level institution in a country where many legal and political competences are either devolved to substate polities (most significantly the Federation of Bosnia and Herzegovina or the RS) or performed by international agencies on the state's behalf (as in the case of the ICTY). While there have been many attempts to renegotiate the GFAP constitution, such as the abortive Butmir Process in 2009, the establishment of a single legal code provides one mechanism through which the significance of ethnonationally aligned territories within BiH may be eroded. Perhaps the most tangible evidence of the threat posed to such established postconflict power bases has been the vociferous and constant criticism of the internationally led judicial efforts by politicians within the RS. For example, Milorad Dodik, President of the Republika Srpska, has described the CBiH as a 'place of injustice, promoting violence and the international community', using a familiar ethno-national matrix to argue that the court has prioritised the investigation of crimes perpetrated by Serbs, rather than on Serbs:

> We feel humiliated and betrayed by the fact that every crime against the Serbs, wherever it might be and wherever it is needed to process, was obstructed by other levels of government.
> (Milorad Dodik in B92, 2014)

The political implications of the establishment of a single criminal code and state court underscore the point that justice in general, and transitional justice in particular, is more than simply a practice of redress, it is also orientated towards future desires for a reconciled citizenry. Such political considerations were matched by a set of legal implications of the CCBiH because the code was designed to supersede the 1976 Criminal Code of the Socialist Federal Republic of Yugoslavia (CCSFRY), a legal framework that had more lenient sentences for war crimes[39] and

---

[39] The most severe custodial penalty under the CCSFRY is 15 years, though it gave the option to impose the death penalty. However, with the signing of the GFAP in 1995 the death penalty was abolished, an abolition that was formally agreed by the Federation of Bosnia and Herzegovina in 1998 and by the RS in 2000.

no provision for crimes against humanity. Reflecting the devolved complexity of the post-GFAP Bosnian state, the CCSFRY coexisted with more localised criminal codes, such as 1998 Criminal Code for the Federation of Bosnia and Herzegovina. But innovations of the Criminal Code of BiH 2003 extend beyond simply a widening of the forms of the crime or the unification of a fragmented legal landscape; it also marked a move away from a legal system based on civil law, to a system that integrated aspects of common law. As Barria and Roper have identified,[40] the style of civil law encapsulated by the CCSFRY meant that previously judicial rulings were not viewed as precedent and binding on future decisions. The introduction of the new code led to problems of judges refusing to follow precedents established in other courts, while other courts challenged the legitimacy of the CBiH as the court of last instance in war crimes cases.

These concerns regarding the novelty of the CCBiH were reflected during my research, both in terms of the practices of the legal profession and the attitudes of the Bosnian public. In terms of the practice of law, a US legal advisor to the CBiH remarked that unfamiliarity with the CCBiH led to the CCSFRY being used a source of guidance in the CBiH, especially where deliberations took place outside public hearings. Later in the interview, they reflected the enduring significance of legal personality remarking 'these are the same judges as the pre-war system, how are they going to simply switch to a new legal code?' (interview, Sarajevo, 10 December 2011). The operation of an unfamiliar legal system also had consequences for public attitudes towards war crimes trials, particularly when plea agreements were reached and sentences made more lenient for revealing evidence of mass graves and complying with the trial process.[41] One human rights NGO in Bjeljina argued that, the use of plea bargaining was creating confusion and resentment amongst victims and witnesses, who did not regard it as a 'traditional way of behaving' (interview, Bjeljina, 10 May 2012). Under the CCSFRY, judges performed an investigative role, and

---

[40] See Barria, L. A., & Roper, S. D. (2005). How effective are international criminal tribunals? An analysis of the ICTY and the ICTR. *The International Journal of Human Rights* 9(3): 349–368; Roper, S. D., & Barria, L. A. (2007). Donor motivations and contributions to war crimes tribunals. *Journal of Conflict Resolution* 51(2): 285–304.

[41] Balkan Insight (2014). Bosnia War Crimes Plea Bargains Provoke Questions, http://archive.balkaninsight.com/en/article/no-pleas-for-bosnian-war-criminals/1452/37 (accessed 12 July 2019).

would have consequently developed links with trial participants, an element of social contextualising that is lost in a system where prosecution is prepared by a separate legal department. It is, then, not simply a new legal system, but a new form of legal separation. A new edge of law.

EXPLOITING THE LEGAL COMPLEX

But questions as to the social validity of the court and the new criminal code have been overshadowed by challenges to its legal legitimacy. Recalling the preceding discussion of the nature of the rule of law in times of transition, a number of individuals convicted under the Criminal Code of BiH 2003 have appealed their prosecutions and argue they breach Article 7 (Paragraph 1) of ECHR, namely that 'no one shall be held guilty of any criminal offence on account of any act or omission which did not constitute a criminal offence under national or international law at the time when it was committed. Nor shall a heavier penalty be imposed than the one that was applicable at the time the criminal offence was committed'.[42] The case of Abduladhim Maktouf, who was convicted of committing war crimes against civilians under Article 173 of the Criminal Code of BiH 2003, is particularly instructive. First Maktouf appealed the Constitutional Court BiH. The court initially rejected the appeal, (citing Article 7 (Paragraph 2) of the ECHR) because Maktouf's acts were already criminal at the time when they were committed, according to the 'general principles of law recognized by civilized nations'.[43] The case (brought together with that of convicted war criminal Goran Damjanović) was then taken to the ECtHR,[44] which found in their favour:

> Given the type of offences of which the applicants had been convicted (war crimes as opposed to crimes against humanity) and the degree of seriousness (neither of the applicants had been held criminally liable for any loss of life), the Court found that the applicants could have received

---

[42] See Council of Europe (1950). European Convention on Human Rights, www.echr.coe.int/Documents/Convention_ENG.pdf (accessed 12 July 2019).
[43] See Organisation for Security and Cooperation in Europe (2008). Moving towards a harmonized application of the law applicable in war crimes cases before courts in Bosnia and Herzegovina, www.osce.org/mission-to-bosnia-and-herzegovina/314846?download=true (accessed 18 December 2018).
[44] See European Court of Human Rights (2013). Case of Maktouf and Damjanović v. Bosnia and Herzegovina, www.legal-tools.org/doc/5e3c45/pdf/ (accessed 19 December 2018).

lower sentences had the 1976 Code been applied. Since there was a real possibility that the retroactive application of the 2003 Code operated to the applicants' disadvantage in the special circumstances of this case, it held that they had not been afforded effective safeguards against the imposition of a heavier penalty.[45]

As a consequence of this ruling, Maktouf's original sentence of five years in prison was deemed unduly harsh, and in November 2016 he took the BiH government to court for damages resulting from false imprisonment. As an outcome of this legal action, Maktouf was awarded €36,000 to reflect the hardship of spending longer in prison than that which could be expected under the 1976 Code.[46]

There are a number of important implications of this judgement. The first is that while the ECtHR ruling applies to war crimes and genocide, it does not apply to crimes against humanity (which were crimes under international law but were not foreseen by the CCSFRY). As legal analyst Francesco De Sanctis notes, this has the disturbing consequence of 'subjecting those convicted for crimes against humanity to sentences up to 45 years under the Criminal Code of BiH 2003, while leaving those convicted of war crimes and genocide under the more favourable CCSFRY sentencing regime'.[47] The second is that it grants credibility to the argument made in the Supreme Court of the Republika Srpska, made in the acquittal of Dragoje Radanović, that to argue for contraventions of international law – and in particular of the Geneva Conventions – a clear international dimension to the conflict must be demonstrated.[48] This position aligns with a political desire to portray the conflict in BiH as part of a civil war (the fragmentation of Yugoslavia) rather than an example of interstate violence (in particular the remnants of Yugoslavia in conflict with a newly independent BiH). Reflecting a well-established discourse of querying the independence claim of BiH in 1992, this is a political and

---

[45] Ibid.
[46] Balkan Transitional Justice (2016). Bosnia awards Iraqi war crimes convict €36,600, www.balkaninsight.com/en/article/bosnia-awards-iraqi-war-crimes-convict-36-000-11-09-2016 (accessed 12 November 2018).
[47] de Sanctis, F. (2014). Reconciling justice and legality: A quest for fair punishment in cases on Bosnian atrocity crimes. *Journal of International Criminal Justice* 12(4): 847–870.
[48] See Organisation for Security and Cooperation in Europe (2008). Moving towards a harmonized application of the law, www.osce.org/mission-to-bosnia-and-herzegovina/314846?download=true (accessed 18 December 2018).

geographical interpretation that shapes the severity of crimes within RS's court system. One final implication has been the requirement to release those convicted of war crimes or genocide, and retrying their cases under the CCSFRY. In late 2013, 12 convicted war criminals serving sentences in BiH were released, including 6 who were convicted of their role in the genocide at Srebrenica in 1995.[49] The releases were met with complaint and derision by civil society organisations working to support the prosecution of indicted war criminals. The Mothers of Srebrenica were vocal in their protest at the interpretation of human rights law, one member asking, 'is there anything human in those judges who decide to annul their verdicts?'[50]

There are few absolute conclusions that can be drawn from this example of the contested, crisis-ridden and elongated process of applying a new criminal code to crimes of the past. This is neither a story of strict adherence to legal positivism, nor is it a triumph of moral idealism emanating from a common humanity. Similarly, this is neither a tale of legal clarity, (the varied severity of punishments for different atrocity crimes lends considerable legal complexity), nor is it a case of the complete failure of international jurisprudence in the face of a fragmented legal topography. It supports the calls from Mountz[51] and Orzeck[52] for greater attention to the personal effects of law, but also underscores the significance of bodies – and in particular the legacies of previous regimes carried through bodies – on individual perceptions of justice. This is not an arena where a unitary 'international community' has exerted sovereign power to suspend previous law; it is a site of a polyvalent legal complex, starkly illustrating the ultimate fragmentation and incoherence of an imagined global sovereign.

As we have seen in earlier chapters of this book, the edge of law is suggestive of a singular boundary containing a particular jurisdiction. The concept of legal pluralism – the coexistence of a number of centres of legal authority overlapping in a given territory – troubles this

---

[49] See BBC News (2013). Bosnia frees Srebrenica convicts over legal error, www.bbc.co.uk/news/world-europe-25007858 (accessed 12 December 2018).
[50] See The Journal.ie (2013), www.thejournal.ie/bosnia-war-criminals-released-1209704-Dec2013/ (accessed 12 December 2018).
[51] Mountz, A. (2010). *Seeking asylum: Human smuggling and bureaucracy at the border*. Minneapolis: University of Minnesota Press.
[52] Orzeck, R. (2014). Normative geographies and the 1940 land transfer regulations in Palestine. *Transactions of the Institute of British Geographers* 39(3): 345–359.

centralised imaginary. The purpose of this chapter has been to illuminate the production and consequences of a pluralist legal system in BiH. The establishment of the WCC at the CBiH relied upon two competing imaginations of law. The first was a humanitarian impulse that sought to hold individuals to account and render those victims of atrocities during war as rights-bearers. In this respect, CBiH was accommodating a legal commons, a form of legal redress that transcended the sovereignty claims of specific territories and related to normative frameworks based on a common humanity. The second is a more spatialised imaginary of building the coherence of BiH through the establishment of a unified legal structure with jurisdiction over the state. These two competing spatial imaginaries of law were accommodated within the BiH Criminal Code 2003, where the state assumed both legal jurisdiction over the territory of BiH and the facility to try individuals for crimes perpetrated in the past. The troubled conditions surrounding the establishment of this new Criminal Code reveal the limits to international authority where the embodied knowledge of the judiciary and legal legitimacy of previous doctrine limit the ability to make law. By examining the fallacy of 'exit strategies' the penultimate chapter continues this consideration of performing the localisation of legal responsibility and the subsequent separation of BiH from wider geopolitical concerns.

CHAPTER SEVEN

ENTRANCE STRATEGIES

INTRODUCTION

> By the middle of 1996, approximately 300,000 of the total 400,000 to 430,000 soldiers within [BiH] left their respective armed forces voluntarily. Given the substantive lack of governance and institutional capacity in Bosnia at that time, the two ethnic entities did not provide assistance to their ex-combatants. Similarly, during this initial and ad hoc stage of the demobilization process, the OHR, the state government and international organizations did not extend assistance to the demobilizing soldiers. In the absence of any assistance, these former soldiers were forced to immediately and individually seek employment alternatives to support their families. The former combatants re-entered Bosnian society largely unprepared for such a transition, often lacking education and skills and suffering from post-traumatic stress disorder (PTSD). Despite the fact that many soldiers were civilians prior to the onset of the Bosnian war, most were lost in the war-devastated and virtually non-existent Bosnian economy, given that there were little to no employment opportunities available.[1]

The significance of the form and extent of military forces in post-Dayton BiH extends beyond simply the capacity to wage war. As Moratti and Sabic-El-Rayess illustrate, the demobilisation of troops produced a

---

[1] Moratti, M., & Sabic-El-Rayess, A. (2009). Transitional justice and DDR: The case of Bosnia and Herzegovina, International Center for Transitional Justice. June, www.ictj.org/sites/default/files/ICTJ-DDR-Bosnia-CaseStudy-2009-English.pdf (accessed 16 July 2019).

significant social crisis, as working-age (predominantly) men returned to communities with which they were often unfamiliar without employment opportunities or suitable education alternatives. Within the armed forces the story was similarly disjointed, the shrunken BiH military was divided down ethnic lines, reflecting the divisions endorsed at the GFAP, while the various military forces benefitted from material support from sympathetic neighbouring countries. Security-sector reform, then, became a key element of state formation: it was clear that the Weberian imaginary of a monopoly of legitimate violence over a given territory would be a future accomplishment rather than an outcome of a peace treaty. This chapter explores the interventions made in the attempt to reconstruct military forces in BiH, exploring how these processes have enrolled various international and domestic actors in new legal relationships and conflicts. These processes of enrolment have a strong bearing on the overarching argument concerning the edge of law in BiH. The reorganisation of the military was presented by intervening agencies as a central component of an 'exit strategy', performing a separation between the site of intervention and the temporary presence of an intervening agency. In a sense: an enactment of the edge. But this chapter argues these performances would be better framed as 'entrance strategies', heralding new and often covert forms of intervention. It seems an appropriate empirical and theoretical point on which to end the book: that the passage of time does not lead to the inevitable strengthening of state sovereignty and the exit of international influence. Instead we need to carefully trace how imaginations of 'exit' create new forms of dependence, reliance and influence.

This concern for the co-presence of 'exit' and 'entrance' is reflected in literature on the normative framing of international intervention. The term 'exit strategy' has been used by military planners to denote the planned finality of any deployment of troops or international administration in a conflict or post-conflict scenario. It is term borrowed by the military from the world of business (specifically entrance and exit from financial markets) and rose to prominence after the failed US-led Operation Gothic Serpent in Mogadishu, Somalia, in 1993. It is also an inherently spatial term, conjuring an image of a clear border between presence and absence of international agencies (exit) and a vacating authority with a clear plan (strategy). In addition, and perhaps more fundamentally, it asserts the separate identities of an administering authority and a territorial entity under administration. It is no surprise that this pristine story of premeditated departure and separation is hard to sustain in practice. Indeed, they are imaginaries that come from a post–World War II reaction against European colonial administration and the subsequent assertion of the primacy of self-determination within the international state system. In this normative framework, 'exit' becomes an important moral claim, where intervention may be justified on the basis of its temporary nature; it is an exceptional status that will revert to the self-governing norm at a pre-assigned moment.

The challenge within such a narrative of 'exit' becomes one of perception. The designation of criteria to be use in monitoring the departure of an international administration poses a particular challenge. Recognising this, scholars have long argued that exit is a transition rather than an event, where the slow consolidation of domestic territorial sovereignty takes place alongside the graduated withdrawal of international agencies and agendas.[2] In tandem, such work has recognised that the institutional architecture produced through interventions are hybrid in nature. Consequently, discerning between the 'international' and the 'domestic' (in terms of personnel, funding or policy approach) can become an empirical challenge. Rather than self-determination marking the end of international administration, we see new forms of international presence flourish in the transitional process of 'exit'. These performances may not be publicly- performed in the same fashion as the practice of troop withdrawal or the handing over of sovereignty, though their policy impacts could be more profound. As has been illuminated across the chapters of this book, law is a key mechanism for such 'entrance strategies', where the design of new legal codes embeds particular international agendas, while normalising the presence of external agencies and expertise. Such 'entrances' require cross-institutional scrutiny, to establish how influence over particular elements of the state is projected across international borders, challenging the finality enfolded into a language of 'exit'.

The chapter makes this argument across three inter-linked sections. The first explores the military landscape in BiH in the months following the signing of the GFAP. This account traces the fragmented military forces strewn across the territory of the partitioned state, underscoring the significance of security sector reform to the consolidation of the BiH state. The second section examines the interventions made in the name of strengthening the capacity of specific military forces in BiH, and in particular the 'Train and Equip' programme

---

[2] Caplan, R. (Ed.). (2012). *Exit strategies and state building*. Oxford University Press.

launched by the US government and directed towards improving the professionalism and capability of the Federation Army. In contrast to dominant geopolitical discourses of the time, I argue that these acts ensured that US agendas could be pursued through the conditionality attached to the promise of support. But as with other elements of the interventions explored in this book, the spaces of law structure the possibilities of intervention. The desire to train the Federation Army was unsettled through legal challenges made by residents in Serbia against the military contractor, Military Professional Resources Inc. (MPRI), relating to support for Croatian assaults on Serb civilians during Operation Storm in 1995 and pursued in a US District Court. Examining previously unanalysed court documents, the argument explores the competing understandings of the spatiality of law and responsibility in this case, demonstrating how practices of 'entrance' are performed alongside vehement claims of 'exit'. These contestations illuminate the multiple pathways through which an 'entrance strategy' can operate: forms of obligation and connection that lead to the ability to arbitrate on the legal claims of distant plaintiffs.

If the first two sections explore the external construction of the military presence in BiH, the final section examines the experience of outcasts: those with a military past who have found shifting geopolitical allegiances recast their presence on BiH territory. While the GFAP introduced the label of 'foreign fighter', the immediate post-conflict period saw many who have travelled to BiH to fight in the war granted citizenship and residential rights by the BiH government as a reward for their military service. While fighters on all sides received such rewards, the presence of Islamist fighters who had naturalised in BiH has become a focal point for intervening agencies in recent years. Drawing on legal documents, previously classified diplomatic cables and human rights reports, this section traces how legal processes have been used to remove rights from these individuals, supported by US government resources and personnel. These covert 'entrances' into the heart of BiH state practice represent a new edge of law, where external governmental power is used to reconfigure the normative model of citizenship in BiH. But as with all edges of law: this is a relational encounter, where those suffering deportation and incarceration have sought legal redress both through the Court of BiH and international human rights courts. These tensions illuminate how legal frameworks in post-conflict settings can both act to incorporate and exclude, often with a bewildering co-presence.

THE MILITARY LANDSCAPE

Understanding the entrance strategies of intervening agencies in BiH requires a return to the discourses of security that have circulated from the GFAP onwards, discussions that have framed many of the arguments concerning transitional justice explored over the chapters of this book. These are, as Toal and Dahlman note, inherently geopolitical stories, as differently positioned actors attempt to frame the BiH state as variously divided, distant, threatening or consolidating.[3] But the central geopolitical storyline provided within the Dayton Accords is framed around building the capacity of the BiH state to govern itself, a rubric that has been countered in the years since as underplaying the considerable international supervisory role in achieving this aim.[4] Reflecting a Weberian understanding of legitimate force as central to the exercise(?) of sovereignty, the integration of BiH security – and in particular security-sector reform aiming to establish a single army and integrated police force – has been a key spar of state-building efforts. There are both internal and external aspects to aspects to these processes. Internally, this was a process of establishing and performing internal sovereignty; to underscore BiH stateness by establishing a singular military force with a monopoly of legitimate violence.[5] This objective involved two processes, each enfolded within a discursive framing of the legitimacy granted to particular forms of embodied violence. The first was the removal of 'foreign fighters' from the territory of BiH, an objective conveyed through Article III of Annex 1 of the GFAP:

> All Forces in Bosnia and Herzegovina as of the date this Annex enters into force which are not *of local origin*, whether or not they are legally and militarily subordinated to the Republic of Bosnia and Herzegovina, the Federation of Bosnia and Herzegovina, or Republika Srpska, shall be withdrawn together with their equipment from the territory of Bosnia and Herzegovina within thirty (30) days. Furthermore, all Forces that remain on the territory of Bosnia and Herzegovina must act consistently with the territorial integrity, sovereignty, and political independence of Bosnia and Herzegovina. In accordance with Article II, paragraph 1, this

---

[3] Toal, G., & Dahlman, C. T. (2011). *Bosnia remade: Ethnic cleansing and its reversal.* Oxford: Oxford University Press.
[4] Chandler, D. (2000). *Bosnia: Faking democracy after Dayton.* London: Pluto Press.
[5] Bose, S. (2005). The Bosnian state a decade after Dayton. *International Peacekeeping* 12(3): 322–335.

paragraph does not apply to UNPROFOR, the International Police Task Force referred to in the General Framework Agreement, the IFOR or other elements referred to in Article I, paragraph 1 (c).[6]

Of course, there is considerable interpretative work required to identify what constitutes 'not of local origin', while the necessary exemption of UNPROFOR and IFOR points to fissures in the category of foreign fighter between valid and invalid forms. Indeed, one of the profound questions confronting the analyst of the post-conflict military landscape in BiH is how the category of local/domestic is understood and, in tandem, how the label international/foreign is constructed as its antonym. This geographical conundrum is only amplified by the phrasing of the delegation of military authority in the GFAP: no mention is made to 'defence', rather issues relating to authority over the army are referred to through the more abstract notion of 'military matters'. For Vetschera and Damian this unspoken elision of 'defence' with 'military matters' ignores how 'defence' is a 'political function related to external security policy, and thus primarily of a foreign policy character, which the [GFAP] constitution assigned to the state-level'.[7]

In the absence of an explicit engagement with issues of defence, security issues in the GFAP are devolved to the two entities. Notionally, then, the division of the armed forces reflected the wider territorial division of the BiH state, with an Army of the FBiH (*Vojska Federacije*, or VF) and the Army of the Republika Srpska (*Vojska Republike Srpske*, or VRS). But under this neat military distinction lay a more complex, and avowedly transnational, picture. In the case of the VF, it was an umbrella structure that brought together two armies that had intermittently been in conflict with one another between 1992 and 1994: the Army of the Republic of Bosnia and Herzegovina (*Armija Republike Bosne i Herzegovine*, ARBiH) and the Croatian Defense Council (*Hrvatsko vijeće obrane*, HVO). Despite the allegiance formed between these military forces at the Washington Agreement in 1994, the post-Dayton VF did not resemble a unified army, rather a joint military force at the corps level upwards but the 'lower units remaining totally

---

[6] Dayton General Framework Agreement for Peace, Annex 1 Article III; emphasis added.
[7] Vetschera, H., & Damian, M. (2006). Security sector reform in Bosnia and Herzegovina: The role of the international community. *International Peacekeeping* 13(1): 28–42, p. 26.

separate'.[8] This separation, and the transnational character of this military project, is illustrated through its funding: an International Crisis Group report in 1999 asserts that 40 per cent of the budget for the Bosnian-Muslim part of the army came from countries in the Persian Gulf.[9] In contrast, the entirety of the Bosnian-Croat funds came from beyond the territory of BiH, with 83 per cent originating in Croatia and the rest from emigres and the Gulf states. In the circumstances of such significant military support from external sources the very line between 'domestic' and 'foreign' forces blurs.[10]

Similarly, the VRS was, from the outset, an international invention emerging from the military structures of the fragmenting Yugoslav state. When fighting in BiH broke out in May 1992, and despite claims of an official withdrawal, the majority of the Yugoslav People's Army (*Jugoslovenska narodna armija*, or JNA) on BiH territory reconstituted themselves as the VRS. This was a careful piece of military choreography that was significant for both those loyal to Serb causes within Bosnia but also for the remaining Yugoslav state. For Karadžić and the Bosnian Serbs, the performance of statehood and the legitimacy of claims of independence within BiH rested on the autonomy of the VRS army. For Slobodan Milošević, then President of Serbia, the public claims of non-involvement were crucial to his international standing. As we have seen, the conflict involved paramilitary and military units that had crossed international borders to join the violence in BiH. Like many aspects of the conflict in BiH, these actions were highly varied and complex, shifting over the four years of fighting both in location and prevalence. But alongside the El Mujahid, fighters within Croatian and Serbian paramilitary groups also played a prominent role within the unfolding violence. James Ron has traced the ebb and flow of Serbian paramilitary groups and their involvement in the Bosnian war, seeing their involvement as a product of international prohibition of Serbian military action beyond

---

[8] P. 128 in Hoare, M. A. (2004). *How Bosnia armed*. London: Saqi Books.
[9] International Crisis Group (1999). Is Dayton failing? Bosnia four years after the peace agreement, www.crisisgroup.org/europe-central-asia/balkans/bosnia-and-herzegovina/dayton-failing-bosnia-four-years-after-peace-agreement (accessed 20 December 2018).
[10] See p. 40 in Short, E. (2018). The Orao affair: The key to military integration in post-Dayton Bosnia and Herzegovina. *The Journal of Slavic Military Studies* 31(1): 37–64.

its borders.[11] For Ron, this stipulation led to Bosnian-Serb officials entering into subcontracting relationships in both BiH and Serbia, an approach that allowed involvement of paramilitary groups 'without directly incriminating the Belgrade regime'.[12]

Peter Andreas,[13] drawing on the dramaturgical language of Erving Goffman,[14] argues that these military and paramilitary manoeuvres reflect a well-established distinction between the appearance of non-involvement and separation on the 'front stage', while engaging in covert facilitation 'backstage'. Evidence of such covert facilitation is not hard to find. The VRS largely comprised the 2nd Military District Command of the JNA with the 'old command structures in Sarajevo withdrawn to the wartime command location of Han Pijesak and transformed into a General Staff'.[15] The existence of an international arms embargo over the territory of the former Yugoslav Republics (UN Security Council Resolution 713) heightened the ideological and material significance of retaining connections with the JNA, and such connections came in numerous clandestine forms. In terms of infantry, arms and ordnance, the VRS inherited somewhere in the region of 60,000 troops, 300 tanks and more than 55 aircraft from the JNA.[16] In addition, a supply line from Serbia through Eastern BiH and across the Drina River provided ammunition, fuel and provisions to the VRS army, while a return route allowed VRS soldiers to receive treatment in Serbia.[17] Consequently, the international blockade gave a significant advantage to the VRS as the military imbalance with other groups in BiH could be retained: a reason for Slobodan Miloševic's support for the continued embargo.[18] The close links between the RS and its neighbour continued after the conflict ended, reflected by the statistic that by 1998 'about 40 per cent of VRS funding came directly from

---

[11] Ron, J. (2000). Territoriality and plausible deniability: Serbian paramilitaries in the Bosnian war, in B. Campbell & A. Brenner (eds.), *Death squads in global perspective*. New York: Palgrave Macmillan, pp. 287–312.
[12] P. 287 in ibid.
[13] Andreas, P. (2008). *Blue helmets and black markets: The business of survival in the siege of Sarajevo*. Ithaca, NY: Cornell University Press.
[14] Goffman, E. (1959). *The presentation of self in everyday life*. New York: Doubleday.
[15] P. 77 in Gow, J. (2003). *The Serbian project and its adversaries*. London: Hurst and Company.
[16] Ibid.
[17] P. 44 in Short, The Orao affair.
[18] See p. 23 in Andreas, *Blue helmets and black markets*.

Yugoslavia, and until 2002 its officers' wages were still being paid from Belgrade'.[19]

TRAIN AND EQUIP

While there is a tendency to view 'foreign' assistance solely through the prism of BiH's position as a client state to its Yugoslav neighbours, security-sector reform, and the associated material and training support for the various military forces operating in BiH, was also shaped by wider geopolitical dynamics. In the post-Dayton years, interventions in BiH's military capacity became geopolitical technologies: mechanisms through which specific allegiances could be strengthened and enmities stabilised. One of the central traits of such technologies is their plurality and mutability, where circumstance, audience and materials shape the geopolitical stories surrounding military reform. Of course, at their heart these processes shared with other aspects of the GFAP an explicit commitment to the construction of a territorially bound and democratic sovereign state. As with many international state-building concerns following World War II, the central stated objective was establishing the capacity of the state to govern its own population and territory. This creates a series of paradoxes, not least that invasive international action is made in the name of stabilising local democratic control over a given territory.[20]

The co-presence of exit narratives and entrance strategies can be traced in the post-GFAP international intervention in the BiH state. As discussed in earlier chapters, the form and agenda of early interventions in the wake of the GFAP were focused squarely on the cessation of violence and the implementation of the institutions and borders established at Dayton, putting the quest for justice through legal redress as a second-order concern.[21] This was a consequence of the quest for a clear completion of international responsibility: in the eyes of the International Crisis Group an 'exit strategy' became a 'preoccupation'

---

[19] Short, The Orao affair, p. 44; see also Gow, J., & Zverzhanovski, I. (2013). *Security, democracy and war crimes: Security sector transformation in Serbia*. London: Springer.
[20] Elden, S. (2009). *Terror and territory: The spatial extent of sovereignty*. Minneapolis: University of Minnesota Press.
[21] P. 88 in Witte, E. (2009). Beyond 'peace vs. justice': Understanding the relationship between DDR programs and the prosecution of international crimes, in A. C. Patel, P. De Greiff & L. Waldorf (eds.), *Disarming the past: Transitional justice and ex-combatants*. New York: Social Science Research Council, pp. 86–107.

amongst the US administration in the immediate aftermath of the signing of the GFAP, sending 'a confusing and destabilising message to Bosnians' and encouraging hardliners to 'sit tight and wait NATO out'.[22] As O Tuathail identifies, the international military response to the conflict was shaped by a fear of a Vietnam-style 'quagmire', where troops are bogged down in a lengthy and ill-defined engagement.[23] The Peace Implementation Council (PIC) used three strategies to avoid such an open-ended commitment to military involvement in post-GFAP BiH. The first, which has been discussed in previous chapters, was to scale down the initial attempts to establish legal processes of transitional justice; in the clichéd binary between peace and justice, the early attempts to implement the GFAP settled on the side of peace.[24] The second was to put a strict time limit on the presence of troops: Annex I-a of the GFAP provided the mandate for the deployment of a NATO-led Implementation Force (I-FOR) for one year only, comprising around 54,000 soldiers in BiH (with others stationed in neighbouring countries). While this served to communicate the temporary nature of the initial engagement it did not foreclose the possibility of renewal in a different guise. While I-FOR's mandate ceased in December 1996, the UN Security Council (through Resolution 1088) immediately redeployed the international force as a stabilisation force (S-FOR) with a similar role but a reduced troop deployment of around 32,000 soldiers.[25] The third strategy was to emphasise the significance of self-determination through the holding of multi-party elections in September 1996. That these were scheduled only nine months after the cessation of violence points to a rather optimistic imagination of the duration of state formation in the wake of the conflict.[26] As the election embedded wartime leaders, or parties, into the power structures

---

[22] International Crisis Group (1997). A peace, or just a cease-fire? The military equation in post-Dayton Bosnia and Herzegovina. ICG Bosnia Project Report 28, 15 December.
[23] Ó Tuathail, G. (1996). *Critical geopolitics*. Abingdon: Routledge.
[24] Waldorf, L. (2009). Linking DDR and Transitional justice, in A. C. Patel, P. De Greiff & L. Waldorf (eds.), *Disarming the past: Transitional justice and ex-combatants*. New York: Social Science Research Council, pp. 14–35.
[25] S-FOR was replaced in December 2004 by the European Union military force EUFOR Althea.
[26] For a discussion of the failings of the September 1996 BiH election process see Riley, C. A. (1997). Neither free nor fair: The 1996 Bosnian elections and the failure of the UN election-monitoring mission. *Vanderbilt Journal of Transnational Law* 30: 1173.

of the nascent BiH state, intervening agencies looked to other levers to assist with the strengthening of the BiH state with a view to the exit of international agencies. At the top of this list was the reform and integration of the BiH military.

From the perspective of 'entrance strategies', security-sector reform offered a number of mechanisms for embedding internationally mediated agendas within the BiH state. In particular, it encouraged the BiH state to reorient its geopolitical allegiances from Iran and towards Euro-Atlantic security structures.[27] The formative moment for such initiatives came during the Dayton negotiations, where Bosnian Muslim parties made military assistance a key requirement for their signature on the nascent agreement.[28] This granted an opportunity to US interlocutors: the provision of military resources could be used to demand strengthened cooperation between the two armies of the Federation while also providing the leverage to sever military and financial ties with other third-party states. A particular, and ongoing, concern for the United States was the continued connections between Bosnian Muslim political elites, and in particular that of SDA President Alija Izetbegović, and Islamist politics.[29]

By placing such an emphasis on these connections, US officials were articulating an ingrained fear of Islamist factions in the emergent BiH state, a concern that had strengthened through the assistance offered to BiH by Iran during the years of the arms embargo and the presence of mujahidin during the conflict. Certainly, the religious conviction of Alija Izetbegović, and its role in shaping his geopolitical objectives, has been a point of ongoing contestation. These deliberations illuminate differing imaginations of the role of Islam in the modern European state. In this vein, Izetbegović's 1970 essay *The Islamic Declaration*, a meditation on Islam and modernity, has been the focus of sustained analysis in both scholarly and policy circles. The text seeks to foster the

---

[27] See Aybet, G., & Bieber, F. (2011). From Dayton to Brussels: The impact of EU and NATO conditionality on state building in Bosnia and Hercegovina. *Europe-Asia Studies* 63(10): 1911–1937; Ó Tuathail, G. (2005). Embedding Bosnia-Herzegovina in Euro-Atlantic structures: From Dayton to Brussels. *Eurasian Geography and Economics* 46(1): 51–67.

[28] Singer, P. W. (2003). *Corporate warriors: The rise of the privatized military industry*. Ithaca, NY: Cornell University Press.

[29] See, e.g., Bardos, G. N. (2013). Iran in the Balkans: A history and a forecast. *World Affairs* 175(5): 59–66.

'implementation of Islam in all areas of personal individual life, in the family and in society, through the renewal of Islamic religious thought and the creation of a unified Islamic community'.[30] But this general geopolitical objective can be read in different ways. For some the writing stands as evidence of Izetbegović's 'Islamic fixation',[31] where the suggestion that there could be 'no peace or co-existence between Islamic faith and non-Islamic social and political institutions'[32] was a clear sign of the inevitability of religious conflict, providing a forerunner to more recent calls for jihad in the name of international Islamic caliphate.[33] Encapsulating this view, Radovan Karadžić cited the text in closing remarks during his trial at the ICTY as evidence of the fascistic objectives of Izetbegović's regime, remarking 'it is one of the key points to the Islamic Declaration ... that only 5% of Serbs can remain [in BiH].'[34] Others refute the violence of the document, suggesting it was an 'esoteric text' designed as 'a work of scholarship, not politics, intended to promote philosophical discourse amongst Muslims'.[35] Rather than a caliphate, Izetbegović was imagining an international Islamic Federation analogous to the European Union.[36] From this perspective it is the prominence given to the Islamic Declaration by external commentators, in contrast to Izetbegović's other more explicitly liberal writings such as 1984's *Islam between East and West*, that points to a desire to forcibly align his position with radical Islamist politics.

It is, then, the fear of stronger connections between a post-Dayton BiH and certain aspects of the Islamic world that motivated peace negotiators to attempt to reorientate the geopolitical compass: to shift the nascent state towards Euro-Atlantic security and political structures

---

[30] Knežević, A. (1997). Alija Izetbegović's 'Islamic Declaration': Its substance and its western reception. *Islamic Studies* 36(2/3): 483–521.
[31] P. 3 in O'Ballance, E. (1995). *Civil war in Bosnia*. London: Macmillan.
[32] Cited in ibid.
[33] P. 61 in Bardos, Iran in the Balkans.
[34] See Balkan Transitional Justice (2010). Karadžić talks Izetbegović in cross-examination, www.balkaninsight.com/en/article/karadzic-talks-izetbegovic-in-cross-examination (accessed 16 July 2019); ICTY (2014). Defense closing statement, www.icty.org/x/cases/karadzic/trans/en/141001ED.htm (accessed 16 July 2019).
[35] P. 208 in Silber, L., & Little, A. (1996). *The death of Yugoslavia*. London: Penguin; for further discussion on the varying interpretations of Izetbegović's Islamic Declaration see Campbell, D. (1998). MetaBosnia: Narratives of the Bosnian War. *Review of International Studies* 24(2): 261–281.
[36] Knežević, Alija Izetbegović's 'Islamic Declaration', pp. 483–521.

through the promise of security-sector support. At the heart of this package of support was the 'Train and Equip' (T&E) programme, initiated by the United States to strengthen the capabilities of the VF in the face of the better-resourced VRS. The significance of this shift in Western strategy towards the military in BiH – from arms embargo to military re-arming – should not be understated, and created unease amongst many Western European powers. The United Kingdom was a prominent critic, continuing to argue for arms reductions in the post-Dayton period, perhaps reproducing a message of 'putting weapons beyond use' that characterised responses to paramilitary violence in Northern Ireland. Debates in the UK House of Commons also reveal a fear of dwindling US involvement in the NATO-led international troop deployment I-FOR: an anxiety over US 'exit'. In a debate on UK military deployment in BiH on July 1996, then Labour MP David Clark explained the fears surrounding T&E:

> So far, this mission [in BiH] has been a success, but the peace is fragile. Indeed, it may become more fragile in the light of the news that the United States has given authority to start training Bosnian Government troops and Croatian troops. If we walk away in December, there is every chance that the war will begin again. There must be some form of IFOR 2. I hope that our United States allies will stay in Bosnia. We shall use our best endeavours, as will the Government, to persuade the Americans that they must remain.[37]

Unlike the disarming of paramilitary groups, in BiH it was not a zero-sum game of the presence or absence of weaponry, it remained an asymmetrical military environment where the VRS, continuing to exploit its established links with the Serbian security infrastructure, held a far greater arsenal of weaponry than the hastily and imperfectly integrated VF. Consequently, the opening justification for T&E was the need for 'military balance', that equivalence in military capability would prevent the further outbreak of violence. As former US ambassador and US Director of Train and Equip, James Pardew, explained at the time:

> The U. S. concept for security in Bosnia is simple and straightforward. Stability in southern Europe requires peace in Bosnia. Long-term peace in Bosnia requires the creation of a military balance, and a military

---

[37] Hansard (1996). British Forces (Bosnia), https://api.parliament.uk/historic-hansard/commons/1996/jul/18/british-forces-bosnia (accessed 7 November 2018).

balance is achieved by a combination of arms control and adequate training and equipment for the Bosnian Federation.[38]

But while the 'front stage' may have performed this increase in military capacity through the language of parity in the monopoly of legitimate violence, the more 'backstage' operation focused on the positioning of Islamist politicians within the architecture of the BiH state. This reorientation was not an abstract commitment but rather a highly embodied practice that sought to alter the makeup of the inner circle of advisers and ministers surrounding Izetbegović. In particular, the dismissal of the Deputy Defence Minister in the Federation, Hasan Čengić, was a key demand of the US administration prior to the launching of the T&E programme.[39] Čengić was a prominent Bosnian Muslim cleric with strong connections to Iran, including allegedly arranging arms transfers during the war. In memoirs of the events, James Pardew recollects dining at Izetbegović's apartment in central Sarajevo and the strain that fulfilling the requirements of T&E was placing on his host: '[r]emoving Čengić and breaking the security link with Iran meant rejecting a hero of the Bosnian Muslims' cause during the war and those who supported Sarajevo when others did not. It was a painful choice for the Bosnian president'.[40] On June 26, 1996, US President Clinton confirmed that the criteria for the launching of T&E had been met, moves that in Ambassador Pardew's view 'greatly reduc[ed] the influence of radical Iranian and other foreign elements in Bosnia'.[41] But as with the GFAP, the designation of 'foreign elements' articulates an imagined geography of the state, where foreignness stands as a simple signifier of illegitimacy and other forms of non-local intervention are either celebrated, naturalised or erased.

---

[38] US State Department (1996). Briefing on train-and-equip program for the Bosnian Federation, https://1997-2001.state.gov/regions/eur/bosnia/724brief_bosnia_federation.html (accessed 20 December 2018).
[39] P. 184 in Bieber, F. (2001). Arming the Muslim-Croat Federation: Failed realpolitik with moralistic justifications?, in Albrecht Schnabel (ed.), *Southeast European security: Threats, responses, challenges*. Huntington, NY: Nova Science Publishers, pp. 177–192.
[40] No page number, Pardew, J. W. (2017). *Peacemakers: American leadership and the end of genocide in the Balkans*. Lexington: University Press of Kentucky.
[41] US State Department, Briefing on train-and-equip program for the Bosnian Federation, https://1997-2001.state.gov/regions/eur/bosnia/724brief_bosnia_federation.html (accessed 26 July 2019).

One specific act of erasure involves the role of US military expertise in the enactment of T&E. While the dominant narrative of security-sector reform related to an overarching desire for 'exit', the process of T&E required a new form of 'entrance'. But where the peace negotiations and NATO presence were publicised through political speeches and policy reports, the involvement of US actors in T&E remained less open to examination. This was not simply an act of political omission: the institutional form and makeup of T&E was designed to place US involvement at a remove from public scrutiny (either in BiH or the US). This was both a financial and institutional performance. In financial terms, the architects of T&E were keen to point to the distance of US involvement in the scheme, promoting it as an 'international' initiative and one that drew in approved Islamic states:

> The funds used to pay for the Federation MPRI contract are provided not by U. S. tax dollars but by international donor countries who want to help create peace through military balance in Bosnia. Those countries who strongly support the U. S. in this concept are Turkey, Saudi Arabia, Kuwait, the United Arab Emirates, Malaysia and Brunei. We hope others will join us as this project moves forward.[42]

In institutional terms, T&E was delivered through a private military consultancy, reflecting the more 'outsourced' model of military assistance that grew in prevalence over the 1990s.[43] The Federation government granted the contract for the T&E programme to MPRI, a US firm based in the state of Virginia with experience of working in the former Yugoslavia. Offering the cheapest package of support, MPRI were a 'lean alternative compared to the other companies and had a great deal of credibility with the Bosnians and particularly the Croats'.[44] While experience and economy are clearly benefits, MPRI's suitability for this function has been questioned on the basis of their alleged involvement in training Croatian Forces for 1995's Operation Storm offensive that drove more than 100,000 Serb residents out of Croatia's Krajina

---

[42] Ibid.
[43] Shearer, D. (1998). Outsourcing war. *Foreign Policy 112*(Autumn): 68–81.
[44] Lamb, C., Arkin, S. & Scudder, S. (1994). *The Bosnian train and equip program: A lesson in interagency integration of hard and soft power strategic perspectives 15*, Center for Strategic Research Institute for National Strategic Studies National Defense, https://inss.ndu.edu/Portals/68/Documents/stratperspective/inss/Strategic-Perspectives-15.pdf (accessed 20 December 2018).

region.[45] This involvement has always been refuted by MPRI, though as the journalist David Isenberg notes, the conduct of the offensive bore similarities with US military techniques:

> [T]he August 1995 Operation Storm which resulted in Croatia recapturing its previously Serb-held Krajina region utilized typical American operational tactics, including integrated air, artillery and infantry movements, and the use of maneuver warfighting techniques to destroy Serbian command and control networks. Many observers at the time claimed the Croatians never could have done that without the training provided by MPRI[46]

The use of a private military contractor provided some distance for the US government from these allegations, a crucial buffer when the entire territory of the former Yugoslavia was at the time under a UN arms embargo (UN Security Council Resolution 713). But MPRI's registration on US territory was not without consequence. In subsequent years, former Krajina residents have sought legal redress through US courts for the alleged crimes carried out during Operation Storm. Specifically, L-3 MPRI[47] was the target of a class action brought to the Northern District of Illinois Eastern Division Court by Milena Jović and Zivka Mijić in August 2010. Both had been expelled with their families from the Krajina during the Croatian military assault and subsequently taken up residence in Serbia. The plaintiffs alleged that the company's involvement in 'an aggressive, systematic military attack and bombardment on a demilitarized civilian population that had been placed under the protection of the United Nations'.[48] The legal scholar Chia Lehnardt also reports allegations that someone referred to as 'the American general', assumed to be one of the retired American generals on MPRI's

---

[45] Lehnardt, C. (2008). Individual liability of private military personnel under international criminal law. *European Journal of International Law* 19(5): 1015–1034, p. 1022.
[46] Isenberg, D. (2010). MPRI couldn't read minds, let's sue. HuffPost Blog, 19 August, www.huffingtonpost.com/david-isenberg/mpri-couldnt-read-minds-l_b_ 688000.html (accessed 20 December 2018).
[47] MPRI was acquired by L-3 Communications in 2000; L-3 and MPRI are joint defendants in the court proceedings (though some court materials refer to joint defendants of L-3 Services and Engility Holdings, the latter a spin-off from L-3).
[48] Case 1:10-cv-05197 In the US District Court Northern District of Illinois Eastern Division Filed 08/17/10, www.veritas.org.rs/wp-content/uploads/2011/08/tuzba-usa .pdf (accessed 12 November 2018).

payroll, had planned the operation.[49] One of the key allegations related to a historic ethnic enmity of which MPRI should, in the plaintiffs' eyes, have been aware:

> MPRI knew or reasonably should have known the open facts of the genocide at the Jasenovac Concentration Camp. MPRI knew or reasonably should have known of the intense hatred the Croats felt toward the Serbs. MPRI knew or reasonably should have known that the Croatian leaders with whom it was negotiating had been key figures in the Ustasha Party that fomented, organized and led the massacres at Jasenovac and other killing camps in Croatia during World War Two.[50]

Either through intent or by wilful ignorance, the defendants accuse L-3 MPRI of 'complicity to genocide', a crime that differs from genocide in that it does not require participation in the targeted killing of a group on the basis of religious, national, ethnic or racial identity, rather that the defendants were aware 'that the perpetrator has that specific intent'.[51] Of course, complicity to genocide requires a burden of proof that both genocide took place and the defendants were aware that their interventions facilitated these crimes.

The legal basis of the accusation stemmed from US Alien Tort Statute (ATS), 28 U.S.C. § 1350, a statute that grants US district courts 'original jurisdiction of any civil action by an alien for a tort [infringement of rights] only, committed in violation of the law of nations or a treaty of the United States'.[52] Considering the distance between the location of the alleged crimes and the site of legal judgement, the choice of court is justified by the plaintiffs in two, potentially contradictory, ways. The first is to assign the aspatial nature of crimes of this significance (complicity to genocide). It is a crime against

---

[49] Lehnardt, Individual liability of private military personnel under international criminal law, p. 1022.
[50] Case 1:10-cv-05197, www.veritas.org.rs/wp-content/uploads/2011/08/tuzba-usa.pdf (accessed 26 July 2019).
[51] Ibid.
[52] U.S. Code Title 28-Judiciary and Judicial Procedure (1940). Alien Action for Tort (Alien Tort Statute) June 25, 1948, ch. 646, 62 Stat. 934, https://h2o.law.harvard.edu/collages/41749 (accessed 16 July 2019). The ATS defines the liable party as '[a]n individual who, under actual or apparent authority, or color of law, of any foreign nation – (1) subjects an individual to torture shall, in a civil action, be liable for damages to that individual or (2) subjects an individual to extrajudicial killing shall, in a civil action, be liable for damages to the individual's legal representative, or to any person who may be a claimant in an action for wrongful death'.

humanity and therefore any site of legal deliberation is qualified to hear the case. The complaint describes ATS as a 'jurisdiction-conferring statute', considering the crimes of such magnitude that the location of their judgement is immaterial to the legal case. Such an argument recalls an idealistic imagination of transitional justice, where the location of crime or the existence of a specific law is immaterial in the case of such profound criminality.

Conversely, the second justification is based on the specific location of the Northern District of Illinois Eastern Division Court:

> This Court has personal jurisdiction over Defendant L-3 because L-3 maintains a division within this judicial district and conducts substantial business within this judicial district. Venue is proper because L-3 resides in this district and MPRI can be found in this district. Additionally, numerous plaintiffs reside in this district.[53]

Here, it is the bodily presence of class-action plaintiffs in Illinois that provides the justification for court selection, a territorialised imaginary of legal responsibility based on residence. But this latter claim served to undermine their first justification, drawing attention to more appropriate venues for adjudication through territorial connection. Exploiting this point, in January 2011 the defendants attempted to force a change in venue for the trial to the US District Court for the Southern District of New York (SDNY). They rejected the Illinois Court on the grounds of irrelevance to the specifics of the trial: 'the only connection to this District is that one named Plaintiff in a putative class whose members may span the entire globe allegedly resides here. This fact is insufficient to overcome Defendants' meaningful connections to the SDNY.... Neither corporation is organized under the laws of Illinois. Nor does either have continuous and systematic contacts with Illinois'. In this optic, proximity and presence retain a significant role in justifying the legitimacy of a legal regime, regardless of the scale of crime.

The court judgement came in September 2014 and, reflecting one of the challenges in the case of lengthy court proceedings, the material facts of the case had changed. In the years between the complaint and its legal outcome, two key Croatian military officials found guilty at the ICTY of genocide during Operation Storm, Ante Gotovina and

---

[53] Case 1:10-cv-05197, www.veritas.org.rs/wp-content/uploads/2011/08/tuzba-usa.pdf (accessed 26, July 2019).

Mladen Markač had won their appeals against their sentences.[54] Following this outcome, the possibility of a guilty verdict in the Illinois case was reduced: the existence of genocide is a prerequisite of a case for complicity to genocide. But in making its judgement the court focused on geography of jurisdiction, and specifically whether a US District Court was the appropriate venue for the trial. The presiding judge, Judge John Z. Lee, agreed with the defendants and dismissed the case for a lack of subject matter jurisdiction, arguing that the 'mere corporate presence' of the defendant in the United States was insufficient to confer jurisdiction over the claim.[55] Although plaintiffs allege that MPRI negotiated its contract with the Croatian leadership in Virginia and conducted some planning and development activities in Virginia, defendants' involvement occurred 'also within and from Croatia itself', culminating in 10 different trips to Croatia, with MPRI 'plac[ing] its personnel on the ground' in Croatia.[56] The subtext to this judgement is consistent with the post-ICTY approach to transitional justice in the former Yugoslavia: if there is a case to be heard then the appropriate jurisdiction is the venue of the crime as opposed to any other node within the wider network of military, legal and political relationships within which they were embedded. The edge of law is reasserted as the territorial boundaries of the jurisdiction within which the crimes took place.

THE PRODUCTION OF OUTSIDERS

If the case surrounding MPRI points to forms of complicity across international boundaries, the subsequent production of legislation around citizenship in BiH points to continued lines of influence from external actors within the BiH state. Of course, speaking of the subtle projection of international influence seems rather obscure in a context where the constitution of the state was produced through an internationally brokered peace agreement and an international authority

---

[54] Balkan Insight (2015). Operation Storm: Croatia's triumph, Serbia's grief, www.balkaninsight.com/en/article/operation-storm-croatia-s-triumph-serbia-s-grief-07-31-2015 (accessed 16 July 2019).
[55] 1:10-cv-05197 Document #: 100 Filed: 09/24/14, Jovic vs. L3-Holdings, in the US District Court for the Northern District of Illinois Eastern Division, Memorandum Opinion and Order, https://law.justia.com/cases/federal/district-courts/illinois/ilndce/1:2010cv05197/246538/100/ (accessed 16 July 2019).
[56] Ibid.

(the OHR) has, since 1997, had executive and legislative powers over the BiH state. But the processes under scrutiny point to the covert mechanisms through which agendas stemming from external sovereign states are expressed through citizenship legislation in BiH. I argue that this clandestine enactment of 'entrance' has required the careful production of insiders and outsiders, a move that was less a reflection of spatial location than an ideological designation of legitimacy onto specific racialised bodies. Specifically, through material support for new citizenship laws, the United States has sought to enrol BiH into its wider agenda to confront Islamic extremism. This process has involved the expulsion of individuals who were granted BiH citizenship in the wake of the conflict and the internment of those considered a potential terror threat. At the same time, the Russian state has lent diplomatic support to the separatist aspirations of the Republika Srpska through strengthened ties between Milorad Dodik (President of RS) and Vladmir Putin.

I want to consider the lingering significance of material support and discursive agendas in the establishment of citizenship legislation through the lens of a single coordinated action between police and military in BiH. In the autumn of 2014, officials of BiH's State Investigation and Protection Agency (SIPA) initiated Operation 'Damask' ('Damascus'), a nationwide search for individuals considered by the BiH government to be involved in terror-related activities. This operation was a response to a changing legislative climate in the country; earlier in the year, the BiH government had adopted amendments to the country's Criminal Code that both extended the prison terms for convicted terrorists to up to 10 years while widening the definition of *terror* to include recruiters working for radical Islamist organisations.[57] This legislative shift was the culmination of a number of years work by the US government, in particular by International Criminal Investigative Training Assistance Program (ICITAP), a body that provided both strategic and material support to the BiH state. The specific focus of ICITAP was the operation and agendas of the BiH Foreigners Affairs Service (FAS), the body tasked with adjudicating the citizenship rights of immigrants both during and after the BiH conflict. The account of

---

[57] Library of Congress (2017); www.loc.gov/law/help/foreign-fighters/country-surveys .php#_ftnref51 (accessed 16 July 2019), see also Criminal Procedure Code of Bosnia and Herzegovina, www.sudbih.gov.ba/files/docs/zakoni/en/Criminal_Procedure_ Code_of_BH_-_Consolidated_text.pdf (accessed 16 July 2019).

anthropologist Daryl Li paints a picture of growing pressure of BiH legislators to cohere to the agendas of the US state:

> Through the ICITAP program, the USG provides the Foreigners Affairs Service (FAS) an advisor, who provides technical assistance to the FAS as they continue to develop their organizational and operational capacities as a state-level law enforcement agency. The FAS Advisor recommended legislative changes and has assisted in the development of Book of Rules and Policies and Procedures. He also helped the FAS develop policies and procedures for BiH's first alien detention center, which opened recently and is patterned on similar facilities in the U.S. Following a security assessment of the new alien detention center, the FAS Advisor made recommendations to increase the safety and security of the alien detention center, including the development of a Book of Rules for the Sector for Readmission, Admission and Accommodating of Foreigners. He has also worked closely with all of the directorates within the FAS in the development of an Operational Requirements Based Budget Process for long range planning and provided guidance to the FAS regarding the development of a classified information security program.[58]

Diplomatic cables corroborate Li's account, where the US government donated material resources to support the work of the FAS:

> To date (2009), ICITAP has donated automobiles, office equipment – including computers, combination printer/fax/copy machines and UPS units – for FAS Headquarters and each of the 16 Field Centers. Additional equipment consisting of binoculars, night vision binoculars, ASP batons, hand held radios, radio remotes, office scanners and routers were also donated to FAS investigators. ICITAP's total support for the FAS including equipment and specialized training is approximately USD 700,000. In regular meetings with Embassy staff, FAS Director Dragan Mektic and Deputy Director Izet Nizam have stressed that without USG assistance the FAS could never have become operational so quickly.[59]

In the course of Operation Damask, 16 people were arrested after searches that included locations in the Federation, RS and Brčko

---

[58] Li, D. (2015). Welcome to Bosnatanamo: Migrant detention in Bosnia, www.law.ox.ac.uk/research-subject-groups/centre-criminology/centreborder-criminologies/blog/2015/10/welcome (accessed 20 December 2018).

[59] US Government (2009). INL-managed seed-funded projects update: Focus on the Foreigners Affairs Service, https://wikileaks.org/plusd/cables/09SARAJEVO563_a.html (accessed 20 December 2018).

District: including Sarajevo, Kiseljak, Zenica, Maglaj, Gornja Maoča, Zvornik, Tuzla, Kalesija, Banovići, Bužim and Teslić. According to SIPA, the arrested individuals were suspected of committing 'criminal offences of financing terrorist activities, public incitement to terrorist activities, recruitment for terrorist activities, organising a terrorist group, all in conjunction with the criminal offence of terrorism'. While in addition some were also accused of being linked to 'financing, organising and recruiting BH nationals for departure to Syria and Iraq', as well as taking part in 'armed conflicts in Syria and Iraq, while fighting for radical terrorist groups and organisations'.[60] While this outcome was in itself considered a success, the scale of the operation also demonstrated cooperation between agencies in BiH, including the Intelligence Security Agency BH, the RS Interior Ministry, Brčko District Police and the interior ministries of Zenica-Doboj Canton, Tuzla Canton, Una-Sana Canton and Sarajevo Canton[61].

The most prominent target of Operation Damask was Hussein 'Bilal' Bosnić, an Islamic preacher based in the northwestern Bosnian municipality of Bužim. Bosnić had fought during the BiH war in the *El Mujahid*,[62] a detachment containing both domestic and foreign Islamist fighters officially located within the 7th Battalion of the 3rd Corps of the ARBiH. But it was not his military past that led to his arrest: during the subsequent years, Bosnić had risen to prominence as a leading proponent of Salafist Islam within BiH, a strict form of Islam that challenges the more moderate mixture of nondenominational and Sunni Islam generally practiced in BiH.[63] Bosnić was accused of supporting young men to fight for Islamic State in Syria and Iraq through his teachings. At his subsequent trial at the CBiH, six individuals were found to have died as a result of Bosnić's encouragement to fight overseas: Emrah Filipović, Samir Begić, Amir Crnjeković, Ismar Mesinović, Azmir Alisić, and Muaz Sabić. In court, the prosecution played

---

[60] SIPA (2014); see www.sipa.gov.ba/en/news/operation-damask-sipa-arrested-16-individuals-linked-to-terrorism/12107 (accessed 16 July 2019).
[61] Balkan Insight (2014), www.balkaninsight.com/en/article/bosnia-arrests-15-alleged-terrorists (accessed 16 July 2019).
[62] In line with conventions in ICTY reporting, I will use the term *El Mujahid* to refer to the formal inclusion of Islamist fighters in the ARBiH, while I will use the term *mujahidin* to refer to the wider phenomenon of Islamic fighters committed to jihad.
[63] Shatzmiller, M. (2002). *Islam and Bosnia: Conflict resolution and foreign policy in multi-ethnic states*. Montreal and Kingston: McGill-Queen's Press.

excerpts from his popular YouTube sermons, where Bosnić espoused jihad and particularly encouraged martyrdom: 'with explosives on our chests we pave the way to paradise' he claimed in one video; 'what makes the Lord of the servant, Allah, most happy is when his servant like that, without armour, jumps into a group of infidels and fights until he is killed', he suggested in another. In November 2015 Bosnić was found guilty and sentenced to seven years imprisonment.

As with other aspects of legal reform in BiH, we need to see these political and martial strategies within the wider mappings of danger in the twenty-first century. In this vein, the case of Operation 'Damask' and its judicial outcome for Bilal Bosnić could be inserted into the wider narrative of the global 'war on terror' which unfolded in the years following the 9/11 attacks in the United States.[64] In this scripting, new security imperatives, particularly emanating from the US government, elevate Islamic extremism as the key threat facing the global state system. BiH has long been considered a prime site for the emergence of Islamic terror, on account of its weak state structures, the presence of Islamic communities and its relatively porous borders, which permit transnational migration.[65] The intersection of these factors plays into an imaginative geography of BiH as a focal point for Islamic terror, prompting claims of 'mountain village where locals fly the black flag of ISIS above their homes as jihadists' influence spreads',[66] 'remote sharia villages'[67] and the country acting as a "recruitment hotbed" for ISIS.'[68] In many respects there is nothing new in these projections of malevolence onto BiH's territory and topography. There is no shortage of commentaries exploring the invocation of intrinsic deviance, difference and distance in Western accounts of the Balkans, where Said's

---

[64] See Gregory, D. (2004). *The colonial present*. Oxford: Malden Blackwell; Morrissey, J. (2017). *The long war: CENTCOM, grand strategy, and global security* (Vol. 34). Athens: University of Georgia Press.

[65] See Innes, M. A. (2005). Terrorist sanctuaries and Bosnia-Herzegovina: Challenging conventional assumptions. *Studies in Conflict and Terrorism* 28(4): 295–305; Shay, S. (2017). *Islamic terror and the Balkans*. Abingdon: Routledge.

[66] Daily Mail (2015), www.dailymail.co.uk/news/article-2940244/A-far-welcoming-village-Entrance-Bosnian-mountain-hamlet-branded-Islamic-State-emblem-homes-fly-terrorists-flag-group-s-influence-spreads.html#ixzz4zpn8P5Gr (accessed 16 July 2019).

[67] Der Spiegel (2016), www.spiegel.de/international/europe/islamic-state-presence-in-bosnia-cause-for-concern-a-1085326.html (accessed 20 July 2019).

[68] Business Insider (2015), http://uk.businessinsider.com/bosnia-isis-recruitment-hotbed-2015-12 (accessed 16 July 2019).

critique of Orientalism[69] is modified and appropriated to the geographical and historical specificities of the Balkan peninsula.

There are two conclusions that can be drawn from the example of Operation 'Damask'. The first is that it has rested upon a resurgent *Balkanism*, where a self-congratulatory image of the Western observer is reproduced through invocations of the primitive and violent nature of BiH culture and society.[70] The structure of knowledge production concerning social difference in BiH invites a historical narrative of Muslim presence as anomalous to an imagined indigenous Christian population. This storyline has been the dominant pejorative representation of the Islamic community in BiH both before and after the conflict 1992–1995. Of course, the maintenance of a social cleft, what elsewhere I have referred to as a 'fault line',[71] was an important explanatory narrative for the violence for both perpetrator and international intervening agencies, where the close proximity of difference was seen to cause the subsequent eruption of violence and killing. Stripping these representative strategies of their detail, we see an enduring two-stage approach to understanding legitimacy and violence: firstly, that the static body (the indigenous community) constitutes safety, in contrast to the threatening mobile or mutable body. Histories of the Ottoman Empire provide the narrative framework for these fearmongering tales, laced with stories of invasion and forced conversion. The significance of such images in fomenting conflict in the 1980s is well known, Slobodan Milosevic's Gazimestan speech at the site of the 1389 Battle of Kosovo is often cited as a key example. The speech, made to mark the 600th anniversary of the conflict, included repeated allusions to Serb victimhood, the illegitimacy of the Ottoman invasion and the requirement for violence to correct historic wrongs. Stark reminders of this trope can be found in modern-day representations of international migration in pathogenic terms, where varying levels of the legitimacy of presence are conveyed through the rubric of 'host' and 'invader'.

---

[69] Said, E. (1978). Orientalism. London: Penguin.
[70] See Jeffrey, A. (2008). Contesting Europe: The politics of Bosnian integration into European structures. *Environment and Planning D: Society and Space* 26(3): 428–443.
[71] See Bakić-Hayden, M. (1995). Nesting orientalisms: The case of former Yugoslavia. *Slavic Review* 54(4): 917–931; Jeffrey, A. (2013). *The improvised state: Sovereignty performance and agency in Dayton Bosnia*. Oxford: Wiley-Blackwell; Todorova, M. (2009). *Imagining the Balkans*. Oxford: Oxford University Press.

The second conclusion relates to the use of citizenship law as a mechanism of exclusion. Across the chapters of this book we have seen an example of international intervening authorities legitimising legal reform on the basis of, firstly, the strengthening of sovereignty and, secondly, on the fostering of democratic structures of law. These laudable aims have been publicly performed – often with considerable pomp and circumstance[72] – and championed through media and civil society initiatives.[73] In contrast, the reform of citizenship law, involving the tracking down of individuals who fought in the BiH war and their expulsion on the grounds of terror threat, has been clandestine in its organisation; the role of the US government only becoming evident through declassified diplomatic material and political anthropologies. While the image of law as a mechanism for strengthening state sovereignty is weakened (in the sense that US government agendas are transposed to the heart of the BiH state), the use of law as a tactic for bolstering the project of sovereign power across global space is emboldened.

CONCLUSION

There is a popular impression that the passage of time heals the divisions of war. This is a physiological imagination that views the geopolitical landscape as the human body, the cuts in the map as the scars of a wound. But the experience of BiH defies this analogy, the years since the Dayton GFAP have seen widening divisions between former antagonists, greater stagnation of federal-level institutions (such as the CBiH) and increased calls for international mediation to break the deadlock. One cause of this situation that received considerable scrutiny is the failing of the post-Dayton constitution: a political resolution that embedded structures of 'ethnocracy' despite provisions to retain a multi-ethnic state and permit displaced peoples and refugees to return to their homes.[74] Attempts to reform the Dayton state have

---

[72] See United Nations (2005). Bosnia and Herzegovina gets own war crimes court to help UN tribunal, https://news.un.org/en/story/2005/03/131222-bosnia-and-herzegovina-gets-own-war-crimes-court-help-un-tribunal (accessed 20 December 2018).
[73] See Chapters 4 and 5.
[74] See Toal, G., & Dahlman, C. T. (2011). *Bosnia remade*. Oxford: Oxford University Press.

proved ineffective to date, reflecting the advantageous nature of these arrangements for some in BiH, in particular in the RS. Scores of studies have gone on to show how the divisions contained at Dayton have been reflected in the social structures of the state, be that education,[75] media,[76] the social landscape,[77] amongst many others.

The purpose of this chapter is to contribute to this growing field of work to study how law has been utilised as a tactic through which geopolitical agendas can be pursued in the post-conflict period. The concept of 'entrance strategies' is used to both challenge an imagination of increasing withdrawal of international agencies from the BiH state and to, consequently, undermine the imagination of the *edge of law* examined in earlier chapters. We see in these discussions the plural and multifaceted nature of legal regimes, where the purported empowerment of the CBiH is taking place alongside the prominent role of US government agencies and resources in the reformulation of BiH citizenship law. In this sense, the chapter is particularly interested in the use of law as a means of exclusion, countering the examples found elsewhere in the book where new judicial processes have been designed to foster a sense of civic inclusion in the BiH state.

One of the key insights that stems from these discussions for the wider concern with the edge of law is that it foregrounds mobility and change. The geopolitical context within and beyond the borders of the BiH state is constantly shifting, reframing the legitimacy of certain actors and changing the eligibility of citizenship for specific bodies. The edge then appears not as a fixed limit, but a moving frontier where laws are made, enacted, superseded and renounced. It is a constant dance of creation, enactment and destruction, where bodies and things, their meaning, identity and inter-relation, are in a constant process of

---

[75] Hromadžić, A. (2008). Discourses of integration and practices of reunification at the Mostar Gymnasium, Bosnia and Herzegovina. *Comparative Education Review* 52(4): 541–563; Weinstein, H. M., Freedman, S. W. & Hughson, H. (2007). School voices: Challenges facing education systems after identity-based conflicts. *Education, Citizenship and Social Justice* 2(1): 41–71.

[76] Reljic, D. (2004). The news media and the transformation of ethnopolitical conflicts, in A. Austin, N. Ropers & M. Fischer (eds.), *Transforming ethnopolitical conflict*. Wiesbaden: VS Verlag für Sozialwissenschaften, pp. 321–339.

[77] Jeffrey, A., Staeheli, L. A., Buire, C. & Čelebičić, V. (2018). Drinking coffee, rehearsing civility, making subjects. *Political Geography* 67: 125–134.

remaking. The edge of law is better thought of as a spatial ethos of law, where the distinction between law and non-law, the territories, materials and things brought within law's gaze is constantly being reconstituted. It is thinking through judicial practices in these terms that law is revealed not an encompassment but rather it is a practice of limitation, exclusion and bounding.

CHAPTER EIGHT

CONCLUSION

The Edge of Law is a study of the relationship between (and entanglement of) law and society in a post-conflict, state-building scenario. I have argued that studying the establishment of war crimes trials at the Court of Bosnia and Herzegovina helps explain the limits to legal redress and the subsequent challenges of using law as an instrument to establish justice after conflict. Following Galligan, the book directly engages with two facets of the law and society field: understanding law as a social formation (tracing its origins, institutionalisation and performance) while also exploring its implications for other social formations (such as associative life, identity formation and understandings of citizenship).[1] This analytical approach contributes to a growing field of research that has adopted a law and society perspective to examine the establishment and operation of international, humanitarian or transitional legal processes; instances in which the innovative or *ad hoc* nature of the institutions of law makes studying its social consequences all the more pressing.[2] A particular focus has been placed on the social legacy of law, either by studying the effectiveness of a particular legal

---

[1] Galligan, D. (2006). *Law in modern society*. Oxford: Oxford University Press.
[2] See, e.g., Hughes, R. (2015). Ordinary theatre and extraordinary law at the Khmer Rouge Tribunal. *Environment and Planning D: Society and Space* 33(4): 714–731; Lundy, P., & McGovern, M. (2008). Whose justice? Rethinking transitional justice from the bottom up. *Journal of Law and Society* 35(2): 265–292; McEvoy, K. (2007). Beyond legalism: Towards a thicker understanding of transitional justice. *Journal of Law and Society* 34(4): 411–440.

reform,[3] measuring attitudinal changes brought about through a specific legal innovation[4] or reflecting on the opportunities for popular participation and local agency in new institutions of law.[5]

By focusing on the 'edge' of law the book has sought to foreground the ways in which the production of legal institutions directed towards transitional justice is always a spatial practice. The discourses surrounding the production of the Court were of state consolidation, of localising the responsibility for legal redress and emphasising the virtue of proximity between crime and punishment. Such spatial assertions are, at once, also normative claims – the edge of law marks the limits of responsibility, absolving external agencies of their role in the previous violence while also setting a limit to investigations of culpability. The central concluding point to such observations is the illusory nature of such claims: the edge of law is an ideal rather than a material reality. As we have seen, the production of a new legal institution cannot escape the legacies of the past, whether the past violence enacted on the sites of the new court (Chapter 3), the enduring ethno-national attachments that shape engagement with the legal process (Chapters 4 and 5), the significance of embodied attachments to a previous criminal code (Chapter 6) or the culpability of external actors for training military forces (Chapter 7). By reaching for law's sense of closure, its imagined separation from these plural and shifting legacies and contexts, the localisation of war crimes trials performs the edge of law. To expand on the intellectual implications of these empirical observations I want to briefly think through the edge of law in three ways: the production of law, legal communication and legal performance.

THE PRODUCTION OF LAW

A law and society perspective allows a focus on law as both plural and mutable: as Galligan notes, 'contemporary societies may have several legal orders running in parallel'.[6] This orientates scholarly attention to

---

[3] Hazan, P. (2006). Measuring the impact of punishment and forgiveness: A framework for evaluating transitional justice. *International Review of the Red Cross* 88(861): 19–47.
[4] Nettelfield, L. (2010). *Courting democracy in Bosnia and Herzegovina: The Hague Tribunal's impact in a postwar state*. Cambridge: Cambridge University Press.
[5] Lundy, P., & McGovern, M. (2008). Whose justice? Rethinking transitional justice from the bottom up. *Journal of Law and Society* 35(2): 265–292.
[6] P. 17 in Galligan, D. (2006). *Law in modern society*. Oxford: Oxford University Press.

the social and political forces through which certain legal systems come into being and lay claim to authority and, in tandem, how complex social and political worlds are made 'legible' to administrators and jurists. This language shares much with work on the establishment of bureaucracy as a means of governing a complex and unruly world, a process often connected to the emergence of the modern state from seventeenth century onwards.[7] The argument presented in the previous chapters suggests that as a legal institution renders a social context legible to law's categorisations so it also performs processes of exclusion. What has been evidenced is legal 'bracketing'[8] at multiple spatial scales, where the deliberation of law privileges certain understandings of identity and social relations, fixing these to territory. But in addition to these geographical consequences, there is also a concurrent assumption of a linear temporailty, where the production of a new legal system can supersede previous legal and moral institutions and norms.

Using this style of critical analysis, the creation of the CBiH cannot be easily understood as a process of 'localisation' because the creation of the Court required a series of international interventions, not least in the OHR imposing the laws necessary to create the CBiH, thereby rendering the territory of Bosnia 'legible' to certain forms of legal investigation and 'bracketing' other forms of deviance as beyond the jurisdiction of the new legal instrument. But, of course, this is more than simply a case of overlooking certain crimes and focusing on the activities of specific groups. It is also a mechanism that individualises punishment and lacks a truth-telling component. In this retributive sense, crime is considered to be the pathology of the single body and the resolution its constraint and correction. There are, of course, alternative forms of judicial instrument that could have focused on restorative approaches, perhaps modelled on the Truth and Reconciliation Commission in South Africa.[9] For example, there was an

---

[7] See Scott, J. C. (1998). *Seeing like a state: How certain schemes to improve the human condition have failed*. New Haven, CT: Yale University Press; Tilly, C. (1992). *Coercion, capital, and European states, AD 990–1992*. Oxford: Wiley-Blackwell.

[8] P. 133 in Blomley, N. (2014). Disentangling law: The practice of bracketing. *Annual Review of Law and Social Science* 10: 133–148.

[9] For a discussion of the limits of retribution in BiH see Clark, J. N. (2009). The limits of retributive justice: Findings of an empirical study in Bosnia and Hercegovina. *Journal of International Criminal Justice* 7(3): 463–487; for discussion the possibility of a truth commission in BiH see Dragovic-Soso, J. (2016). History of a failure: Attempts to create a national truth and reconciliation commission in Bosnia

CONCLUSION

ultimately unsuccessful civil society-led initiative *Za Rekom* that sought create a transnational truth commission across the states of the former Yugoslavia.[10] Reflecting the durability to the edge of law, one of the key objections for the establishment of such a civil society initiative stemmed from concerns regarding the threats posed to state sovereignty over such a transnational movement.

But the narrative of localisation also obscures the continued role of international agencies, in particular third-party states, in funding and regulating the work of the Court. As we have seen, multilateral funding has supported the operation of the Court and, between 2005 and 2012, international representatives were present within the judiciary. Indeed, the presence of international judges became a focal point for domestic criticisms of the court and invocations of the spectre of neo-imperialism. In a sense, this tangible presence detracts from the more plural role of international financial and regulatory frameworks in the operation of the judicial instruments in BiH. In Chapters 6 and 7 the role of both international courts and external government agendas was traced through legal deliberations that illuminated a tension between the goals of transitional justice and enforcing human rights law. The presence of such legal pluralism ensures that sovereignty over the judicial process is not confirmed by the relocation of legal activity because external involvement takes many normative, material and bodily forms.

LEGAL COMMUNICATION

One of the key findings of *The Edge of Law* is that, in practice, localising transitional justice is more complex than simply shifting the site of legal deliberation. The ability to establish a new court requires practices of *legal communication*, work that seeks to establish the legitimacy of a new Court.[11] Often framed in terms of 'public outreach', the enrolment of

---

and Herzegovina, 1997–2006. *International Journal of Transitional Justice* 10(2): 292–310; Kritz, N. J., & Finci, J. (2001). A truth and reconciliation commission in Bosnia and Herzegovina: An idea whose time has come. *International Law FORUM du droit international* 3(1): 50–58.

[10] For a discussion of this initiative see Jeffrey, A., & Jakala, M. (2012). Beyond trial justice in the former Yugoslavia. *The Geographical Journal* 178(4): 290–295.

[11] This observation echoes wider work in international relations and political geography over the contested nature of state legitimacy, how it is 'earnt' and the mechanisms used by non-state actors to perform their legitimacy, see Jeffrey, A.,

non-state, non-legal agencies in the communication of law is thus expected to foster public understanding of legal processes and cultivate a sense of the rights protected through law. Reflecting established post-Cold War normative discourses of civil society, such human rights organisations have often been perceived as a 'bridge' between legal authority and wider society, capable of providing an arena where issues of minority rights, social justice and citizenship may be deliberated.[12] As Merry notes, '[I]ntermediaries such as community leaders, nongovernmental organization participants, and social movement activists play a critical role in translating ideas from the global arena down and from local arenas up'.[13] While Merry is referring to the operation of global human rights courts, a similar case could be made for the translation of legal regimes in conditions (such as the CBiH) where a new criminal procedure code and court has been imposed by external agencies. Reflecting the complexity of this intermediary role, civil society agencies in development and post-conflict arenas have been viewed as more heterogeneous than simply a link between governmental authority and social life. Consequently, scholars have focused on the role of funding agencies, regulatory authority, sectarian interests and narrow economic gain as forces that can shape the democratising potential of civic associations.[14]

Rather than reading off the existence of civil society as an inherently democratising force within a given context, *The Edge of Law* focused on the plural motivations that these organisations hold and their potential to produce a variety of social and legal effects. The discussion in Chapter 4 used the classification of 'invited' and 'invented' spaces of justice to highlight the agency of civil society actors in shaping the judicial process. This is not to suggest the process was problem free: the operation of communication strategies from the court were often ineffective or inappropriate, actions that emphasised a disconnect between the

---

McConnell, F. & Wilson, A. (2015). Understanding legitimacy: Perspectives from anomalous geopolitical spaces. *Geoforum* 66: 177–183.

[12] Fagan, A. (2011). EU assistance for civil society in Kosovo: A step too far for democracy promotion? *Democratization* 18(3): 707–730; Jeffrey, A. (2007). The geopolitical framing of localized struggles: NGOs in Bosnia and Herzegovina. *Development and Change* 38(2): 251–274.

[13] P. 38 in Merry, S. E. (2006). *Translating international law into local justice*. Chicago and London: University of Chicago.

[14] Howell, J. (2000). Making civil society from the outside: Challenges for donors. *The European Journal of Development Research* 12(1): 3–22.

operation of law and the needs of wider social formations. But the enrolment of civil society actors did work to recognise the ways in which the 'invited' and 'invented' spaces of justice were interconnected in practice: that the successful completion of a trial (an 'invited' space) required the informal connections and support structures between individuals within civil society ('invented' practices). It is perhaps these benefits that explain the ICTY's investment in public outreach since 1999, even as its jurisdiction over the trials in the former Yugoslavia was reduced and ultimately transferred to the successor states of Yugoslavia.

The significance of communication was also a key aspect of the discussion of citizenship and transitional justice in Chapter 5. These discussions focused specifically on the tensions between the state-building intensions of the political architects of the Court and the subsequent requirement to enrol civil society agencies in the operation of the court. There was a disconnect between message and media: the imagination of a coherent and unified state required the devolution of communication to patchwork of civil society actors, many of which operated with alterative normative imaginations of the state. One of the key findings of this element of the research, and emphasised vociferously when discussed at a dissemination workshop in Sarajevo in 2012, was a nostalgia for a form of modernity where the state played a key role in provisioning rights, even voiced by members of NGOs and civil society organisations that were involved in encouraging participation in the Court's activities. In these terms locality is not understood as the site of more virtuous or authentic politics, but the contested site of struggles over territory, identity and justice.

LEGAL PERFORMANCE

To understand legal processes as social formations attention needs to be paid to the enactment of trials, recognising that trial processes have a greater series of effects than simply producing outcomes of guilt or innocence. Hannah Arendt's account of the trial of Adolf Eichmann in Jerusalem in 1961 was a touchstone for a wealth of work exploring the theatrical aspects of trial processes, that their performance may serve a purpose in bolstering wider narratives of history, geography and victimhood.[15] In terms of transitional justice (such as that of the

---

[15] Arendt, H. (1963). *Eichmann in Jerusalem*. London: Penguin.

Eichmann trial), Shoshana Felman has argued that trials bring 'a conscious closure to the trauma of the war', in doing so demarcating a 'suffering that seemed both unending and unbearable'.[16] Felman's analysis goes on to examine the psychological and legal effects of giving testimony, of recalling traumas of the past within an arena of law. Structured around the example of a witness (Yehiel De-Nur also known as K-Zetnik) who lost consciousness while trying to recount his memories of the Holocaust, Felman's argument centres on the essential 'unnarratability' of trauma, of the impossibility of rendering into legal language the horror and violence of the past. By raising the issue of bodily limits and frailty, Felman's work provides an entry point for thinking about the impacts of the trial process on those called upon to participate, where the recalling of traumatic events serves to repeat the trauma visited upon the body during the original violence (a process that is often referred to as 'retraumatisation'). There are a number of directions that such a focus on the embodied nature of evidence could lead. It reminds us of the centrality of bodies to the enactment of law, as sites of investigation, materialisations of evidence, expressions of property and loci of deviance.[17] A focus on embodiment also orientates attention to the expectations of certain forms of bodily comportment during the trial process, whether the penitent accused, the assured defence lawyer or distraught witness. The production of legal subjects, then, extends beyond the declaration of guilt or innocence, projecting wider judgements concerning expertise, consequence and trauma.

An embodied and materialist perspective on the performance of legal processes poses a fundamental challenge to the spatial imagination of law's 'edge'. Rather than thinking about the implications of law 'on' the individual body, we start to consider the entanglement of bodily and materialist arrangements with the performance of law. We therefore cannot separate the embodied experience of individuals within court spaces from the unfolding of the legal process. Turning the equation the other way: the production of what we understand as 'law' cannot be

---

[16] P. 107 in Felman, S. (2002). *The juridical unconscious: Trials and traumas in the twentieth century*. Cambridge, MA: Harvard University Press.

[17] See Arsenijević, D. (2011). Gendering the bone: The politics of memory in Bosnia and Herzegovina. *Journal of Cultural Research* 15: 193–205; Hyde, A. (1997). *Bodies of law*. Princeton, NJ: Princeton University Press; Weizman, E. (2014). Introduction: Forensis, in forensic architecture (eds.), *Forensis: The architecture of public truth*. Berlin: Sternberg Press, pp. 9–32.

separated from the immanent and improvised presence of bodies and materials within spaces understood as 'the court'. This imagination of co-production has been a key feature of recent works on law and space, where neologisms of *nomosphere*,[18] *lawscape*[19] or *jurispadence*[20] have been coined to avoid privileging law or space in our understanding of the production of the world. It is not the place of this book to add to this list but rather to illuminate how the production of the edge of law has the effect of erasing this hybrid and co-produced understanding of social life. As reflected in the discussions in Chapter 3 and 7, this conclusion is not simply one of nuance, where attention to the embodied and material qualities of law helps give a sense of the intricacies of a legal system. Instead, these observations help to explain the social and cultural restrictions on trial processes, shaped as they are by the absence of willing witnesses, missing material evidence, political attacks and the reticence of individuals to come forward to report historic crimes. As time passes, witnesses die and evidence degrades, the possibility of completing the judicial processes connected to war crimes trials in BiH becomes more remote. Performing the edge of law seeks to remove war crimes processes from these material and embodied considerations, but it is these social restrictions that, ultimately, shape the possibility for trial justice.

[18] Delaney, D. (2010). *The spatial, the legal and the pragmatics of world-making: Nomospheric investigations*. Abingdon: Routledge-Cavendish.
[19] Philippopoulos-Mihalopoulos, A. (2014). *Spatial justice: Body, lawscape, atmosphere*. Abingdon: Routledge.
[20] Kedar, A. (2000). The legal transformation of ethnic geography: Israeli law and the Palestinian landholder 1948–1967. *New York University Journal of International Law and Politics* 33: 923–1000.

BIBLIOGRAPHY

Abulof, U. (2016) We the peoples? The strange demise of self-determination. *European Journal of International Relations* 22(3), 536–565.

Abrahamsen, R. (2000) *Disciplining democracy: Development discourse and good governance in Africa.* London: Zed Books.

Agamben, G. (1998) *Homo sacer: Sovereign power and bare life.* Palo Alto, CA: Stanford University Press.

Agnew, J. (1994) The territorial trap: The geographical assumptions of international relation theory. *Review of International Political Economy* 1: 53–80.

Allman, T. L., Mittelstaedt, R. D., Martin, B., & Goldenberg, M. (2009) Exploring the motivations of BASE jumpers: Extreme sport enthusiasts. *Journal of Sport & Tourism* 14(4): 229–247.

Andreas, P. (2004) The clandestine political economy of war and peace in Bosnia. *International Studies Quarterly* 48(1): 29–51.

(2008) *Blue helmets and black markets: The business of survival in the seige of Sarajevo.* Ithaca, NY: Cornell University Press.

Anghie, A. (2007) *Imperialism, sovereignty and the making of international law.* Cambridge: Cambridge University Press.

Arendt, H. (1963) *Eichmann in Jerusalem: A report on the banality of evil.* London: Penguin Books.

Arsenijević, D. (2011) Gendering the bone: The politics of memory in Bosnia and Herzegovina. *Journal of Cultural Research* 15: 193–205.

Aybet, G., & Bieber, F. (2011) From Dayton to Brussels: The impact of EU and NATO conditionality on state building in Bosnia and Hercegovina. *Europe-Asia Studies* 63(10): 1911–1937.

Bakić-Hayden, M. (1995) Nesting orientalisms: The case of former Yugoslavia. *Slavic Review* 54(4): 917–931.

Bakker, K. (2007) The 'commons' versus the 'commodity': Alter-globalization, anti-privatization and the human right to water in the Global South. *Antipode* 39(3): 430–455.

Balkan Insight. (2014) Bosnia war crimes plea bargains provoke questions, http://archive.balkaninsight.com/en/article/no-pleas-for-bosnian-war-criminals/1452/37.

(2014) Bosnia arrests 16 suspected jihad recruiters, www.balkaninsight.com/en/article/bosnia-arrests-15-alleged-terrorists.

BIBLIOGRAPHY

(2015) Operation Storm: Croatia's triumph, Serbia's grief, www.balkaninsight.com/en/article/operation-storm-croatia-s-triumph-serbia-s-grief-07-31-2015.

Balkan Transitional Justice. (2010) Karadžić talks Izetbegović in cross-examination, www.balkaninsight.com/en/article/karadzic-talks-izetbegovic-in-cross-examination.

(2016) Bosnia awards Iraqi war crimes convict €36,600, www.balkaninsight.com/en/article/bosnia-awards-iraqi-war-crimes-convict-36-000-11-09-2016.

Baltic, N. (2007) Theory and practice of human and minority rights under the Yugoslav communist system, www.eurac.edu/en/research/institutes/imr/Documents/ReportontheTheoryandPracticeofHumanRightsandMinorityRightsundertheYugoslavCommunistS.pdf.

Bardos, G. N. (2013) Iran in the Balkans: A history and a forecast. *World Affairs* 175(5): 59–66.

Barnett, C., & Low, M. (eds.) (2004) *Spaces of democracy: Geographical perspectives on citizenship, participation and representation*. London: Sage.

Barria, L. A., & Roper, S. D. (2005) How effective are international criminal tribunals? An analysis of the ICTY and the ICTR. *The International Journal of Human Rights* 9(3): 349–368.

Barry, A. (2013) *Material politics: Disputes along the pipeline*. Oxford: John Wiley & Sons.

Bartel, R., Graham, N., Jackson, S., Prior, J. H., Robinson, D., Sherval, M. & Williams, S. (2013) Legal geography: An Australian perspective. *Geographical Research* 51(4): 339–353.

Baudrillard, J. (1995) *The Gulf War did not take place*. Bloomington: Indiana University Press.

Baxter, J. (2013) Surrealist vertigo in Schwindel. Gefühle. In Baxter, J., Henitiuk, V. & Hutchinson, B. (eds.) *A literature of restitution: Critical essays on WG Sebald* (pp. 77–93). Oxford: Oxford University Press.

BBC News. (2013) Bosnia frees Srebrenica convicts over legal error, www.bbc.co.uk/news/world-europe-25007858.

Bell, D. (1995) Pleasure and danger: The paradoxical spaces of sexual citizenship. *Political Geography* 14(2): 139–153.

Bell, J. E., & Staeheli, L. A. (2001) Discourses of diffusion and democratization. *Political Geography* 20(2): 175–195.

Belloni, R. (2001) Civil society and peacebuilding in Bosnia and Herzegovina. *Journal of Peace Research* 38: 163–180.

Bellott, H. (1922) Some early courts and the English Bar. *Law Quarterly Review* 38: 168–84.

Benhabib, S. (2004) *The rights of others: Aliens, residents, and citizens*. Cambridge: Cambridge University Press.

Bieber, F. (2001) Arming the Muslim-Croat Federation: Failed realpolitik with moralistic justifications? In Schnabel, A. (ed.), *Southeast European security: Threats, responses, challenges* (pp. 177–192). Huntington, NY: Nova Science Publishers.

Binnie, J., & Valentine, G. (1999) Geographies of sexuality – A review of progress. *Progress in Human Geography* 23(2): 175–187.
Blomley, N. (1994) *Law, space, and the geographies of power*. New York: Guilford Press.
(2003) Law, property, and the geography of violence: The frontier, the survey, and the grid. *Annals of the Association of American geographers* 93(1): 121–141.
(2008) Making space for law. In Cox, K., Low, M. & Robinson, J. (eds.) *The Sage Handbook of Political Geography* (pp. 155–168). London: Sage
(2014) Disentangling law: The practice of bracketing. *Annual Review of Law and Social Science* 10: 133–148.
(2014) Making space for property. *Annals of the Association of American Geographers* 104(6): 1291–1306.
(2015) The ties that blind: Making fee simple in the British Columbia treaty process. *Transactions of the Institute of British Geographers* 40(2): 168–179.
Boas, G. (2000) Comparing the ICTY and the ICC: Some procedural and substantive issues. *Netherlands International Law Review* 47(3): 267–291.
Bose, S. (2005) The Bosnian State a decade after Dayton. *International Peacekeeping* 12(3): 322–335.
Bourdieu, P. (1987) The force of law: Toward a sociology of the juridical field. *Hastings Law Journal* 38(5): 814–853.
Boyle, M., & Kobayashi, A. (2015) In the face of epistemic injustices? On the meaning of people-led war crimes tribunals. *Environment and Planning D: Society and Space* 33(4): 697–713.
Braverman, I., Blomley, N., Delaney, D. & Kedar, A. (eds.) (2014) *The expanding spaces of law: A timely legal geography*. Palo Alto, CA: Stanford University Press.
Brickell, K., & Cuomo, D. (2019) Feminist geolegality. *Progress in Human Geography* 43(1), 104–122.
Brljavac, B. (2017) Barrier to the EU membership: The institutional discrimination of minority groups in Bosnia and Herzegovina. *Geografia-Malaysian Journal of Society and Space* 8(1): 30–37.
Broomhall, B. (2003) *International justice and the International Criminal Court: Between sovereignty and the rule of law* (Vol. 1) Oxford: Oxford University Press.
Brown, W. (2009) *Edgework: Critical essays on knowledge and politics*. Princeton, NJ: Princeton University Press.
(2010) *Walled states waning sovereignty*. Cambridge, MA: MIT Press.
Business Insider (2015) An under-the-radar European country has become a 'recruitment hotbed' for ISIS, http://uk.businessinsider.com/bosnia-isis-recruitment-hotbed-2015-12.

BIBLIOGRAPHY

Butler, J. (2013) *Excitable speech: A politics of the performative*. Abingdon: Routledge.
Campbell, D. (1998) MetaBosnia: Narratives of the Bosnian War. *Review of International Studies* 24(2): 261–281.
——— (1998) *National deconstruction: Violence, identity and justice in Bosnia*. Minneapolis: University of Minnesota Press.
——— (1999) Apartheid cartography: The political anthropology and spatial effects of international diplomacy in Bosnia. *Political Geography* 18: 395–435.
Caplan, R. (Ed.). (2012). *Exit strategies and state building*. Oxford: Oxford University Press.
Chandler, D. (2000) *Bosnia: Faking democracy after Dayton*. London: Pluto Press.
Chomsky, N. (1999) *The new military humanism: Lessons from Kosovo*. London: Pluto Press.
Clark, J. N. (2009) The limits of retributive justice: Findings of an empirical study in Bosnia and Hercegovina. *Journal of International Criminal Justice* 7(3): 463–487.
Clark, P. (2007) Hybridity, holism and 'traditional' justice: The case of the Gacaca community courts in post-genocide Rwanda. *George Washington International Law Review* 39: 765–838.
Clarkson, C. (2014) *Drawing the line: Towards an aesthetics of transitional justice*. New York: Fordham University Press.
Comaroff, J., & Comaroff, J. (2006) Law and disorder in the postcolony: An introduction. In Comaroff, J., & Comaroff, J. (eds.) *Law and disorder in the postcolony* (pp. 1–56). Chicago: University of Chicago Press.
Comaroff, J., & Comaroff, J. L. (eds.) (2008) *Law and disorder in the postcolony*. Chicago: University of Chicago Press.
Cornwall, A. (2002) Locating citizen participation. *Institute of Development Studies Bulletin* 33: i–x.
Council of Europe (1950) European Convention on Human Rights, www.echr.coe.int/Documents/Convention_ENG.pdf.
Cover R. M. (1983) Foreword: Nomos and narrative. *Harvard Law Review* 97: 4–68.
Cresswell, T. (1992) *In place-out of place: Geography, ideology, and transgression*. Minneapolis: University of Minnesota Press.
Dahlman, C., & Ó Tuathail, G. (2005) Broken Bosnia: The localized geopolitics of displacement and return in two Bosnian places. *Annals of the Association of American Geographers* 95: 644–662.
Daily Mail (2015) Inside the Bosnian mountain village where locals fly the black flag of ISIS above their homes as jihadists' influence spreads, www.dailymail.co.uk/news/article-2940244/A-far-welcoming-village-Entrance-Bosnian-mountain-hamlet-branded-Islamic-State-emblem-homes-fly-terrorists-flag-group-s-influence-spreads.html#ixzz4zpn8P5Gr.

David, D. (2015) Legal geography I: Constitutivities, complexities, and contingencies. *Progress in Human Geography* 39(1): 96–102.
Delaney, D. (2001) Introduction: Globalization and law. In Blomley, N., Delaney, D. & Ford, R. T. (eds.) *The legal geographies reader: Law, power and space* (pp. 252–255). Oxford: Blackwell.
(2004) Tracing displacements: Or evictions in the nomosphere. *Environment and Planning D: Society and Space* 22(6): 847–860.
(2010) *The spatial, the legal and the pragmatics of world-making: Nomospheric investigations*. Abingdon: Routledge-Cavendish.
(2014) At work in the nomosphere: The spatio-legal production of emotions at work. In Braverman, I., Blomley, N., Delaney, D. & Kedar, A. (eds.) *The expanding spaces of law: A timely legal geography* (pp. 239–262). Palo Alto, CA: Stanford University Press.
(2015) Legal geography I: Constitutivities, complexities, and contingencies. *Progress in Human Geography* 39(1): 96–102.
Delpla, I. (2007) In the midst of injustice: The ICTY from the perspective of some victim associations. In Bougarel, X., Helms, E. & Duijzings, G. (eds.) *The new Bosnian mosaic: Identities, memories and moral claims in a post-war society* (pp. 211–234) Aldershot: Ashgate.
Derrida, J. (1994) *Specters of Marx: The State of the Debt, the Work of Mourning and the New*. New York: Routledge.
Der Spiegel (2016) Bosnia's Islamic state problem, www.spiegel.de/international/europe/islamic-state-presence-in-bosnia-cause-for-concern-a-1085326.html.
de Sanctis, F. (2014) Reconciling justice and legality: A quest for fair punishment in cases on Bosnian atrocity crimes. *Journal of International Criminal Justice* 12(4): 847–870.
DeSilvey, C. (2006) Observed decay: telling stories with mutable things. *Journal of material Culture* 11(3): 318–338.
Desforges, L., Jones, R. & Woods, M. (2005) New geographies of citizenship. *Citizenship Studies* 9(5): 439–451.
Dittmer J. (2014) Geopolitical assemblages and complexity. *Progress in Human Geography* 38(3): 385–401.
Dogra, N. (2011) The mixed metaphor of 'third world woman': Gendered representations by international development NGOs. *Third World Quarterly* 32: 333–348.
Donais, T. (2000) Division and democracy: Bosnia's post-Dayton elections. In Spencer, M. (ed.) *The Lessons of Yugoslavia* (pp. 229–258). London: JAI Elsevier Science.
Dragovic-Soso, J. (2016) History of a failure: Attempts to create a national truth and reconciliation commission in Bosnia and Herzegovina, 1997–2006. *International Journal of Transitional Justice* 10(2): 292–310.

Duffield, M. (2001) Governing the borderlands: Decoding the power of aid. *Disasters* 25(4): 308–320.
Dwyer, M. B. (2014) Micro-geopolitics: Capitalising security in Laos's golden quadrangle. *Geopolitics* 19(2): 377–405.
Elden, S. (2009) *Terror and territory: The spatial extent of sovereignty*. Minneapolis: University of Minnesota Press.
(2013) *The birth of territory*. Chicago: University of Chicago Press.
Eliot, G. (1965) *Middlemarch*, London: Penguin. Cited in Fitzpatrick, P. (2001) *Modernism and the Grounds of Law*. Cambridge University Press, p. 11.
Engvall, L. (2007) The future of extended joint criminal enterprise: Will the ICTY's innovation meet the standards of the ICC. *Nordic Journal of International Law* 76(2/3): 241.
European Court of Human Rights (2013) Annual Report 2013, www.echr.coe.int/Documents/Annual_report_2013_prov_ENG.pdf.
(2013) Case of Maktouf and Damjanović vs. Bosnia and Herzegovina, https://hudoc.echr.coe.int/app/conversion/pdf/?library=ECHR&id=002-7636&filename=002-7636.pdf&TID=ihgdqbxnfi.
Fagan, A. (2005) Civil society in Bosnia ten years after Dayton. *International Peacekeeping* 12: 406–419.
(2011) EU assistance for civil society in Kosovo: A step too far for democracy promotion? *Democratization* 18(3): 707–730.
Fassin, D. (2011) *Humanitarian reason: A moral history of the present*. Berkeley: University of California Press.
Felman, S. (2002) *The juridical unconscious: trial and traumas in the twentieth century*. Cambridge, MA: Harvard University Press.
Ferrell, J. (2016) Foreword: Graffiti, street art and the politics of complexity. In Ross, J. I. (ed.) *Routledge handbook of graffiti and street art* (pp. xxx–xxxviii). London: Routledge.
Foucault, M. (1977) *Discipline and punish – The birth of the prison* (trans. Alan Sheridan). London: Penguin.
(1979) Governmentality. *Ideology and Consciousness* 6: 5–21.
Fuller, L. L. (1958) Positivism and fidelity to law: A reply to Professor Hart. *Harvard Law Review* 71: 630–672.
Galligan, D. (2006) *Law in modern society*. Oxford: Oxford University Press.
Gieryn, T. F. (1983) Boundary-work and the demarcation of science from non-science: Strains and interests in professional ideologies of scientists. *American Sociological Review* 48 6): 781–795.
Glenny, M. (1996) *The fall of Yugoslavia: The third Balkan war*. London: Penguin Books.
Goddard, S. E. (2009) When right makes might: How Prussia overturned the European balance of power. *International Security* 33(3): 110–142.
Goffman, E. (1959) *The presentation of self in everyday life*. New York: Doubleday.

Goldring, L. (2001) The gender and geography of citizenship in Mexico-US transnational spaces. *Identities Global Studies in Culture and Power* 7(4): 501–537.
Goldstone, R. (2000) *For humanity: Refections of a war crimes investigator.* New Haven, CT: Yale University Press.
Government of Bosnia and Herzegovina (2003) Criminal Procedure Code of Bosnia and Herzegovina, www.sudbih.gov.ba/files/docs/zakoni/en/Criminal_Procedure_Code_of_BH_-_Consolidated_text.pdf.
Gow, J. (2003) *The Serbian Project and its adversaries.* London: Hurst and Company.
Gow, J., & Zverzhanovski, I. (2013) *Security, democracy and war crimes: Security Sector transformation in Serbia.* Basingstoke: Palgrave.
Grayling, A. C. (2006) *Among the dead cities: Was the Allied bombing of civilians in WWII a necessity or a crime?* London: Bloomsbury Publishing.
Gregory, D. (2004) *The colonial present: Afghanistan, Palestine, Iraq.* Malden, MA: Blackwell.
(2007) Vanishing points. In Gregory, D., & Pred, A. (eds.) *Violent Geographies Fear, Terror and Political Violence* (pp. 205–236). New York: Routledge.
(2010) War and peace. *Transactions of the Institute of British Geographers* 35(2): 154–186.
Griffiths, J. (1979) Is law important. *New York University Law Review* 54: 339–374, p. 343.
(1986) What is legal pluralism? *The Journal of Legal Pluralism and Unofficial Law* 18(24): 1–55.
Hagan, J. (2003) *Justice in the Balkans.* Chicago: Chicago University Press.
Hansard (1996) British Forces (Bosnia), https://api.parliament.uk/historic-hansard/commons/1996/jul/18/british-forces-bosnia.
Hart, H. L. A. (1958) Positivism and the separation of law and morals. *Harvard Law Review* 71: 593–629.
(2012) *The concept of law.* Oxford: Oxford University Press.
Hazan, P. (2004) *Justice in a time of war: The true story behind the international criminal tribunal for the former Yugoslavia.* College Station: Texas A&M University Press.
(2006) Measuring the impact of punishment and forgiveness: A framework for evaluating transitional justice. *International Review of the Red Cross* 88(861): 19–47.
Helms, E., Bougarel, X. & Duijzings, G. (eds.) (2007) *The new Bosnian mosaic.* London: Routledge.
Herbert, S. (2009) *Citizens, cops, and power: Recognizing the limits of community.* Chicago: University of Chicago Press.
Hoare, M. A. (2004) *How Bosnia armed.* London: Saqi Books.

Hodžić, R. (2010) Living the legacy of mass atrocities: Victims' perspectives on war crimes trials. *Journal of International Criminal Justice* 8: 113–136.
Hoffe, O. (1994) *Immanuel Kant*. New York: SUNY Press.
Holbrooke, R. (2008) *The face of evil*. London: The Guardian.
Holston, J. (2009) *Insurgent citizenship: Disjunctions of democracy and modernity in Brazil*. Princeton, NJ: Princeton University Press.
Howell, J. (2000) Making civil society from the outside: Challenges for donors. *The European Journal of Development Research* 12(1): 3–22.
Hromadžić, A. (2008) Discourses of integration and practices of reunification at the Mostar Gymnasium, Bosnia and Herzegovina. *Comparative Education Review* 52(4): 541–563.
Hubbard, P. (2001) Sex zones: Intimacy, citizenship and public space. *Sexualities* 4(1): 51–71.
Hughes, R. (2015) Ordinary theatre and extraordinary law at the Khmer Rouge Tribunal. *Environment and Planning D: Society and Space* 33(4): 714–731.
Human Rights Watch (1992) *War crimes in Bosnia-Hercegovina*. New York: Human Rights Watch.
(2012) Key lessons from Bosnia's war crimes prosecutions, www.hrw.org/news/2012/03/12/bosnia-key-lessons-war-crimes-prosecutions.
Hyde, A. (1997) *Bodies of law*. Princeton, NJ: Princeton University Press.
Hyndman, J. (2004) Mind the gap: Bridging feminist and political geography through geopolitics. *Political Geography* 23(3): 307–322.
ICTY (2018) Address of the Prosecutor at the Inauguration of the War Crimes Chamber of the Court of BH, www.icty.org/en/press/address-prosecutor-inauguration-war-crimes-chamber-court-bh.
Ingram, A., & Dodds, K. (2016) *Spaces of security and insecurity: Geographies of the war on terror*. London: Routledge.
Innes, M. A. (2005) Terrorist sanctuaries and Bosnia-Herzegovina: Challenging conventional assumptions. *Studies in Conflict and Terrorism* 28(4): 295–305.
International Criminal Tribunal for the former Yugoslavia (2016) IT-95-5/18: Karadžić and Mladić submission of accurate transcript of Radovan Karadžić's closing argument.
International Crisis Group (1997) A peace, or just a cease-fire? The military equation in post-Dayton Bosnia and Herzegovina. ICG Bosnia Project Report 28, 15 December.
(1999) Is Dayton failing? Bosnia four years after the peace agreement, www.crisisgroup.org/europe-central-asia/balkans/bosnia-and-herzegovina/dayton-failing-bosnia-four-years-after-peace-agreement.
(2007). Ensuring Bosnia's Future: A New International Engagement Strategy. International Crisis Group, Sarajevo/Brussels.

Isenberg, D. (2010) MPRI couldn't read minds, let's sue, *HuffPost Blog*, 19, August, www.huffingtonpost.com/david-isenberg/mpri-couldnt-read-minds-l_b_688000.html.
Isin, E. F. (2002) *Being political geneaologies of citizenship*. Minneapolis: University of Minnesota Press.
Isin, E. F., & Nielsen, G. M. (eds.) (2013) *Acts of citizenship*. London: Zed Books Ltd.
Jacobs, J. M. (2006) A geography of big things. *Cultural Geographies* 13(1): 1–27.
Jansson, E (2005) Risk of instability remains a factor, *The Financial Times*, 14 November.
Jeffrey, A. (2007) The geopolitical framing of localized struggles: NGOs in Bosnia and Herzegovina. *Development and Change* 38(2): 251–274.
(2008) Contesting Europe: The politics of Bosnian integration into European structures. *Environment and Planning D: Society and Space* 26(3): 428–443.
(2009) Containers of fate: Labelling states in the 'war on terror'. In Dodds, K., & Ingram, A. (eds.) *Spaces of security and insecurity: Geographies of the war on terror* (pp. 43–64) Aldershot: Ashgate.
(2009) Justice incomplete: Radovan Karadžić, the ICTY and the spaces of international law. *Environment and Planning D: Society and Space* 27: 387–402.
(2013) *The improvised state: Sovereignty, Performance and Agency in Dayton Bosnia*. Oxford: Wiley-Blackwell;
Jeffrey, A., & Jakala, M. (2012) Beyond trial justice in the former Yugoslavia. *The Geographical Journal* 178(4): 290–295.
(2014) The hybrid legal geographies of a war crimes court. *Annals of the Association of American Geographers* 104(3): 652–667.
Jeffrey, A., McConnell, F. & Wilson, A. (2015) Understanding legitimacy: Perspectives from anomalous geopolitical spaces. *Geoforum* 66: 177–183.
Jeffrey, A., McFarlane, C. and Vasudevan, A. (2012) Rethinking enclosure: Space, subjectivity and the commons. *Antipode* 44(4): 1247–1267.
Jeffrey, A., Staeheli, L. A., Buire, C. & Čelebičić, V. (2018) Drinking coffee, rehearsing civility, making subjects. *Political Geography* 67: 125–134.
Jones, B., Jeffrey, A. & Jakala, M. (2013) The transitional citizen: Civil society, political agency and hopes for transitional justice in Bosnia-Herzegovina. In Simić, O., & Volčić, Z. (eds.) *Transitional justice and civil society in the Balkans* (pp. 87–104). New York: Springer Publishing.
Jones, C. A. (2016) Lawfare and the juridification of late modern war. *Progress in Human Geography* 40(2): 221–239.
Kadrić, J. (1998) *Brcko: Genocide and testimony*. Sarajevo: Institute for the Research of Crimes Against Humanity and International Law.

Kafka, F. (2014 [1925]) *The Trial* (trans. David Wyllie). Dublin: Roads Publishing.
Katz, V. (2018) The position of national minorities in Bosnia and Hercegovina before and after the breakup of Jugoslavia. *Studia Środkowoeuropejskie i Bałkanistyczne, 2017* (Tom XXVI): 193–204.
Kedar, A. (2000) The legal transformation of ethnic geography: Israeli law and the Palestinian landholder 1948–1967. *New York University Journal of International Law and Politics* 33: 923–1000.
Kerr, R., & Mobekk, E. (2007) *Peace and justice seeking accountability after war.* Cambridge: Polity Press.
Klemenčić, M. (2009) The international community and the FRY/Belligerents 1989–1997. In Ingrao, C., & Emmert, T. (eds.) *Confronting the Yugoslav controversies: A scholar's initiative* (pp. 152–199). Washington, DC: United States Institute for Peace Press.
Knežević, A. (1997) Alija Izetbegović's 'Islamic Declaration': Its substance and its western reception. *Islamic Studies* 36(2/3): 483–521.
Kofman, E. (1995) Citizenship for some but not for others: Spaces of citizenship in contemporary Europe. *Political Geography* 14(2): 121–137.
Koopman, S. (2011) Alter-geopolitics: Other securities are happening. *Geoforum* 42(3): 274–284.
Kritz, N. J., & Finci, J. (2001) A truth and reconciliation commission in Bosnia and Herzegovina: An idea whose time has come. *International Law FORUM du droit international* 3(1): 50–58.
Kuus, M. (2007) *Geopolitics reframed: Security and identity in Europe's eastern enlargement.* New York and Houndmills: Palgrave Macmillan.
(2013) *Geopolitics and expertise: Knowledge and authority in European diplomacy.* Oxford: John Wiley & Sons.
(2015) Transnational bureaucracies: How do we know what they know? *Progress in Human Geography* 39(4): 432–448.
Lamb, C., Arkin, S. & Scudder, S. (1994) The Bosnian train and equip program: A lesson in interagency integration of hard and soft power strategic perspectives 15. Center for Strategic Research Institute for National Strategic Studies National Defense, https://inss.ndu.edu/Portals/68/Documents/stratperspective/inss/Strategic-Perspectives-15.pdf.
Lambourne, W. (2009) Transitional justice and peacebuilding after mass violence. *International Journal of Transitional Justice* 3(1): 28–48.
(2012) Outreach, inreach and civil society participation in transitional justice. In Palmer, N., Clark, P. & Granville, D. (eds.) *Critical perspectives in transitional justice* (pp. 235–261). Cambridge: Intersentia.
Latour, B. (2004) Scientific objects and legal objectivity. In Pottage, A., & Mundy M. (eds.) *Law, anthropology, and the constitution of the social making persons and things* (pp. 73–114). Cambridge: Cambridge University Press.

(2010) *The making of law: An ethnography of the Conseil d'État*. Cambridge: Polity.
Lehnardt, C. (2008) Individual liability of private military personnel under international criminal law. *European Journal of International Law* 19(5): 1015–1034, p. 1022.
Leitner, H., & Strunk, C. (2014) Spaces of immigrant advocacy and liberal democratic citizenship. *Annals of the Association of American Geographers* 104(2): 348–356.
Li, D. (2015) Welcome to Bosnatanamo: Migrant detention in Bosnia, www.law.ox.ac.uk/research-subject-groups/centre-criminology/centrebordercriminologies/blog/2015/10/welcome.
Library of Congress (2017) Treatment of foreign fighters in selected jurisdictions: Country surveys, www.loc.gov/law/help/foreign-fighters/country-surveys.php#_ftnref51.
Lister, R. (1997) Citizenship: Towards a feminist synthesis. *Feminist Review* 57: 28–48.
Lundy, P., & McGovern, M. (2008) Whose justice? Rethinking transitional justice from the bottom up. *Journal of Law and Society* 35(2): 265–292.
Lyng, S. (1990) Edgework: A social psychological analysis of voluntary risk taking. *American Journal of Sociology* 95(4): 851–886.
(2005) Edgework and the risk-taking experience. In Lyng, S. (Ed.) *Edgework: The Sociology of Risk-Taking* (pp. 3–16). London: Routledge.
Major, J. (1999) *John Major: The autobiography*. London: Harper Collins.
Mallinder, L. (2009) Retribution, restitution and reconciliation: Limited amnesty in Bosnia-Herzegovina. Queen's University Belfast, unpublished thesis.
Marshall, T. H. (1950) *Citizenship and social class*. Cambridge: Cambridge University Press.
Marston, S. (2004) Space, culture, state: Uneven developments in political geography. *Political Geography* 23: 1–16.
Massey, D. (2004) Geographies of responsibility. *Geografiska Annaler B* 86: 5–18.
Matthews, D. (2016) Book review: Robert P. Burns: Kafka's Law: The trial and american criminal justice. *International Journal for the Semiotics of Law* 29: 237–241.
McConnell, F. (2009) De facto, displaced, tacit: The sovereign articulations of the Tibetan government-in-exile. *Political Geography* 28: 343–352.
McEvoy K. (2007) Beyond legalism: Towards a thicker understanding of transitional justice. *Journal of Law and Society* 34: 411–440.
McMurtry, J. (2011) Human rights versus corporate rights: Life value, the civil commons and social justice. *Studies in Social Justice* 5(1): 11–61.
McNamara, R. S. N., & Morse, S. (2004) Voices from the aid 'chain': The personal dynamics of care. *Social and Cultural Geography* 5(2): 253–270.

Megoran, N. (2006) For ethnography in political geography: Experiencing and re-imagining Ferghana Valley boundary closures *Political Geography* 25: 622–640.
(2008) Militarism, realism, just war, or nonviolence? Critical geopolitics and the problem of normativity. *Geopolitics* 13(3): 473–497.
Merry, S. E. (1988) Legal pluralism. *Law and Society Review* 22: 869.
(2006) *Translating international law into local justice.* Chicago and London: University of Chicago.
Miraftab, F. (2009) Insurgent planning: Situating radical planning in the Global South. *Planning Theory* 8(1): 32–50.
Miraftab, F., & Wills, S. (2005) Insurgency and spaces of active citizenship. *Journal of Planning Education and Research* 25: 200–17.
Mohan, G. (2002) The disappointments of civil society: The politics of NGO intervention in northern Ghana. *Political Geography* 21(1): 125–154.
Moratti, M., & Sabic-El-Rayess, A. (2009) Transitional Justice and DDR: The case of Bosnia and Herzegovina, International Center for Transitional Justice, June, www.ictj.org/sites/default/files/ICTJ-DDR-Bosnia-Case Study-2009-English.pdf.
Morris, R. C. (2011) In the name of trauma: Notes on testimony, truth telling and the secret of literature in South Africa. *Comparative Literature Studies* 48(3): 388–416.
Morrissey, J. (2017) *The long war: CENTCOM, grand strategy, and global security* (Vol. 34) Athens: University of Georgia Press.
Mountz, A. (2010) *Seeking asylum: Human smuggling and bureaucracy at the border.* Minneapolis: University of Minnesota Press.
Mulcahy, L. (2011) *Legal architecture: Justice, due process and the place of law.* Abingdon: Routledge.
(2013) Putting the defendant in their place: Why do we still use the dock in criminal proceedings? *British Journal of Criminology* 53(6): 1139–1156.
Müller, M. (2012) Opening the black box of the organization: Socio-material practices of geopolitical ordering. *Political Geography* 31(6): 379–388.
Nagy, R. (2008) Transitional justice as global project: Critical reflections. *Third World Quarterly* 29(2): 275–289.
Nettelfield, L. (2010) *Courting democracy in Bosnia and Herzegovina: The Hague Tribunal's impact in a postwar state.* Cambridge: Cambridge University Press.
O'Ballance, E. (1995) *Civil war in Bosnia.* London: Macmillan.
O'Brien, J. (1993) The international tribunal for violations of international humanitarian law in the former Yugoslavia. *American Journal of International Law* 87(4): 639–659.
Office of the High Representative (2002) Remarks by the High Representative, Paddy Ashdown, at the inaugural session of the BiH State Court, www.ohr.int/ohr-dept/presso/presssp/default.asp?content_id=8657.

(2003) Criminal code of Bosnia and Herzegovina 'Official Gazette' of Bosnia and Herzegovina, March, www.ohr.int/ohr-dept/legal/oth-legist/doc/criminal-code-of-bih.doc.
(2018) Speech by High Representative for BiH Lord Paddy Ashdown to the United Nations, www.ohr.int/?p=47391.
Olson, E., & Sayer, A. (2009) Radical geography and its critical standpoints: Embracing the normative. *Antipode* 41(1): 180–198.
O'Neill, J. (1986) The disciplinary society: From Weber to Foucault. *British Journal of Sociology* 37(1): 42–60.
Oomen, B. (2005) Donor-driven justice and its discontents: The case of Rwanda. *Development and Change* 36(5): 887–910, p. 887.
Organisation for Security and Cooperation in Europe (2004) OSCE Trial Monitoring Report, www.oscebih.org/documents/osce_bih_doc_2010122310535111eng.pdf.
(2008) Moving towards a harmonized application of the law applicable in war crimes cases before courts in Bosnia and Herzegovina, www.osce.org/mission-to-bosnia-and-herzegovina/314846?download=true.
Orzeck, R. (2014) Normative geographies and the 1940 Land Transfer Regulations in Palestine. *Transactions of the Institute of British Geographers* 39(3): 345–359.
Ó Tuathail, G. (1996) *Critical geopolitics*. Abington: Routledge.
(2002) Theorizing practical geopolitical reasoning: The case of the United States' response to the war in Bosnia. *Political Geography* 21: 601–628.
(2005) Embedding Bosnia-Herzegovina in Euro-Atlantic Structures: From Dayton to Brussels. *Eurasian Geography and Economics* 46(1): 51–67.
Owen, D. (1998) Five wars in the former Yugoslavia. Abu Dhabi: The Emirates Center for Strategic Studies and Research, www.ecssr.ae/en/publication/five-wars-in-the-former-yugoslavia-1991-98/.
Painter, J. (2006) Prosaic geographies of stateness. *Political Geography* 25: 752–774.
Painter, J., & Philo, C. (1995) Spaces of citizenship: An introduction. *Political Geography* 14: 107–120.
Pardew, J. W. (2017) *Peacemakers: American leadership and the end of genocide in the Balkans*. Lexington: University Press of Kentucky.
Patel, A. C., De Greiff, P. & Waldorf, L. (eds.) (2009) Disarming the past: Transitional justice and ex-combatants (Vol. 4) *Social Science Research*. New York: Social Science Research Council.
Pearson, Z. (2008) Spaces of international law. *Griffith Law Review* 17(2008): 489–514.
Philippopoulos-Mihalopoulos, A. (2014) *Spatial justice: Body, lawscape, atmosphere*. Abingdon: Routledge.
Portillo, S., Rudes, D. S., Viglione, J. & Nelson, M. (2013) Front-stage stars and backstage producers: The role of judges in problem-solving courts. *Victims and Offenders* 8(1): 1–22.

Prpa-Jovanović, B. (1997) The making of Yugoslavia: 1830–1945. In Udovički, J., & Ridgeway, J. (eds.) Burn this house the making and unmaking of Yugoslavia (pp. 43–63). Durham, NC: Duke University Press.

Pykett, J. (2009) Making citizens in the classroom: An urban geography of citizenship education? Urban Studies 46(4): 803–823.

Rancière, J. (2004) The politics of aesthetics: The distribution of the sensible. London: Continuum.

Reljic, D. (2004) The news media and the transformation of ethnopolitical conflicts. In Austin, A., Ropers, N. & Fischer, M. (eds.) Transforming ethnopolitical conflict (pp. 321–339). Wiesbaden: VS Verlag für Sozialwissenschaften.

Rich, R. (1993) Symposium: Recent developments in the practice of state recognition. European Journal of International Law 36: 36–65.

Ridgeway, J., & Udovički, J. (2000) Burn this house: The making and unmaking of Yugoslavia. Durham, NC: Duke University Press.

Riding, J. (2018) A new regional geography of a revolution: Bosnia's plenum movement. Territory, Politics, Governance 6(1): 16–41.

Rieff, D. (2003) A bed for the night: Humanitarianism in crisis. London: Vintage.

Riley, C. A. (1997) Neither free nor fair: The 1996 Bosnian elections and the failure of the UN election-monitoring mission. Vanderbilt Journal of Transnational Law 30: 1173.

Ron, J. (2000) Territoriality and plausible deniability: Serbian paramilitaries in the Bosnian war. In Campbell, B., & Brenner, A. (eds.) Death squads in global perspective (pp. 287–312) New York: Palgrave Macmillan.

Roper, S. D., & Barria, L. A. (2007) Donor motivations and contributions to war crimes tribunals. Journal of Conflict Resolution 51(2): 285–304.

Rosenbloom, J. D. (1997) Social ideology as seen through courtroom and courthouse architecture. Columbia-VLA Journal of Law and the Arts 22: 463–524.

Rossner, M. (2016) In the dock: The placement of the accused at court and the right to a fair trial. LSE Law – Policy Briefing Paper No. 18.

Said, E. (1978) Orientalism. London: Penguin.

Saxon, D. (2005) Exporting justice: Perceptions of the ICTY among the Serbian, Croatian, and Muslim communities in the former Yugoslavia. Journal of Human Rights 4(4): 559–572.

Schabas, W. (2012) Unimaginable atrocities: Justice, politics, and rights at the war crimes tribunals. Oxford: Oxford University Press.

Schmitt C (1950 [2003]) The Nomos of the earth. New York: Telos Press.

Scott, J. C. (1998) Seeing like a state: How certain schemes to improve the human condition have failed. New Haven, CT: Yale University Press;

Sebald, W. G. (2001) Austerlitz. London: Penguin Books.

Shapiro, S. J., & Shapiro, S. (2011) Legality (p. 54). Cambridge, MA: Harvard University Press.

Shatzmiller, M. (2002) *Islam and Bosnia: Conflict resolution and foreign policy in multi-ethnic states*. Montreal: McGill-Queen's Press.

Shaw, R., Waldorf, L. & Hazan, P. (eds.) (2010) *Localizing transitional justice: Interventions and priorities after mass violence*. Palo Alto, CA: Stanford University Press.

Shay, S. (2017) *Islamic terror and the Balkans*. London: Routledge.

Shearer, D. (1998) Outsourcing war. *Foreign Policy* 68–81.

Shklar J. N. (1986) *Legalism: law, morals, and political trials*. London: Harvard University Press

Short, E. (2018) The Orao affair: The key to military integration in post-Dayton Bosnia and Herzegovina. *The Journal of Slavic Military Studies* 31(1): 37–64.

Silber, L., & Little, A. (1996) *The death of Yugoslavia*. London: Penguin Books.

Silbey, S. (1997) Presidential address: 'Let them eat cake': Globalization, postmodern colonialism, and the possibilities of justice. *Law and Society Review* 31: 207–235.

Simms, B. (2001) *Unfinest hour: Britain and the destruction of Bosnia*. London: Penguin Books Ltd.

Singer, P. W. (2003) *Corporate warriors: The rise of the privatized military industry*. Ithaca, NY: Cornell University Press.

SIPA (2014) Operation 'Damask': SIPA arrested 16 individuals linked to terrorism, www.sipa.gov.ba/en/news/operation-damask-sipa-arrested-16-individuals-linked-to-terrorism/12107.

Sparke, M. B. (2006) A neoliberal nexus: Economy, security and the biopolitics of citizenship on the border. *Political Geography* 25: 151–180.

Sriram, C., & Ross, A. (2007) Geographies of crime and justice: Contemporary transitional justice and the creation of 'zones of impunity'. *The International Journal of Transitional Justice* 1: 25–65.

Staeheli, L. A. (2011) Political geography: Where's citizenship? *Progress in Human Geography* 35(3): 393–400.

Staeheli, L. A., & Hammett, D. (2010) Educating the new national citizen: Education, political subjectivity and divided societies. *Citizenship Studies* 14(6): 667–680.

Staeheli, L., & Nagel, C. R. (2013) Whose awakening is it? Youth and the geopolitics of civic engagement in the 'Arab Awakening'. *European Urban and Regional Studies* 20(1): 115–119.

Staeheli, L. A., Ehrkamp, P., Leitner, H. & Nagel, C. R. (2012) Dreaming the ordinary daily life and the complex geographies of citizenship. *Progress in Human Geography* 36(5): 628–644.

Štiks, I., & Horvat, S. (2014) The new Balkan revolts: From protests to plenums, and beyond, *openDemocracy*, www.opendemocracy.net/can-europe-make-it/igor-%C5%A1tiks-sre%C4%87ko-horvat/new-balkan-revolts-from-protests-to-plenums-and-beyond.

BIBLIOGRAPHY

Sumner, B. T. (2003) Territorial disputes at the International Court of Justice. *Duke Law Journal* 53: 1779.
Superbosna (2003) Spomen ploča Srbima donešena i odnešena, www.super bosna.com/vijesti/ostalo/spomen_plo%E8a_srbima_done%B9ena_i_odne%B9ena/.
Taylor, M., & Kent, M. L. (2000) Media transitions in Bosnia from propagandistic past to uncertain future. *International Communication Gazette* 62(5): 355–378.
Teitel, R. G. (2000) *Transitional justice*. Oxford: Oxford University Press.
 (2003) Transitional justice genealogy. *Harvard Human Rights Journal* 69: 69–94.
The Journal.ie (2013) Hundreds of Bosnian war criminals to be released and retried, www.thejournal.ie/bosnia-war-criminals-released-1209704-Dec2013/.
Thompson, E. P. (1975) *Whigs and hunters: The origins of the Black Act*. New York: Pantheon.
Tilly, C. (1990) *Coercion, capital, and European states, AD 990*. Oxford: Basil Blackwell.
 (1992) *Coercion, capital, and European states, AD 990–1992*. Oxford: Wiley-Blackwell
Toal, G., & Dahlman, C. T. (2011) *Bosnia remade: Ethnic cleansing and its reversal*. Oxford: Oxford University Press.
Todorova, M. (2009) *Imagining the Balkans*. Oxford: Oxford University Press.
TRIAL (2018) The War Crimes Chamber of the Court of Bosnia and Herzegovina, www.trial-ch.org/en/resources/tribunals/hybrid-tribunals/war-crimes-chamber-in-bosnia-herzegovina.html.
Turner, B. (2013) Religious subtleties in disputing: Spatiotemporal inscriptions of faith in the nomosphere in rural Morocco. In von Benda-Beckmann, F., von Benda-Beckmann, K., Ramstedt, M. & Turner, B. (eds.) *Religion in dispute: Pervasiveness of religious normativity in disputing processes* (pp. 55–73). Basingstoke: Palgrave Macmillan.
Udovicki, J., & Stikovac, E. (2000) Bosnia and Hercegovina: The second war. In Udovicki, I., & Ridgeway, J. (eds.) *Burn this house: The making and unmaking of Yugoslavia* (pp. 175–216). Durham, NC: Duke University Press.
United Nations (2005) Bosnia and Herzegovina gets own war crimes court to help UN tribunal, https://news.un.org/en/story/2005/03/131222-bosnia-and-herzegovina-gets-own-war-crimes-court-help-un-tribunal.
United Nations Development Programme (2013) Access to justice and rule of law, www.undp.org/content/undp/en/home/ourwork/democraticgovernance/focus_areas/focus_justice_law/.
United Nations Security Council (2004) *The rule of law and transitional justice in conflict and post-conflict societies* (pp. 1–24). New York: United Nations.

US Government (2009) INL-managed seed-funded projects update: Focus on the Foreigners Affairs Service, https://wikileaks.org/plusd/cables/09SARAJEVO563_a.html.
US State Department (1996) Briefing on train-and equip program for the Bosnian Federation, https://1997-2001.state.gov/regions/eur/bosnia/724brief_bosnia_federation.html.
Valentine, G., & Skelton, T. (2007) The right to be heard: Citizenship and language. *Political Geography* 26: 121–140.
Valverde, M. (2009) Jurisdiction and scale: Legal technicalities' as resources for theory. *Social and Legal Studies* 18(2): 139–157.
Van Leeuwen, M. (2001) Rwanda's Imidugudu programme and earlier experiences with villagisation and resettlement in East Africa. *The Journal of Modern African Studies* 39(4): 623–644.
Vasudevan, A. (2015) *Metropolitan preoccupations: The spatial politics of squatting in Berlin.* Oxford: John Wiley & Sons.
Vetschera, H., & Damian, M. (2006) Security sector reform in Bosnia and Herzegovina: The role of the international community. *International Peacekeeping* 13(1): 28–42, p. 26.
von Benda-Beckmann, F. (2002) Who's afraid of legal pluralism? *The Journal of Legal Pluralism and Unofficial Law* 34(47): 37–82.
Waldorf, L. (2018) Legal empowerment and horizontal inequalities after conflict. *The Journal of Development Studies* 55(3) 437–455.
Walker, N. (2010) Surface and depth: The EU's resilient sovereignty question. University of Edinburgh School of Law Working Paper 2010/10.
Weber, M. (1958) Politics as a vocation. In Gerth, H. H., & Wright Mills, C. (eds.) *Max Weber: Essays in sociology* (pp. 77–128). New York: Oxford University Press.
Weinstein, H. M., Freedman, S. W. & Hughson, H. (2007) School voices: Challenges facing education systems after identity-based conflicts. *Education, citizenship and social justice* 2(1): 41–71.
Weizman, E. (2011) *The least of all possible evils: Humanitarian violence from Arendt to Gaza.* London: Verso Books.
(2014) Introduction: Forensis. In Forensic Architecture (eds.) *Forensis: The architecture of public truth* (pp. 9–32). Berlin: Sternberg Press.
Whatmore, S. (2002) *Hybrid geographies: Natures cultures spaces.* London: Sage.
Williams, S. (2013) Licit narcotics production in Australia: Legal geographies nomospheric and topological. *Geographical Research* 51(4): 364–374.
Wilson, W. (1918) President's address to Congress. *The Washington Post*, 12 February.
Witte, R. (2009) Beyond 'peace vs. justice': Understanding the relationship between DDR programs and the prosecution of international crimes. In Patel, A. C., De Greiff, P. & Waldorf, L. (eds.) *Disarming the past:*

Transitional justice and ex-combatants (Vol. 4, pp. 86–107). New York: Social Sicence Research Council.

Zilcosky, J. (2004) Sebald's uncanny travels: The impossibility of getting lost. In Long, J. J., & Whitehead, A. (eds.) *W. G. Sebald – A critical companion* (pp. 102–120). Seattle: University of Washington Press.

Zimmerman, W. (1996) *Origins of a catastrophe Yugoslavia and its destroyers – America's last amabssador tells what happened and why.* London: Times Books.

INDEX

Access to Justice programmes, 103–104, 116–117
activist citizenship, 109–110
'actual existing' citizenship, 111
'aesthetic acts,' legal systems as, 17, 61, 63, 65
agency, 84
Alien Action for Tort Statute, U.S., 169–170
Alien Tort Statute, U.S., 169–170
Alisić, Azmir, 174–175
Amnesty International, 41
Andreas, Peter, 160
Arbour, Louise, 47
Arendt, Hannah, 66
Arsenijevíc, Damir, 20
Ashdown, Paddy, 48–49, 54–55, 93, 106
Austin, John, 15–16

Balkanism, 176
Bassiouni, Cherif, 46
Baudrillard, Jacques, 32–33
Begić, Samir, 174–175
Benhabib, Seyla, 38
BiH. *See* Bosnia and Herzegovina
Bijeljina stamp, 72–73
Bodies of Law (Hyde), 20
Bosnia and Herzegovina (BiH). *See also* Court of Bosnia and Herzegovina
  Access to Justice programme in, 103–104
  Bijeljina stamp, 72–73
  CCBiH, 146–149
  consolidation of, 6–7
  in Council of Europe, 136–138
  critical legal geography and, 5–6
  under Dayton Agreement, 6
  after dissolution of Yugoslavia, 42
  ECHR and, 136–138
  under ECtHR jurisdiction, 136–138
  I-FOR in, 162
  international relations in, judicialisation of, 6
  Islam in, 163–164
  mass graves in, classification of human remains from, 20
  ontolopological characteristics of, 53

Operation 'Damask' and, 172–177
  Balkanism as result of, 176
  citizenship law and, 177
  ICITAP and, 172–173
  Republic Srpska and, 43
  residential fieldwork in, 21–22
  rule of law in, 6, 146–149
  transitional justice in, manipulation of, 98
  violence in, 43–44
  causes of, 44–45
Bosnian War. *See also* Court of Bosnia and Herzegovina; International Criminal Tribunal for the Former Yugoslavia; War Crimes Chamber
  accountability as frame for, 90–91
  GFAP and, 106, 111–112
  humanitarianism as frame for, 89–90
  national security as frame for, 89, 91–92
Bosnić, Hussein 'Bilal,' 174–176
Brammertz, Serge, 47
Brown, Wendy, 17, 35
Bucher, Claude, 66
Bush, George H. W., 44–45
Butler, Judith, 31

Campbell, David, 53
care ethics, 40
CBiH. *See* Court of Bosnia and Herzegovina
CCBiH. *See* Criminal Code of Bosnia and Herzegovina
CCSFRY. *See* Criminal Code of the Socialist Federal Republic of Yugoslavia
citizenship
  activist, 109–110
  actual existing, 111
  civic republican, 107–108
  communication strategies for, 118–123
  characteristics of public and, discernment of, 118
  through CSN, 121–122
  NGOs and, 121, 124–126
  through public outreach, 121–124, 130
  de facto, 109
  de jure, 109
  edgeworks and, 9

206

INDEX

exclusion from, 109–110
  forms of, 108–109
  as form of governmental technique, 107
  inclusion through, 109–110
  international interventions for, 114–118
  invented practices of, 84
  invited practices of, 84–85
  liberal democratic, 107–108
  universalism in, 108–129
  Operation 'Damask' and, 177
  public outreach programmes for, 111
  communication strategies in, 121–124, 130
  Responsibility to Protect initiative and, 114–115
  rights through, 114–118
  spaces of, 123–128
civic republican citizenship, 107–108
Clark, David, 165
Clarkson, Carrol, 61
Clinton, Bill, 44–46
Commission of Experts, CBiH, 46–47
common law, establishment of, 140
Concept of Law (Hart), 15–16
constructivism, edgeworks and, 11
Council of Europe, 136–138
Court of Bosnia and Herzegovina (CBiH), 4–7, 28, 93–94. *See also* Court Support Network; War Crimes Chamber; *specific topics*
  Commission of Experts, 46–47
  critical legal geography and, 5–6
  establishment of, 4, 7
    building construction, 52–53
    location selection and, 27
  functions of, 112–113
  ICTY and, 7
  WCC and, 31
  international judges in, 54
  localisation of judicial processes through, 50–51
  sovereignty surplus and, 50
  objectives of, 4, 111–112
  public outreach programmes for citizenship, 111
  purpose of, 50
  SIPA in, 49, 111–112, 172
  sovereignty surplus and, 50
  war crimes trials at, 11
Court Support Network (CSN)
  citizenship and, 121–122
  establishment of, 95
  Helsinški komitet and, 98–103
  NGOs in, 80, 98–103
    educational components of, 102
    objectives of, 95–96

spaces of justice in, 95–103
  invented, 98–103
  invited, 96–98
  transitional justice through, 99
  war victim pensions through, 97
courts. *See also* specific courts
  edge of law and, 18
Criminal Code of Bosnia and Herzegovina (CCBiH), 146–149
Criminal Code of the Socialist Federal Republic of Yugoslavia (CCSFRY), 147–149
critical legal geography, 5–6
  edge of law and, 19–20
  feminism and, 19–20
Crnjekovic, Amir, 174–175
Croatia, 45
CSN. *See* Court Support Network

Damjanović, Goran, 149–150
Dayton General Framework Agreement for Peace (Dayton Agreement) (DPA) (GFAP), 106, 111–112, 136, 146
  BiH, 6
  ICTY and, 48
  national security factors in, 91–92
de facto citizenship, 109
de jure citizenship, 109
Delaney, David, 60–61, 82
Del Ponte, Carla, 47, 56–57
democracy
  legitimacy and, 31–36
  procedural democracy, 34–35
  through representational strategies, 33–34
  self-determination and, 34
  substantive democracy and, 34–35
  procedural, 34–35
  substantive, 34–35
democratisation, sovereignty and, 30
Dodik, Milorad, 53, 94, 147, 172
DPA. *See* Dayton General Framework Agreement for Peace
Duffield, Mark, 37
Dwyer, Michael, 51–52

ECHR. *See* European Convention on Human Rights
ECtHR. *See* European Court of Human Rights
edge of law, 7–12, 180–181
  academic approaches to, 18–22
  critical legal geography in, 19–20
  embodied nature of political life in, 20
  methodological implications of, 19–20
  normativity in, 21
  aspirational nature of, 3
  components of, 1
  courts and, 18

207

INDEX

edge of law, (cont.)
  enclosure in, 2–3
  jurisdiction in, 1
  as legal concept, 1–2
  material, 15–22
    legal systems in, 15
    in sanction theory, 15
  mechanisms of, 2–3
  prisons and, 18
  production of law and, 181–183
  public outreach and, 82–85
  territorial, 12–15
    authoritative role of state in, 12–13
    IHL and, 14
    sovereignty and, 13–14
  tribunals and, 18
edgeworks, 7–10
  citizenship and, 9
  constructivist approach to, 11
  elements and types of, 8
  residential illegality and, 9
Eichmann, Adolf, 66, 185
Elden, Stuart, 144–145
Eliot, George, 143–144
embodied law, materiality of legal institutions through, 70–73
  bodily performance in trials, 72
  through enactment of trials, 70
  through monitoring of trials, 70–71
  testimony of victims and, gender factors in, 71–72
enclosure, in edge of law, 2–3
entrance strategies, for international interventions
  exit strategies compared to, 154–155
  through legal processes, establishment of, 161–171
  military components in, 157–161
  MPRI, 156, 167–169
  PIC and, 162
  removal of foreign forces, 157–158, 167–169
  T&E programme and, 165–166
  Operation 'Damask,' 172–177
    Balkanism as result of, 176
    citizenship law and, 177
    ICITAP and, 172–173
    production by outsider sovereign states, 171–177
European Commission, 81
European Convention on Human Rights (ECHR), 124, 136–138
  rule of law under, 149–150
European Court of Human Rights (ECtHR), 66, 123–124
  BiH under jurisdiction of, 136–138

ex post facto law, 85
exit strategies, for international interventions, entrance strategies compared to, 154–155

Fassin, Didier, 38
Felman, Shoshana, 185–186
feminism, critical legal geography and, 19–20
Filipović, Emrah, 174–175
Finci, Jakob, 136–137
Fitzpatrick, Peter, 143–144
Foucault, Michel, 16–17
  social theory of, 64
Fuller, Lon, 145–146

Gacaca courts, in Rwanda, 63
  transitional justice in, 86
gender, testimony of victims by, intimidation in, 71–72
Geneva Convention, 115
Gengic, Hasan, 166
genocide, 45–46
geopolitics of justice
  ICTY and, creation of, 41
  national security and, 89
  public outreach through, 88–92
GFAP. *See* Dayton General Framework Agreement for Peace
Goffman, Erving, 64
Goldstone, Richard, 47, 91
Gotovina, Ante, 170–171

Hart, H. L. A., 15–16, 145
Hazan, Pierre, 45–46
Helsinški komitet, of ICTY, 98–103
Holston, James, 9
Human Rights Watch, 41
humanitarian ethics, 40
humanitarianism
  biopolitics of, 37
  care ethics and, 40
  civilian treatment during wartime, 115
  ethics of, 40
  ICTY formation and, 30–31
  idealism in, 38
  through IHL, 39
  in political interventions, 38–39
  pragmatism in, 38
  solidarity and, 36–40
  sovereignty and, 30, 36–40
  ad hoc tribunals, 38
  PLWCTs, 39–40
  UDHR and, 37–38
  through WCC creation, 55
Hyde, Alan, 70

INDEX

ICC. *See* International Criminal Court
ICITAP. *See* International Criminal Investigative Training Assistance Program
ICJ. *See* International Court of Justice
ICTR. *See* International Criminal Tribunal for Rwanda
ICTY. *See* International Criminal Tribunal for the Former Yugoslavia
idealism, in humanitarianism, 38
I-FOR. *See* Implementation Force
IHL. *See* international humanitarian law
Implementation Force (I-FOR), 162
International Court of Justice (ICJ), 14
International Criminal Court (ICC), 86
International Criminal Investigative Training Assistance Program (ICITAP), 172–173
International Criminal Tribunal for Rwanda (ICTR), 116
International Criminal Tribunal for the Former Yugoslavia (ICTY), 40–48
  CBiH and, 7
  WCC and, 31
  completion strategy of, 80
  creation of, 30–31, 40–41
  geopolitical context for, 41
  purpose of, 55
  fragmentation of Yugoslavia and, 41–42
  Helsinški komitet of, 98–103
  as humanitarian response, 30–31
  mandate of, 47–48
  public outreach through, 98, 185
  citizenship programmes, 111
  transfer of cases to, 80
  transitional justice and, 116
  UN Security Council of, 90–91
international human rights law, as legal commons, 138–143
  IHL and, 141–142
  standardisation of law, 140
international humanitarian law (IHL)
  institutionalisation of, 141–142
  territorial edge of law and, 14
international law, *nomos* and, 31–32
international relations
  in BiH, 6
  judicialisation of, 6, 116
invented practices, of citizenship, 84
invented spaces of justice, 98–103
invited practices, of citizenship, 84–85
invited spaces of justice, 96–98
Isenberg, David, 168
Islam, in BiH, 163–164
Islam between East and West (Izetbegović), 164
The Islamic Declaration (Izetbegović), 163
Izetbegović, Alija, 163–164

Jacobs, Jane M., 65
JNA. *See* Yugoslav People's Army
Jović, Milena, 168
jurisdiction. *See also* territorial edge of law
  in edge of law, 1
  in ICJ, 14
  legal scope of, 1
  of WCC, 80–81
jurispadence, 187

Kafka, Franz, 62
Karadžić, Radovan, 43, 91–92, 164
  pre-trial defence of, 86
  SDS and, 89
Kuus, Merje, 88–89

language, in law, centrality of, 31–33
Latour, Bruno, 65
law. *See also* edge of law
  central function of, 139–145
  definition of, 1–2
  disciplinary forms of power and, 16–17
  ex post facto, 85
  language in, centrality of, 31–33
  legal centralism and, 2
  micro-geopolitics of, 51–52
  nomos, 31–32, 59
  origins of, 143–146
  transitional justice and, 145–146
  production of, 181–183
  as retributive system, 16
  in sanction theory, 17–18
  social legacy of, 12
  as social phenomenon, 3
  societal aspects of, 3
  standardisation of, 140
  states as producers of, 13–14
lawscape, 187
Lee, John Z., 171
legal centralism, 2
legal commons, international human rights law as, 138–143
  IHL and, 141–142
  standardisation of law, 140
legal communication, 183–185
legal performance, 185–187
legal positivism, 37
  idealism and, 37
legal systems
  as 'aesthetic acts,' 17, 61, 63, 65
  material edge of law and, 15
legal theory, representation in, 32–33
legalism
  transitional justice and, 79–80
  transnational, 41

209

INDEX

legitimacy
  democracy and, 31–36
  procedural, 34–35
  through representational strategies, 33–34
  self-determination and, 34
  substantive, 34–35
  of modern states, 16, 33
  sovereignty and, 31–36
  inviolability of, 35
  through securitisation, 35
  in state theory, 33
Lehnardt, Chia, 168–169
liberal democratic citizenship, 107–108
  universalism in, 108–129
Lyng, Stephen, 7–10

Major, John, 44
Maktouf, Abduladhim, 149–150
Markač, Mladen, 170–171
Marshall, Penny, 45–46
Marston, Sallie, 82–83
material edge of law, 15–22
  legal systems in, 15
  in sanction theory, 15
materiality, of legal institutions, 59–65
  dynamic nature of, 57–58
  through embodied law, 70–73
    bodily performance in trials, 72
    through enactment of trials, 70
    through monitoring of trials, 70–71
    testimony of victims and, gender factors in, 71–72
  localisation of transitional justice, 57
  nomos and, 59–61
    'aesthetic acts' and, 61, 63, 65
    nomic settings, 61, 65
    nomosphere, 60–61
  passage of time and, 58–59
  in WCC, 66–70, 73–75
    through commemoration, 68–69
    through court space design, 66–68
    forms of resistance to, 68–70
    location of, 68
    Savesa Logoraša RS and, 68–69
McFarlane, Colin, 142–143
Medica Zenica, 111, 122
Mesinovic, Ismar, 174–175
micro-geopolitics of law, 51–52. *See also* geopolitics of justice
Middlemarch (Eliot), 143–144
Mijić, Zivka, 168
Military Professionals Resources Inc. (MPRI), 156, 167–169
Milošević, Slobodan, 44, 159–160
Mladić, Ratko, 91–92

modern states
  bureaucratic power within, 16
  international state-building, 51
  legitimacy of, 16, 33
Modernism and the Grounds of Law (Fitzpatrick), 143–144
Morris, Rosalind, 143–144
MPRI. *See* Military Professionals Resources Inc.
Mulcahy, Linda, 64

national security
  Dayton Agreement and, 91–92
  geopolitics of justice and, 89
NGOs. *See* non-governmental organisations
no crime without a law, no punishment without a law. *See nullum crimen sine lege, nulla peona sine lege*
nomos (law), 31–32, 59
  materiality of legal institutions and, 59–61
  'aesthetic acts' and, 61, 63, 65
  nomic settings, 61, 65
nomosphere, 60–61, 82, 187
non-governmental organisations (NGOs)
  citizenship communication strategies and, 121, 124–126
  in CSN, 80, 98–103
  educational components of, 102
nullum crimen sine lege, nulla peona sine lege (no crime without a law, no punishment without a law), 85
Nuremberg trials, 36–37, 41
  under *ex post facto* law, 85
  nullum crimen sine lege, nulla peona sine lege and, 85

Office of the High Representative (OHR), 81, 92, 146
  WCC and, 93–94
Oomen, Barbara, 63
Operation 'Damask,' 172–177
  Balkanism as result of, 176
  citizenship law and, 177
  ICITAP and, 172–173
Operation Iraqi Freedom, 36
Operation Storm, 168, 170–171

Pardew, James, 165–166
Peace Implementation Council (PIC), 92, 162
pensions. *See* war victim pensions
people-led war crimes tribunals (PLWCTs), 39–40
PIC. *See* Peace Implementation Council
PLWCTs. *See* people-led war crimes tribunals
positivism. *See* legal positivism
power, disciplinary forms of, 16–17
pragmatism, in humanitarianism, 38

prisons, edge of law and, 18
procedural democracy, 34–35
procedural justice, 145–146
public outreach
 for citizenship, 111
 communication strategies for, 121–124, 130
 edge of law and, 82–85
 through geopolitics of justice, 88–92
 through ICTY, 98, 185
  citizenship programmes, 111
 through transitional justice, 85–88
 in WCC, 93–95
Putin, Vladimir, 172

Rancière, Jacques, 17
representation
 democratic legitimacy through, 33–34
 in legal theory, 32–33
Republic Srpska, 43
 Savesa Logoraša RS, 68–69
residential illegality, 9
Responsibility to Protect initiative, 114–115
rights, through citizenship, 114–118
Rogers, Richard, 66, 141
Ron, James, 159–160
rule of law
 in BiH, 146–149
 under ECHR, 149–150
 legal codes under, competition between, 146–149
 legal pluralism and, 136
 social validity of, 149–151
 stare decisis principle, 145–146
Rwanda
 Gacaca courts in, 63
 transitional justice in, 86
 ICTR and, 116
 villagisation programme in, 87

Sabić, Muaz, 174–175
sanction theory, 15–16
 separation between law and obeyers of law in, 17–18
Savesa Logoraša RS, 68–69
Schmitt, Carl, 13
 on *nomos*, 31–32, 59
SDS. *See Srpska demokratksa stranka*
Sebald, W. G., 62–63
Sejdić, Dervo, 136–137
self-determination
 democracy and, 34
 legitimacy through, 34
SIPA. *See* State Investigation and Prosecution Agency
Slovenia, 45
social theory, 64

solidarity, in humanitarianism, 36–40
South Africa, TRC in, 87
sovereignty
 democratisation and, 30
 humanitarianism and, 30, 36–40
 ad hoc tribunals, 38
 PLWCTs, 39–40
 legitimacy of, 31–36
 inviolability of, 35
 through securitisation, 35
 territorial edge of law and, 13–14
spaces of citizenship, 123–128
spaces of justice, 95–103
 invented, 98–103
 invited, 96–98
Srpska demokratksa stranka (SDS), 89
Stabilisation and Association Agreement, 50–51
Stanković, Radovan, 100–101
stare decisis principle, 145–146
State Investigation and Prosecution Agency (SIPA), 49, 111–112, 172
state-law relationships, 83–84
state theory, legitimacy in, 33
Stop Genocide Denial Campaign, 122
substantive democracy, 34–35
substantive justice, 145–146

T&E programme. *See* Train and Equip programme
territorial edge of law, 12–15
 authoritative role of state in, 12–13
 IHL and, 14
 sovereignty and, 13–14
Thompson, E. P., 139–140
Tokyo tribunals, 41
Track Impunity Always (TRIAL), 111, 122
Train and Equip (T&E) programme, 165–166
 U.S. involvement in, 167–169
transitional justice, 37–38, 185–186
 in BiH, manipulation of, 98
 through CSN, 98–100
 definition of, 85
 in Gacaca courts, 86
 in ICC, 86
 ICTR and, 116
 ICTY and, 116
 institutionalisation of, 115
 legalism and, 79–80
 localisation of, 57
 origins of law and, 145–146
 temporal elements of, 85
 WCC mechanisms, 138
TRC. *See* Truth and Reconciliation Commission
TRIAL. *See* Track Impunity Always
The Trial (Kafka), 62

INDEX

trials. *See also* Nuremberg trials; war crime trials
    bodily performance in, 72
    enactment of, 70
    monitoring of, 70–71
    testimony of victims in, gender factors in, 71–72
tribunals. *See also specific tribunals*
    ad hoc, 38
    edge of law and, 18
    PLWCTs, 39–40
    Tokyo tribunal, 41
Truth and Reconciliation Commission (TRC), 87
Tuathail, Ó, 90, 162

U.K. *See* United Kingdom
U.S. *See* United States
UDHR. *See* Universal Declaration of Human Rights
UN. *See* United Nations
UN Development Programme (UNDP), 81
    Access to Justice programmes, 103–104, 116–117
UNDP. *See* UN Development Programme
United Kingdom (U.K.), foreign policy of, 45–46
United Nations (UN)
    Responsibility to Protect initiative, 114–115
    Security Council, 90–91
United States (U.S.)
    Alien Action for Tort Statute, 169–170
    in T&E programme, 167–169
Universal Declaration of Human Rights (UDHR), 37–38
universalism, in liberal democratic citizenship, 108–129

Vasudevan, Alex, 142–143
villagisation programme, in Rwanda, 87
Vulliamy, Ed, 45–46

Walker, Neil, 50
War Crimes Chamber (WCC), in CBiH, 27–29
    creation of, 48–54
    humanitarian purposes of, 55
    ICTY and, 31
    jurisdiction of, 80–81
    materiality of, 66–70. *See also* materiality
        through commemoration, 68–69
        through court space design, 66–68
        forms of resistance to, 68–70
        location of court and, 68
        Savesa Logoraša RS and, 68–69
    OHR and, 93–94
    transitional justice mechanisms in, 138
war crime trials
    at CBiH, 11
    ICTY, 7
war victim pensions, 97
WCC. *See* War Crimes Chamber
Weber, Max, 16
Williams, Ian, 45–46
Wilson, Woodrow, 34

Yugoslavia. *See also* International Criminal Tribunal for the Former Yugoslavia
    BiH and, after dissolution of, 42
    UK foreign policy and, 45–46
    CCSFRY in, 147–149
    ICTY and, after fragmentation of, 41–42
    legal codes in, 29
Yugoslav People's Army (JNA), 43, 49, 89

CAMBRIDGE STUDIES IN LAW AND SOCIETY

Books in the Series
Diseases of the Will: Alcohol and the Dilemmas of Freedom
Mariana Valverde

The Politics of Truth and Reconciliation in South Africa: Legitimizing the Post-Apartheid State
Richard A. Wilson

Modernism and the Grounds of Law
Peter Fitzpatrick

Unemployment and Government: Genealogies of the Social
William Walters

Autonomy and Ethnicity: Negotiating Competing Claims in Multi-Ethnic States
Yash Ghai

Constituting Democracy: Law, Globalism and South Africa's Political Reconstruction
Heinz Klug

The Ritual of Rights in Japan: Law, Society, and Health Policy
Eric A. Feldman

Governing Morals: A Social History of Moral Regulation
Alan Hunt

The Colonies of Law: Colonialism, Zionism and Law in Early Mandate Palestine
Ronen Shamir

Law and Nature
David Delaney

Social Citizenship and Workfare in the United States and Western Europe: The Paradox of Inclusion
Joel F. Handler

Law, Anthropology, and the Constitution of the Social: Making Persons and Things Edited by
Alain Pottage and Martha Mundy

Judicial Review and Bureaucratic Impact: International and Interdisciplinary Perspectives Edited by
Marc Hertogh and Simon Halliday

Immigrants at the Margins: Law, Race, and Exclusion in Southern Europe
Kitty Calavita

Lawyers and Regulation: The Politics of the Administrative Process
Patrick Schmidt

Law and Globalization from Below: Toward a Cosmopolitan Legality Edited by
Boaventura de Sousa Santos and Cesar A. Rodriguez-Garavito

Public Accountability: Designs, Dilemmas and Experiences Edited by
Michael W. Dowdle

Law, Violence and Sovereignty among West Bank Palestinians
Tobias Kelly

Legal Reform and Administrative Detention Powers in China
Sarah Biddulph

The Practice of Human Rights: Tracking Law between the Global and the Local Edited by
Mark Goodale and Sally Engle Merry

Judges beyond Politics in Democracy and Dictatorship: Lessons from Chile
Lisa Hilbink

Paths to International Justice: Social and Legal Perspectives Edited by
Marie-Bénédicte Dembour and Tobias Kelly

Law and Society in Vietnam: The Transition from Socialism in Comparative Perspective
Mark Sidel

Constitutionalizing Economic Globalization: Investment Rules and Democracy's Promise
David Schneiderman

The New World Trade Organization Knowledge Agreements: 2nd Edition
Christopher Arup

Justice and Reconciliation in Post-Apartheid South Africa Edited by
François du Bois and Antje du Bois-Pedain

Militarization and Violence against Women in Conflict Zones in the Middle East: A Palestinian Case-Study
Nadera Shalhoub-Kevorkian

Child Pornography and Sexual Grooming: Legal and Societal Responses
Suzanne Ost

Darfur and the Crime of Genocide
John Hagan and Wenona Rymond-Richmond

Fictions of Justice: The International Criminal Court and the Challenge of Legal Pluralism in Sub-Saharan Africa
Kamari Maxine Clarke

Conducting Law and Society Research: Reflections on Methods and Practices
Simon Halliday and Patrick Schmidt

Planted Flags: Trees, Land, and Law in Israel/Palestine
Irus Braverman

Culture under Cross-Examination: International Justice and the Special Court for Sierra Leone
Tim Kelsall

Cultures of Legality: Judicialization and Political Activism in Latin America
Javier Couso, Alexandra Huneeus, and Rachel Sieder

Courting Democracy in Bosnia and Herzegovina: The Hague Tribunal's Impact in a Postwar State
Lara J. Nettelfield

The Gacaca Courts, Post-Genocide Justice and Reconciliation in Rwanda: Justice without Lawyers
Phil Clark

Law, Society, and History: Themes in the Legal Sociology and Legal History of Lawrence M. Friedman Edited by
Robert W. Gordon and Morton J. Horwitz

After Abu Ghraib: Exploring Human Rights in America and the Middle East
Shadi Mokhtari

Adjudication in Religious Family Laws: Cultural Accommodation, Legal Pluralism, and Gender Equality in India
Gopika Solanki

Water on Tap: Rights and Regulation in the Transnational Governance of Urban Water Services
Bronwen Morgan

Elements of Moral Cognition: Rawls' Linguistic Analogy and the Cognitive Science of Moral and Legal Judgment
John Mikhail

Mitigation and Aggravation at Sentencing Edited by
Julian V. Roberts

Institutional Inequality and the Mobilization of the Family and Medical Leave Act: Rights on Leave
Catherine R. Albiston

Authoritarian Rule of Law: Legislation, Discourse and Legitimacy in Singapore
Jothie Rajah

Law and Development and the Global Discourses of Legal Transfers
Edited by
John Gillespie and Pip Nicholson

Law against the State: Ethnographic Forays into Law's Transformations Edited by
Julia Eckert, Brian Donahoe, Christian Strümpell, and Zerrin Özlem Biner

Transnational Legal Ordering and State Change Edited by
Gregory C. Shaffer

Legal Mobilization under Authoritarianism: The Case of Post-Colonial Hong Kong
Waikeung Tam

Complementarity in the Line of Fire: The Catalysing Effect of the International Criminal Court in Uganda and Sudan
Sarah M. H. Nouwen

Political and Legal Transformations of an Indonesian Polity: The Nagari from Colonisation to Decentralisation
Franz von Benda-Beckmann and Keebet von Benda-Beckmann

Pakistan's Experience with Formal Law: An Alien Justice
Osama Siddique

Human Rights under State-Enforced Religious Family Laws in Israel, Egypt, and India
Yüksel Sezgin

Why Prison? Edited by
David Scott

Law's Fragile State: Colonial, Authoritarian, and Humanitarian Legacies in Sudan
Mark Fathi Massoud

Rights for Others: The Slow Home-Coming of Human Rights in the Netherlands
Barbara Oomen

European States and Their Muslim Citizens: The Impact of Institutions on Perceptions and Boundaries Edited by
John R. Bowen, Christophe Bertossi, Jan Willem Duyvendak, and Mona Lena Krook

Environmental Litigation in China: A Study in Political Ambivalence
Rachel E. Stern

Indigeneity and Legal Pluralism in India: Claims, Histories, Meanings
Pooja Parmar

Paper Tiger: Law, Bureaucracy and the Developmental State in Himalayan India
Nayanika Mathur

Religion, Law and Society
Russell Sandberg

The Experiences of Face Veil Wearers in Europe and the Law
Edited by
Eva Brems

The Contentious History of the International Bill of Human Rights
Christopher N. J. Roberts

Transnational Legal Orders Edited by
Terence C. Halliday and Gregory Shaffer

Lost in China? Law, Culture and Society in Post-1997 Hong Kong
Carol A. G. Jones

Security Theology, Surveillance and the Politics of Fear
Nadera Shalhoub-Kevorkian

Opposing the Rule of Law: How Myanmar's Courts Make Law and Order
Nick Cheesman

The Ironies of Colonial Governance: Law, Custom and Justice in Colonial India
James Jaffe

The Clinic and the Court: Law, Medicine and Anthropology Edited by
Ian Harper, Tobias Kelly, and Akshay Khanna

A World of Indicators: The Making of Government Knowledge through Quantification Edited by
Richard Rottenburg, Sally Engle Merry, Sung-Joon Park, and Johanna Mugler

Contesting Immigration Policy in Court: Legal Activism and Its Radiating Effects in the United States and France
Leila Kawar

The Quiet Power of Indicators: Measuring Governance, Corruption, and Rule of Law Edited by
Sally Engle Merry, Kevin Davis, and Benedict Kingsbury

Investing in Authoritarian Rule: Punishment and Patronage in Rwanda's Gacaca Courts for Genocide Crimes
Anuradha Chakravarty

Contractual Knowledge: One Hundred Years of Legal Experimentation in Global Markets Edited by
Grégoire Mallard and Jérôme Sgard

Iraq and the Crimes of Aggressive War: The Legal Cynicism of Criminal Militarism
John Hagan, Joshua Kaiser, and Anna Hanson

Culture in the Domains of Law Edited by
René Provost

China and Islam: The Prophet, the Party, and Law
Matthew S. Erie

Diversity in Practice: Race, Gender, and Class in Legal and Professional Careers Edited by
Spencer Headworth and Robert Nelson

A Sociology of Constitutions: Constitutions and State Legitimacy in Historical-Sociological Perspective
Chris Thornhill

A Sociology of Transnational Constitutions: Social Foundations of the Post-National Legal Structure
Chris Thornhill

Shifting Legal Visions: Judicial Change and Human Rights Trials in Latin America
Ezequiel A. González Ocantos

The Demographic Transformations of Citizenship
Heli Askola

Criminal Defense in China: The Politics of Lawyers at Work
Sida Liu and Terence C. Halliday

Contesting Economic and Social Rights in Ireland: Constitution, State and Society, 1848–2016
Thomas Murray

Buried in the Heart: Women, Complex Victimhood and the War in Northern Uganda
Erin Baines

Palaces of Hope: The Anthropology of Global Organizations Edited by
Ronald Niezen and Maria Sapignoli

The Politics of Bureaucratic Corruption in Post-Transitional Eastern Europe
Marina Zaloznaya

Revisiting the Law and Governance of Trafficking, Forced Labor and Modern Slavery Edited by
Prabha Kotiswaran

Incitement on Trial: Prosecuting International Speech Crimes
Richard Ashby Wilson

Criminalizing Children: Welfare and the State in Australia
David McCallum

Global Lawmakers: International Organizations in the Crafting of World Markets
Susan Block-Lieb and Terence C. Halliday

Duties to Care: Dementia, Relationality and Law
Rosie Harding

Insiders, Outsiders, Injuries, and Law: Revisiting "The Oven Bird's Song" Edited by
Mary Nell Trautner

Hunting Justice: Displacement, Law, and Activism in the Kalahari
Maria Sapignoli

Injury and Injustice: The Cultural Politics of Harm and Redress
Edited by
Anne Bloom, David M. Engel, and Michael McCann

Ruling Before the Law: The Politics of Legal Regimes in China and Indonesia
William Hurst

The Powers of Law: A Comparative Analysis of Sociopolitical Legal Studies
Mauricio García-Villegas

A Sociology of Justice in Russia Edited by
Marina Kurkchiyan and Agnieszka Kubal

Constituting Religion: Islam, Liberal Rights, and the Malaysian State
Tamir Moustafa

The Invention of the Passport: Surveillance, Citizenship and the State, Second Edition
John C. Torpey

Law's Trials: The Performance of Legal Institutions in the US "War on Terror"
Richard L. Abel

Law's Wars: The Fate of the Rule of Law in the US "War on Terror"
Richard L. Abel

Transforming Gender Citizenship: The Irresistible Rise of Gender Quotas in Europe Edited by
Eléonore Lépinard and Ruth Rubio-Marín

Muslim Women's Quest for Justice: Gender, Law and Activism in India
Mengia Hong Tschalaer

Children as "Risk": Sexual Exploitation and Abuse by Children and Young People
Anne-Marie McAlinden

The Legal Process and the Promise of Justice: Studies Inspired by the Work of Malcolm Feeley
Jonathan Simon, Rosann Greenspan, Hadar Aviram

Sovereign Exchanges: Gifts, Trusts, Reparations, and Other Fetishes of International Solidarity
Grégoire Mallard

Measuring Justice: Quantitative Accountability and the National Prosecuting Authority in South Africa
Johanna Mugler

Negotiating the Power of NGOs: Women's Legal Rights in South Africa
Reem Wael

Indigenous Water Rights in Law and Regulation: Lessons from Comparative Experience
Elizabeth Jane Macpherson